Young Children's Literacy Development and the Role of Televisual Texts

Naima Browne

First published 1999 by Falmer Press
11 New Fetter Lane, London EC4P 4EE

Simultaneously published in the USA and Canada
by Falmer Press
Routledge Inc., 29 West 35th Street, New York, NY 10001

Falmer Press is an imprint of the Taylor & Francis Group

A catalogue record for this book is available from the British Library

ISBN 0 7507 0855 7 cased
ISBN 0 7507 0856 5 paper

Library of Congress Cataloging-in-Publication Data are available on request

Jacket design by Caroline Archer

Typeset in 10/12pt Times by
Graphicraft Ltd., Hong Kong

Printed in Great Britain by Biddles Ltd., Guildford and King's Lynn on paper which has a specified pH value on final paper manufacture of not less than 7.5 and is therefore 'acid free'.

Every effort has been made to contact copyright holders for their permission to reprint material in this book. The publishers would be grateful to hear from any copyright holder who is not here acknowledged and will undertake to rectify any errors or omissions in future editions of this book.

Young Children's Literacy Development and the Role of Televisual Texts

This book is dedicated to Rehana with love

Contents

List of Figures

Notes about Transcriptions

All the names have been changed to protect interviewees' anonymity. The following symbols have been used in the transcriptions:

...	Indicates a pause
...	At end of speech indicates speaker interrupted
...	At beginning of speech indicates interrupted comment continued
[...]	Section from transcript omitted because conversation moved away from point initially being discussed
[Text]	Within transcript provides additional information (e.g. context, child's physical response, age of child etc.)
[ ]	At end of each transcript includes details about speaker and transcript reference (see Appendix C)
NB	The author and researcher
NT	Nursery teacher
Teacher	Names removed for anonymity
QR	Indicates written response to questionnaire

Acknowledgments

I should like to thank all the children who talked so enthusiastically about what they enjoyed reading and watching and also their parents and teachers who so generously gave their time to answer all my questions.

Thanks also to Sue Pidgeon with whom I discussed many of my ideas and who kindly took the time to read and comment on what I had written. Thanks to Neil and Sally Dhruev for their on-going interest and useful comments and questions.

Special thanks to Phil for his support and encouragement throughout the writing of this book.

Finally, thanks to Rehana, without whom this book would not have been written.

Chapter 1

Introduction

At the dawn of the twenty-first century, with the attendant developments in techno-logy and the British government's concern about children's literacy, it is perhaps timely to consider how young children's literacy development may be influenced and shaped by their experiences of written and televisual texts. For the past 50 years concerns have been articulated about the impact of television on children's lives and development. From the 1950s onwards there has been a significant amount of research focusing on children and television. These varied research studies have explored the amount of time young children spend watching television (e.g. Chambers et al., 1998; Himmelweit, Oppenheim and Vince, 1958; Shastri and Mohite, 1997; Truglio et al., 1996), the content of what they watch and the effects of this on their behaviour (e.g. Bandura, Ross and Ross, 1963; Boyatzis, Matillo and Nesbitt, 1995; Drabman and Thomas, 1975; Weigman, Kuttschreuter and Baarda, 1992), the links between children's achievement in school and their television viewing habits and the effect of television on children's social, emotional and cognitive development (Brooks et al., 1997; Schramm, Lyle and Parker, 1961; Young, 1998). Given this wealth of research a reader may conclude that further study of the area is unneces-sary, but I would contend that three important issues need consideration. Firstly, how changes in technology have influenced people's lives and viewing patterns, secondly how the theories of childhood and development and the realities of chil-dren's lives have altered during the past few decades and, finally, how conceptions and definitions of literacy have changed since televisions became a common feature in the majority of homes in Britain.

Reflections on incidental observations of very young children's responses to television, videos and books at home provided the catalyst for the research upon which this book is based. Initially, I was struck by the *active* way in which these very young children watched television and videos: they danced, sang, asked ques-tions, kissed the screen, attempted to mirror what was happening on the screen, and made effective use of the remote control to ensure that they watched what *they* wanted to watch. The children did not necessarily respond to explicit invitations to 'sing along' or 'join in and clap hands' made by adult presenters on shows such as Playdays or Sesame Street, instead the children made their own decisions about when they wanted to participate and when they wanted to adopt the role of an onlooker. I was also intrigued by the fact that many parents of two and three-year-olds reported that their children frequently watched the same video over and over again and I wondered about the reasons for this. What connection, if any, is there between watching a favourite video repeatedly and rereading a well-loved book? Reflecting on how my daughter's literacy development appeared to be influenced by her experiences of both books and television led me to examine the possible links between literacy development and children's experiences of written and televisual texts.

Impact of technology

This study has taken place at a time when the vast majority of children have access to televisions and videos. Whilst carrying out the research only one child did not have a television and the overwhelming majority of the children not only had video recorders at home but were also confident and independent users of them. Furthermore, some of the young children involved in the study had televisions and videos in their bedrooms:

> *William*: Yeah, I got a television and video in my room, I got *Toy Story* . . .
> *NB*:   Mmmm.
> *Alicia*:   I got *Toy Story*.
> *William*: Me too!
> *NB*:   When you want to watch a video . . .
> *William*: You turn it on and put 9 on it and then it, you put in *Toy Story* and it starts.
> [Boy and girl aged 4, TSO, p. 4]

The impact of new technologies on children's lives means that research findings of 30, 20 or even 10 years ago may have only a limited applicability to current contexts. This is certainly the case when examining young children, television and literacy. Parents, for example, spoke of how they videotaped their children's favourite programmes if they were going out, whilst children talked about how they liked to watch and rewatch their favourite videos. Depending on one's stance, it is possible to argue that the opportunity to videotape television programmes encourages adults and children to allow television to assume too great an importance in their lives. Does it really matter if a child misses their favourite programme occasionally? Alternatively, it is possible to argue that videotaping programmes decreases the tyranny of television in that the viewer or, in the case of very young children, the parent decides when the child will watch, and for how long, rather than being at the mercy of the programme schedulers. A key point is that such discussion would not have occurred 10 or 15 years ago. Young children of today can be described as the 'video generation', as for them the presence and use of a video is commonplace.

   In the past, criticisms about television have included the fact that, unlike when reading a book, it is not possible to control the pace:

When we view, the pace of television programs cannot be controlled, only its beginning and end are within our control by clicking the knob on and off. We cannot slow down a delightful program or speed up a dreary one. We cannot 'turn back' if a word or phrase is not understood. The program moves inexorably forward and what is lost or misunderstood remains so.
(Winn, 1985, pp. 60–1)

Marks Greenfield, writing in the mid 1980s, also highlighted that the pace of the television programme determines the pace at which viewers have to process what they view, although she recognized that the use of videos may help overcome this problem (Marks Greenfield, 1984, p. 83). By the late 1990s, as experienced and confident users of video recorders, young children are indeed able to exert much more control over their experience of televisual texts as later chapters demonstrate (see Chapters 3, 4 and 5). Not only are children able to pause a video, rewind or fast forward but they are also able to return again and again to a video, much as they do with a favourite book.

Marie Winn was strongly opposed to children watching television and, in her book, *The Plug-in Drug: Television, Children and the Family*, she argued that television was addictive for children and parents. Twenty years later, adults continue to worry about the addictive properties of certain forms of technology. A mother of an 8-year-old girl was quoted as saying 'I think computers are a good thing but the Mega Drive is the worrying one. It's addictive. It's almost like a drug' (Sanger, et al., 1997). What is interesting is that a parent's anxieties about a relatively new form of technology, in this case a computer games console, are expressed in the same language used to describe the effects of television by a previous generation of parents. It is possible to argue that children's access to and confident use of new technologies and the pleasures that the children gain from television, videos and computer games do not accord with idealized views of childhood.

Concepts of childhood, children's actual lives and theories of learning

Cary Bazalgette and David Buckingham (1995) argue that throughout history, 'new' media including the theatre, the press, cinema and radio have been viewed with suspicion. When children are involved there is an on-going fear that their 'innocence' will be tainted and media such as television will 'rob' children of their childhood. One problem with such views is that the adults tend to conceptualize childhood in terms of the childhoods that they know most about — their own. This in turn means that adults' perceptions of the realities of childhood are likely to be at least 20 years out of date. Most parents in their thirties and forties, for example, will remember the spread of colour television, the introduction of three new terrestrial channels (BBC 2, and the independent Channels 4 and 5), the advent of general interest daytime schedules, all night programming and the introduction of cable and satellite television along with the increase of video recorders in homes. Adults who were born in the 1950s and 60s may recall the first time their family owned a television set and may remember that as a young child, they only had two channels to choose from. Many 5-year-olds today may have numerous terrestrial, cable and satellite television channels to choose from, some of which are dedicated to children's programmes (e.g. Fox Kids, Disney Channel, Cartoon Network). The changes in the availability and use of technology in the home have been accompanied by a shift in children's patterns of play, partly induced by an increase in fears for children's safety outside the home. The free, adventurous and unsupervised play outside the home that was a feature of many adults' own childhoods is no longer a 'normal' part of many young children's lived experience. For example, children living in the 1950s in England were likely to have far more physical freedom to roam with their peers and explore the environment than do their counterparts living in the late 1990s when, 'to be a child outside adult supervision, visible on city centre streets is to be out of place' (Connolly and Ennew, 1996; p. 133 quoted in James, et al., 1998). The change in the patterns and location of play has meant that children are more likely to be playing at home and possibly exploiting the entertainment potential of new technologies. An increase in the numbers and proportion of mothers in work has altered the pattern of parental involvement in many children's lives. In 1994, for example, approximately 20 per cent of children aged 5 to 10 were being left alone after school and in the holidays because both parents were at work (Sanger et al., 1997). Jack Sanger et al. went on to state that 'electronic childminders' (e.g. videos, television and games machines) were used to occupy these young children.

The fact that lived experiences of childhood change over time needs to be taken into account when considering the relevance of research done in the past to children of today. Writing and research framed within a particular conceptualization of childhood cannot automatically be applied to children located in different temporal, cultural, political, social and geographical contexts.

Currently, parents are increasingly concerned about the 'protection' of young children whilst, paradoxically, feeling a loss of control over aspects of their children's lives. On the one hand, children at home may be safe from traffic and strangers, but if playing with their computer games, surfing the internet or watching television and videos, parents worry about the images and information transmitted. Postman described television as 'a total disclosure medium' which diminishes parents' control over what their child is exposed to (Postman, 1984). In March 1998, at the Second World Summit on Television for Children, a keynote speech delivered by the Hon. Edward Markey clarified how, in the United States of America, every television set manufactured must now have a 'V' chip built into it which enables parents to block out 'unsuitable' television programmes even when parents are not physically present to monitor and control their children's viewing. Reportedly, the introduction of the idea was followed by four years of fierce debate in the House of Representatives and in the media. At the summit, one of the delegates suggested that the use of the V chip was an example of 'doing to children what we would not do to adults' in that it was a form of censoring television and raised questions about who decided what was deemed 'appropriate' viewing for children. Comments such as these highlight how attitudes towards television in relation to children cannot be dissociated from conceptions of children and childhood, which draw on the disciplines of sociology and developmental psychology.

Conceptions of childhood are myriad and complex (see Aries, 1962; Coveney, 1957; James, et al., 1998; Pollock, 1983) but there is only space here to look briefly at two opposing views to provide an outline of how models of childhood can impact on views about children and television. One view is that children are inherently evil and the only way of maintaining the existing social structure is to ensure that children's natural propensity for evil is controlled and curtailed. Within this framework, parents have the 'right' to control children's lives whilst children are seen as powerless and without rights. Although this view of children was first articulated in the seventeenth century (Aries, 1962), it still influences contemporary responses to and relationships with children. I would argue that within this framework, anxieties about children seeing violence or other forms of anti-social behaviour on television, videos and computer games rests on the fear that such viewing experiences may result in 'disinhibition'. Children will choose to ignore socially constructed attitudes towards such behaviour and the resulting lack of inhibitions will result in children reverting to their 'natural' state, which will involve anti-social behaviour. Research which focuses on ways in which television may encourage 'bad' or 'good' behaviour are possibly influenced by the view of the child as potentially anti-social. Berkowitz's research findings (1965) could map onto this particular model.

Alternatively, children may be perceived as 'innocent', with rights as people but in need of protection from the evils in society. This romantic vision of children which gained currency following Rousseau's writings in the eighteenth century is still evident today in that parents may feel they have a responsibility for protecting their children from society in order to maintain their 'innocence' and 'childhood'. Although this may also result in parents censoring or controlling children's viewing the intention is not to protect children from themselves but rather to protect them from outside influences and poor examples which they may imitate and in so doing lose their 'innocence'. Research which focuses on the ways in which television may 'serve as an imitative source of behaviour' (Bandura et al., 1963, p. 3) owes more to the view of the innocent child, although it is also interpreted through reference to behavioural learning theories.

A major point to bear in mind when considering both the adults' attitudes to children watching television and the research findings, is the need to be aware of the underlying philosophies and the context. Consequently, analysis of the issues is difficult and complex and does not lead to clear answers. For example, as James, Jenks and Prout highlight, in the current context the need to protect children may not be compatible with the concept of children's right to freedom (James et al., 1998, p. 14) and it would seem that it was this dilemma that the aforementioned delegate raised at the Second World Summit on Television.

As suggested earlier, theories about how children learn are intertwined with concepts of 'the child', which in turn may influence adults' attitudes about the value of television in children's lives. Behaviourists view the child as passively reacting to stimuli and the reinforcements provided by the environment or other people. Alternatively, children may be seen as progressing through a series of developmental stages in which they move from concrete to abstract levels of thinking with society and other people playing a limited role in children's 'natural' cognitive growth. Another model, which stems from the work of Vygotsky and Bruner, acknowledges that the child is located within a social and cultural context and emphasizes the important role played by 'significant others' in 'scaffolding' children's experiences in the social construction of knowledge. The role of adults in facilitating children's learning is different for each of these models and, in terms of children's viewing televisual texts, each of these models has a different role for adults. In the case of the behaviourist mode it could be that adults would need to ensure that they reinforced behaviour deemed to be 'good', either by ensuring children watched programmes in which people behaved 'appropriately', or were punished for 'inappropriate' behaviour or, if watching with the child, ensuring that the child is left in no doubt about the desirability of what is portrayed. In the case of social constructivists it may be more a case of adults helping children to interpret and understand what they are seeing, through discussion and the negotiation of meanings. This brings us on to a consideration of what interpreting television involves and how this relates to concepts of literacy.

Concepts of literacy and theories of literacy development

> Politically, literacy is the term being used but where is the speaking and listening? [Primary teacher, TSW, p. 2]

There are various models of 'literacy'. It could be conceived of as simply reading and writing. Gunther Kress in his book *Before Writing: Rethinking the Paths to Literacy* is very clear that he uses the term literacy 'only for the mode of *lettered representation*, and for the products which result, which are fashioned in its use' (original emphasis) (Kress, 1997, p. 116). In so doing he makes a clear distinction between writing and print and spoken language and other modes of communication and representation.

Margaret Meek, for whom 'literacy is about language', places somewhat more emphasis on speech, arguing that since reading and writing are surrounded by and rooted in spoken language it is important to remember that literacy is more than merely reading and writing (Meek, 1991, pp. 13–17). Meek and others, such as the teacher quoted above, would argue that speaking and listening cannot be excluded from considerations of literacy. The National Curriculum for English includes Programmes of Study for reading, writing and speaking and the National Literacy Framework for Teaching mentions the importance of children's experiences of talk:

> Good oral work enhances pupils' understanding of language in both oral and written forms and of the way language can be used to communicate. It is also an important part of the process through which pupils read and compose texts.
> (DfEE National Literacy Strategy: Framework for Teaching, (1998) p. 3)

Muriel Robinson (*Children Reading Print and Television*, 1997) uses the term 'literacy' to refer exclusively to print literacy rather than encompassing other forms of literacy such as television literacy or computer literacy. For the purposes of her research, 'reading' was defined as 'the interpretation of televisual and print messages' in order to emphasize her view that the interpretation of both printed texts and televisual texts are both active processes (Robinson, 1997, p. 13).

My definition of literacy includes not only the reading and writing of written or printed texts but also the various forms of children's oral storytelling, in acknowledgment of the fact that young children's literacy is supported in the early years by talking, listening, reading and writing.

If literacy is interpreted to include reading, writing and storytelling, then assessing children's literacy development involves more than simply counting the number of books a child reads. Children's development as readers, writers, storytellers, listeners and speakers is supported and stimulated by 'literary' activities other than reading written texts and this book explores how children's experiences of televisual texts support this development. Research by Wells has led him to suggest that, although children's literacy development is advantaged by growing up in 'literate' homes where reading and writing are seen to be an integral and meaningful part of everyday life, it is the sharing of stories that is the most influential factor (Wells, 1987). Wells also postulated that stories are not only important for the development of literacy skills, but have an even more fundamental role to play in children's learning generally. 'Storying', which Wells defines as the construction of stories in the mind, is a key activity in children's search for, and creation of, meaning. Margaret Meek (1991) has stated that in order to understand the relationship between storytelling and literacy it is necessary to acknowledge how narrative enables us to structure our world and experiences and deepen our understandings.

It is misleading to think that narratives and imagined stories are synonymous, since to do so implies that narrative discourse is located in the world of fiction. Narrative is a feature of a wide range of discourses. Both children and adults tell stories as part of every-day life and these stories may be products of the imagination or may be based on truth and real events. Narrative, if defined as the sequencing of events, can be seen to encompass fairy tales, myths, legends, and explanations about every-day occurrences, personal life stories, history and the explanation of scientific happenings (Meek, 1991, p. 105). What is the place of television and videos in the development of understanding of narrative? Meek has likened television to books in that children are introduced to the world through the images and sounds on television. Before the advent of television, children were introduced to objects, living creatures and events that were sometimes a familiar part of their lives and sometimes beyond their personal experiences. Many books still play this role: books about farm animals introduce children living in cities to animals they may never have seen and adults may encourage the children to ask questions, perhaps by initially modelling the questions themselves (e.g. Where is the lamb's mummy? What will the piglet grow up to be? Why did she do that?).

Television is the modern child's *Orbus Pictus*, it brings pictures of the entire world into almost every home. It stimulates children's curiosity about every possible

event, creature and object that can be presented as a *moving* image while, at the
same time, naming what is happening to them.
(Meek, 1991, p. 104)

With the advances in technology referred to earlier, it is possible to state that
television and videos provide numerous opportunities to experience and reflect on a
wide range of narratives. There are those that argue that televisual texts may be a
particularly valuable mode of representing certain meanings. Eisner, for example,
has argued that the value of videos, film and television ought not to be overlooked:

> The senses provide the material for the creation of consciousness, and we, in turn,
> use the content of consciousness and the sensory potential of various materials to
> mediate, transform, and transport our consciousness into worlds beyond ourselves.
> In other words, forms of representations allow us both to create and enhance our
> private life and to give it a public presence. By making it public, we can share that
> life with others. . . . Poetry is used as a language to generate images and other
> forms of meaning through the referents that the language implies and the cadences
> poetic forms display. Film and video exploit vision, text and music to create
> meanings *that no single form of representation could make possible.*
> (Eisner, 1996, pp. 17–18, my emphasis)

Eisner's views are also important if we are to consider the complementary ways in
which written texts and televisual texts may operate in deepening children's understanding of specific texts and developing their literacy, which is a recurring theme
throughout this book (see Chapters 2, 4, 5 and 6).

Models of learning and literacy formulated by policy makers may be very
different from those of parents and teachers, and within each of these groups there
is likely to be a range of views. One reason for this heterogeneity is that models
of literacy connect with theories of cognition, teaching and learning, childhood and
philosophical and political stances about the role of education and schooling. All
of these factors are shaped by prevailing cultural and social influences. Reading a
written text may be conceived of as 'decoding' the meaning which resides in the
text, unchanging and unchanged for all readers. Alternatively, reading could be
seen to involve the creation of meanings which will be unique to each reader as the
interpretation of the marks on the page are shaped by personal life experiences,
cultural and social contexts, expectations the reader brings to the text (some of which
will be based on out-of-text cues such as the type of paper being used or the layout
of the printed words) and the reader's experiences of other texts. The latter model
of reading involves a move away from framing reading merely in terms of the
application of a set of skills or strategies to be learnt (e.g. phonological awareness)
and adds more nebulous but important capabilities (e.g. recognition of intertextuality,
openness to different interpretations, recognition of own response and possible
reasons for this). Furthermore, the child is seen to be an active participant in the
creation of shared meanings and is enabled rather than prevented from negotiating
these meanings within their cultural context.

The model of the learner, as active and involved in the negotiation of meaning,
maps onto Bruner's view of learning as a 'communal activity, a sharing of the

culture' (Bruner, 1986, p. 127) and also onto the theories of Vygotsky, who argued that learning is most effective when a more experienced co-learner works collaboratively with the learner (Vygotsky, 1962). One consequence of such an approach to learning and teaching is that 'knowledge' is seen to be an organic, dynamic construct, constantly changing and open to review and renegotiation. Arguably, societies at different points in their history are able to tolerate such uncertainty and this is what prevents stagnation. Paulo Freire has argued that 'banking education' views learners as 'receptacles to be filled by the teacher' (Freire, 1972, p. 45) whereas 'problem-posing education' acknowledges people as:

> . . . beings in the process of *becoming* — as unfinished, uncompleted beings in and with a likewise unfinished reality . . . The unfinished character of men and the transformational character of reality necessitates that education be an on-going activity. (Freire, 1972, p. 57)

As we move into the twenty-first century, during a period of rapid technological and social change, it would seem that Freire's words are particularly apposite. When one reflects on what is happening in the field of literacy education it would appear that the potential to develop creative, critical thinking is in danger of being stifled. Henrietta Dombey criticized the current Literacy Framework (DfEE, 1998) on the grounds that:

> Texts are to be treated as geological sites from which words and phrases must be quarried in a laborious process. The emphasis is all on drawing the children's attention to the devices by which writers achieve their effects, rather than ensuring that those effects are achieved, much less on taking any account of reader response theory by recognizing the unique nature of each reader's response to the text. (Dombey, 1998, p. 39)

The lack of opportunities to engage with texts at a personally meaningful level may result in children who are walking Treasuries of Children's Literature, being familiar with a wide range of 'rich and varied' texts, with little opportunity to have 'lost' themselves in any of them. Similarly, is there more to learning to write than the development of the ability to produce written texts which are 'accurate, legible and set out in an appropriate way' (DfEE, 1998, p. 5)? What of the author's message and the diverse reasons for writing? Even the development of young children's speaking and listening skills is not straightforward, as Wells (1987) has shown. Is it about learning the language and rules of the classroom, or is it about developing children's ability to talk in different registers, to ask questions and a means by which children can make sense of their own and others' experiences? Is it simply a precursor or an on-going requirement for effective reading and writing development?

The polysemic nature of texts, the active role of the reader and the community have been recognized by a wide range of practitioners and theorists, including Bruner (1986), Meek (1988) and Iser (1974), and the arguments need not be rehearsed here (see Robinson, 1997 for useful discussion of the issues). However, the notion that the reader of a written text is involved in an active process and that the 'meaning' is not a simple construct but one that needs to be created by the reader, may have important implications for thinking about young children viewing televisual texts. If it is assumed that the 'message' of a televisual text can be accessed by applying one's understanding of the forms, codes and devices used by the medium, then it is possible to argue that media literacy is essential because children need to learn how to 'read' an important medium. Observations of young children and discussions with parents would suggest that watching television is a far from passive process and children are actively engaged in the search for meaning. The 'meaning' is not simply transmitted, in other words the visual images and soundtracks of television programmes, videos and films do not provide a neatly parcelled meaning which the viewer, in this case the young child, simply has to register. Televisual texts may be seen to be similar to written texts in that:

> The television text is, like all texts, the site of a struggle for meaning. The structure
> of the text typically tries to limit its meanings to ones that promote the dominant
> ideology but the polysemy sets up forces that oppose this control.
> (Fiske, 1987, p. 93)

Fiske's thesis is that television is essentially polysemic and unstable and suggests that there is no simple, 'right' way of decoding the text. As with written texts, where meaning is not arrived at merely through 'decoding' the black squiggles, but rather through an active process which involves the individual reader, the community and the text itself, drawing meaning from televisual texts also does not depend upon such 'decoding'. The young reader of a televisual text will utilize her growing under-standing of the signs and codes of television to create meaning, but the meanings of screen texts have to be negotiated and are a fusion of the producer's, director's and screenwriter's intentions and the child's past experiences. These past experiences include the child's entire life experiences, not least her previous experiences of watch-ing television, videos and of reading written texts and possibly writing texts. Although there are 'preferred' meanings inherent in every text, many of which coincide with or 'promote the dominant ideology', the polysemic nature of televisual texts ensure that there are 'alternative ways of seeing' (Fiske and Hartley, 1978, p. 18).

If there are parallels between the reading of written and televisual texts it would seem that television and videos may have a rather more positive role to play in children's literacy development than has hitherto been generally acknowledged (Fiske and Hartley, 1978, p. 11) and the extent to which this is true is explored in the latter part of the book.

The patterns of children's television viewing and reading

It is far from widely accepted that television and video viewing may have a positive effect on children's literacy development. The arguments and debates regarding the impact of television on children's academic achievement and cognitive development, and also those exploring children's choices of activities during 'free time', need to be briefly outlined here in order to provide a context for the research. It is common knowledge that children spend far too much time watching television and not enough time reading. Parents, teachers, educationists, development psychologists, writers, authors, politicians and journalists are amongst the groups of adults who agonize about the amount of television young children watch. When asking parents to fill in questionnaires that included a question about the frequency with which children watch television and videos it was not uncommon for parents to hand the completed questionnaire back to me with a slightly apologetic smile and comments such as 'I'm afraid they watch an awful lot of television'. When talking to teachers about the focus for my research, many made unsolicited comments along the lines that, in their view, the children in their class watched 'far too much television' (teachers' views are discussed in more depth in Chapter 2). Articles in newspapers ensure that the topic is regularly revisited. In May 1998, for example, a newspaper article presented 'doing homework' and 'watching television' as mutually antagonistic with the implication that watching television is 'bad' whilst doing homework is 'good' for children's achievement at school:

> Homework is another concern for the government. The fact that 70 per cent of children in their last year of primary school do less than half an hour's homework but watch well over two hours of television a night has to be a concern for parents, especially when there is research evidence that the pupils who do most homework are those that do best at school.
> (Jim Sweetman, *Guardian Education*, 19 May 1998)

No clear references were provided for the research relating to homework but a table created from the DfEE Paper, *Excellence in Schools* was used to highlight the point that children watch too much television and do too little homework. The table was entitled 'Homework vs telly: How long do children spend doing homework and watching TV in their last year in primary school?' As with all statistics and graphs, the DfEE's findings can be interpreted in a number of ways. Using the same data and graph a more positive picture could be presented: that approximately half of the children in their last year at primary school watch two hours or less of television and almost half (42 per cent) of Year 6 children spend up to an hour on homework every night. Chapters 2 and 3 look in more depth at teachers', and parents' perceptions about the amount of television young children watch.

Recent research findings from a study carried out by the National Foundation for Educational Research (NFER) would tend to challenge two commonly held views. Firstly, that television has a negative effect on children's reading and, secondly, that those children who do not watch any television are better readers or are more likely to read than their peers who do watch television. Martin Large powerfully expressed these views in his book, *Who's Bringing Them Up? Television and Child Development: How to Break the TV Habit* (1990). In the book he provides an account of his visit to a class of 8-year-olds and recalled how the teacher pointed out several children who were described as 'lazy readers'. These were children who could read but were not interested in reading or 'found it difficult to get inside what they were reading'. The teacher linked this 'laziness' with the children's tendency to watch television at home. These children were contrasted with children in the class who did not watch television and who, the teacher claimed, not only read regularly at home but also did very well at school. In 1995 the NFER carried out a survey of approximately 5,000 children in Year 3 and the findings challenge the idea that no television results in better readers (Brooks et al., 1997). The NFER research findings certainly showed that children who read 'most days' for fun achieved higher reading test scores than children who 'never' read for fun but, interestingly, children who 'never' watched television or videos had one of the lowest test scores whilst children who watched television and videos 'some days' achieved the same test scores as those who read for fun on most days.

A fair amount of research has been carried out in a number of different countries which has focused on the relationship between children's television viewing habits and their interest in reading and achievement at school (e.g. Furu, 1977; Himmelweit et al., 1958; Hincks and Baldwin, 1988; Murray and Kippax, 1978; Schramm et al., 1961; Shastri and Mohite, 1997; Singer and Singer, 1983). In the mid 1980s, research with more than two million 9, 13 and 17-year-olds in the United States of America found that in the majority of samples, children who watched two to three hours of television a day achieved higher reading scores than those who watched less television (Neuman, 1986) More recently, research conducted in India into the effects of heavy, moderate and light viewing of television on the academic and cognitive achievement of 727 6 to 10-year-olds, as measured by a battery of tests, led the researchers to conclude that 'mean scores were not significantly different for the three groups on the measures of academic performance (except for oral reading) and selected cognitive skills'. Closer analysis of their findings shows that, whilst there was a significant difference between the performance of 'heavy' and 'light' viewers with respect to the oral reading component of the Reading Analysis Test, there was no corresponding difference between the three categories of viewers with respect to the remaining two components of the Reading Analysis Test which were listening, comprehension and silent reading. The researchers explained their findings by arguing that with reading, since many of the children did their homework while watching TV, heavy viewers were less likely to be able to practise oral reading and therefore achieved lowers scores than their peers who watched less television (Shastri and Mohite, 1997).

Moving away from an analysis of children's performance in reading and considering their enjoyment of reading, Neuman found that there was no discernible relationship between television viewing habits and either the children's reading skills or their enjoyment of reading. Interestingly, amongst the youngest children involved in the research, the 9-year-olds, a positive correlation existed between the number of hours spent watching television and the number of hours spent reading. Murray and Kippax's research in Australia investigated the leisure reading patterns of children aged from 5 to 12 in communities with no television, those with access to one channel and those with access to two channels. Their findings at first appear to present a slightly different picture to that of Neuman, in that children with no access to television spent more time reading than those with access to two television channels. Closer examination of the findings, however, reveal that children in communities with access to two television channels read more books than the other two groups, whilst children with no television read the least number of books and the highest number of comics. This pattern had already been noted in the United States in the early 1960s (see for example Schramm et al., 1961). Research cited by Shastri and Mohite includes that of Khurana et al. (1987), Manrow, (1990) and Abrol et al. (1991) all of which suggests that in India children spend most of their time playing and studying. Shastri and Mohite (1997) went on to state that television does not substitute for other activities but becomes one of the many stimulating activities that a child engages in.

Even a brief trawl through the relevant research findings would suggest that the view that watching television has superseded reading by children as a leisure-time activity is questionable. It would be more valid to assert that research has not shown television to have a universally negative effect on young children's literacy development. Instead, the findings suggest that children's literacy development is influenced by the interaction of a diverse range of factors which includes social class, the child's intellectual abilities, the parenting styles, number of consumer durables in the home, the location of the child's school, the age of child, the number of books in the home and the variety and range of children's out-of school activities and television viewing habits. With the interaction of such a wide range of variables it seems unlikely that one particular factor could be identified as being the main influence on a child's literacy development.

An additional problem with attempting to analyse the relationship between children's viewing and reading habits is that causation is unclear. Are the low reading attainments of some of the children in the research samples referred to above caused by those children choosing to watch television rather than read and in so doing not having the same opportunities to develop their reading as those children who choose to read more often? Another possible explanation is that children experiencing difficulties with reading enjoyed reading less and were less likely to read for pleasure and more likely to turn to other easily accessible forms of entertainment such as television. The research of Brooks et al. (1998, p. 30) found that, amongst 8-year-old children, those with a positive attitude towards reading had significantly higher reading scores than those with negative attitudes towards reading. Furthermore, when the average reading scores of children were linked with the frequency with which they chose to read books outside school, it was very apparent that the group of children who 'never' read books for fun had the lowest average reading score.

It is not only the quantity of television watched that causes concern but also the notion that television viewing compares very unfavourably to reading in intellectual terms. Trelease argued that whilst reading requires the active use of a range of skills, television viewing does not require a similar degree of mental activity (Trelease, 1984). Winn stated that reading and television are very different in that reading, unlike viewing television, requires 'complex mental manipulations' (Winn, 1985, p. 60), and as a consequence, reading requires the creation of mental images, whereas television images

> ... do not go through a complex symbolic transformation. The mind does not have
> to decode and manipulate during the television experience.
> (Winn, 1985, p. 59)

Large (1990) expressed the view that television viewing does not facilitate the development of concentration:

> Reading necessitates concentration, focusing, thought, imagination and the ability
> to have 'inner vision'. Television requires little concentration, de-focuses the mind,
> lames the capacity for visualization by the substitution of electronically produced
> images and encourages passivity.
> (Large, 1990, p. 75)

Concerns are also expressed about the fact that many young children watch television alone or without an adult. Young children are likely to experience books in the presence of an adult who may talk to the child about the story or the reading process itself. Large has argued that television for the very young is often an 'anti-social' experience characterized by little conversation and that television 'gives answers all the time' but that children learn by asking questions. (Large, op cit. p. 76). Many parents and teachers, however, would not agree that television does not encourage the asking of questions and are aware of the importance of watching television with young children (see Chapters 2 and 3).

It is also possible to look afresh at what has been written about written texts and consider the extent to which the ideas might also apply to televisual texts. Gregory, for example, has argued that for emergent bilinguals the clearest words are often those in simple storybooks since spoken words are ephemeral as they

> ... disappear suddenly from the mouth of the speaker and return transformed by a
> different context while the text of a book remains constant and can be listened to
> over and over again until it becomes the child's own. In this way we might say a
> dialogue takes place between the child and the text.
> (Gregory, 1996, p. 126)

In view of what has been written earlier in this chapter about the way in which young children are able to revisit televisual texts on video, could it not be argued that both storybooks and videos could support emergent bilinguals' learning? Similarly, it has been argued that it is through discussion that children gain an understanding of a text (e.g. Meek, 1988, 1991) which raises the question whether or not this could also be true for videos and television programmes.

Methodology

This introduction must close with a brief note about the methodology employed. Rather than attempting to provide a quantitative analysis of the positive and negative effects of television and videos on children's literacy development, the research was aimed at providing a qualitative analysis. Subsequent chapters explore issues such as whether watching television discourages children reading; why some children prefer to watch television than read books; how children's writing development may be influenced by television and videos, the impact of gender and children's, parents' and teachers' views on the positive and negative aspects of television and videos.

I surveyed children and parents through questionnaires (Appendices A and B) and conducted semi-structured interviews with children (aged 4 to 7), teachers and parents in order to gain a more in-depth understanding of their ideas and views. I observed young children watching television and reading and, for Chapters 4 and 5, adopted a case study approach. Where possible I attempted to interview and survey parents of children I had interviewed in order to gain another perspective, but this was not always possible. Children, parents and teachers in six schools were involved in the study, three of which were inner urban schools, two were suburban schools and the sixth school was a rural school. One of the inner city schools had a very high proportion of emergent bilinguals, as did one of the suburban schools. Three of the schools catered for children from all social classes. The interviews were audio-taped and transcribed and the interviewees' comments have been utilized throughout the book. As stated early in the introduction, all research involving children is framed by a particular conceptualization of childhood. In this case children have been seen to be active participants in a shared but essentially adult-centred society. Emphasis has been placed on the 'children's voices' in an effort to gain insight into children's views about adults. In sociological terms the children have been researched as a 'minority group' (James et al., 1998).

The majority of the book focuses on children, children's perceptions of adults' views, children's own views, analysis of ways in which children respond to various texts and observations on children's developing literacy. We begin, however, with a necessary look at teachers and schools.

Chapter 2

Teachers and Schools

The previous chapter examined what is 'commonly' known about the deleterious effects of children watching television. This chapter moves into the school setting and examines teacher's views and ideas about the value and use of television programmes in terms of children's literacy development. This book is firmly rooted in 'the real world' in that it looks at what teachers, parents and children have to say about the relationship between watching television and videos and children's literacy development.

Teachers' use of television and videos in the school setting

It was clear that the teachers involved in the study held a range of views about the value of watching television and videos in school in relation to supporting children's literacy development. Some teachers held very positive views:

> The children love *Look and Read*. After the programme they can tell me all sorts of details and notice things I miss. The programme is also really good because it's led to discussions about things like stereotyping. There's a character called Dr. and we talked about whether they thought that it was a man or a woman and the children really became involved and listened to each other, and for this class that *is* something!
> (Year 3 teacher)

Having observed the children's animated response to the programme and heard their groans of disappointment as the week's episode came to yet another cliff-hanging conclusion, the teacher's enthusiasm appeared to be justifiable.

A very experienced early years teacher who felt that certain elements of *Words and Pictures* were valuable for her nursery class talked in more depth about her views:

> *Teacher*: I only use the stories [from *Words and Pictures*] because I think that some of the material is a little too, it's not suitable in the nursery.
> *NB*: Why *stories* in particular?
> *Teacher*: So they can see a story presented in a different way, told by a different person, that they can relate to, they can recognize that they have had that story before and they can go and find it in the book box for

themselves, um, sometimes children are more receptive to television I think, um, what else? You know, I might be using it because I'm focusing on a particular letter, or there's something that I want to draw out of the story, or maybe I don't have that book.

NB: Do children want to read the book after seeing video?

Teacher: Yes, definitely . . .

[. . .]

NB: You keep coming back to narrative, is that what you think television and videos really support?

Teacher: Yeah, sequencing events.

[TSX, p. 4]

Teachers working with emergent bilinguals felt that television and videos were particularly useful for a specific reason:

I use them because I think for second language children the visual stimulus is very important and from that stimulus you can develop a range of skills . . . I found them most useful in conjunction with a book so my book focus entails reading from the book and the additional use of the video.
[Primary teacher, TSV, p. 1]

Another teacher working in a different school echoed this teacher's views:

Yes, watching TV and videos definitely helps children's literacy. It gives them more access to the text, particularly for children in the lower stages of EAL. They get more out of the video than the book. They can follow the plot and it's easier to discuss characters and relationships. Some children read the book, seeing the video gives them added interest in books, I'm not sure if it helped with their reading — probably.
[Primary teacher, TSW, p. 1]

Not all teachers I talked to were convinced about the value of using televisual texts:

I think children would do better to read books. Some children don't have any books at home but they all have a television, maybe more than one! They watch enough television at home; school should be a TV-free zone.
(Year 1 teacher)

Other teachers talked about both the benefits and disadvantages:

I think they *can* be valuable but sometimes used as 'Thank God someone else will run the show and I'll sit back'. They widen the children's knowledge with words *and* images, I *could* do that but it links — it makes school fun. The problem is that videos can very soon become out of date. I think they should be used where appropriate rather than for the sake of it.
[Primary headteacher, TSY, p. 3]

Paul Kelley's research into the use of schools' television carried out on behalf of the Independent Television Commission (Kelley, 1998) highlighted the fact that primary teachers felt that certain television programmes such as *Words and Pictures*, *Storytime* and *Look and Read* were particularly useful in developing various aspects of children's literacy:

> *Look and Read* . . . reinforces phonics in a fun way . . . Key Stage 1 teachers found television programmes useful for developing listening skills . . . Programmes such as *Words and Pictures* and *Storytime*, for example, give an excellent reinforcement to literacy.
> (Kelley, 1998, p. 59)

Some of the teachers I spoke to made it clear that they tailored their use of schools' television programmes in order to suit the needs of their class. Most teachers pre-recorded the programmes and this provided a high degree of flexibility. This flexibility was important, not only because of the difficulties teachers experienced in gaining access to the television and video in school, but also because of the way some of the teachers used the videos. Teachers of younger children stressed the importance of discussing what was seen:

> *Teacher* . . . you have to be very selective with younger children and with younger children you have to break it down into manageable chunks. And quite often when the children are watching I'll keep stopping the tape and I'll point things out to them . . .
> [Nursery teacher TSX, p. 3]

It is interesting to note that this practice is not confined to the early years. Jack Sanger et al. (1997) emphasized how teachers in middle schools stopped the video to allow time for discussion and Paul Kelley (1998) reported that secondary teachers stated that they found that the 'best' way of using educational television was to pause the video at appropriate points and initiate discussions about what the video was saying. Why teachers think it necessary to stop and discuss pertinent points at regular intervals rather than wait until the end of the programme may be related to what they think is happening inside children's heads as they watch. The early years teacher quoted above felt that this regular intervention was necessary in order to encourage the children to think about what they see on the screen:

> Well, I've asked the class at the end of *Words and Pictures*, what did you like about the programme, what did you *see* in the programme? In this school, we used to do this in reception a lot. They hadn't a clue. They couldn't remember what they'd seen which suggested to me that they are quite used to watching television and it must be hitting the back of the brain somewhere you know, but there's no recall.
> [TSX, p. 3]

Alternatively, teachers may believe that the transient nature of television images does not allow children to reflect on or ask questions about things they find new and challenging:

The fleeting and ephemeral quality of television image has been adduced as an explanation for the difficulties experienced by viewers in fully comprehending messages that are intellectually or artistically demanding.
(*Communication Research Trends*, 1985, quoted in Sanger et al., 1997, p. 36)

Unlike a book, in which a passage can be read and reread, the nature, the structure and pace of television programmes do not permit this 'revisiting' of the televisual text. Watching videos, however, allows the viewer to pause, fast forward and rewind and in so doing facilitates the revisiting of the televisual text.

At home, if watching with an adult or older child, young children are likely to ask numerous questions and comment on what they see (see Chapters 5 and 6). Young children in school have to learn to watch television in a different way, they have to learn to behave as a member of an 'audience' and calling out, interrupting and asking questions during the programme is discouraged (Davies, 1989, Sanger et al., 1997). Teachers who believe that children's understanding is enhanced through discussion are likely to provide opportunities for this by stopping the video and talking about what has been seen. This practice provides the opportunity for the teacher to ask questions and check the children's understanding and also for what Gordon Wells describes as 'collaborative, exploratory talk'. The latter involves young children asking their own questions and all participants in the conversation, both adults and children, sharing their ideas rather than merely children searching for the 'right' answer the teacher is looking for (Wells, 1987, p. 92).

In line with the teachers involved in Paul Kelley's study (1998), many of the teachers I spoke to recognized the importance of employing a diverse range of teaching methods in order to cater for different children's learning styles and reported that they frequently used televisual texts and written texts in tandem. A teacher of older children who was very experienced in the use of televisual texts talked about how she combined the use of books and television programmes or videos:

NB: Is it always in that order? Do you always read the book first?
Teacher: Done it both ways. I'm using at the present moment a book called *One Last Lie* and the chapters are quite short — there are five chapters, quite short. It was written by the chap that did *Grange Hill* so again the children already appreciate the kind of style because they have seen it on television . . . Now I didn't know about the video at first, so I was reading the book to them, it's very well illustrated with all kinds of fonts, um, and cartoon character type illustrations and then I found there was a video, but the video I didn't start using until I got to Chapter 3 so the children already had preconceived ideas of their own about the characters so this has set up another type of discussion. It's a bit like the book of the film! So it's set up another sort of discussion but it's very fruitful because if you're looking at characterizations, changes in plot that indicate changes in character, you've got two strands to pull on. You can use the text of the book and you can also use the visual interpretation . . . I've also done it with *The Secret Garden*. Again the characters in that story change quite a lot and it was very good to *see* facial expressions and so on as well as reading the book because for our

> children the nuances of English language are not very well established and it's something you have to work on.
>
> *NB*: It's really interesting you saying this because these are all the sorts of things I've been saying about how videos can help 4 and 5 and 6 year-olds . . .
>
> *Teacher*: I can't see why it wouldn't be true for younger children too.
>
> [Primary teacher, TSV, pp. 2–3]

The teacher went on to talk about how watching videos supported the children's writing development:

> *Teacher*: You've got to broaden children's experiences. Show them different kinds of people, different ways of life which our children don't actually experience. Again, videos can do this, different settings for example . . . If you're thinking about when they're going to write later on and you're talking about settings, *this* is the setting they know but you can draw upon what they've seen elsewhere on video, the setting of the country-side, of the snow, a blizzard. So you've given them a wider experience that they can draw and use within their own context within their own writing. Otherwise, as we were saying before, you're making assumptions and say we start talking about blizzards and snow-covered hillsides they'll think 'So what?' they've never seen one before but at least in that setting for that story they've seen it so they've got a visual picture and they've got more to draw on.
>
> [Primary teacher, TSV, p. 3]

This teacher is clear that using both written and televisual texts can develop children's understanding of author's style, characterization, pivotal points in the plot, inter-pretation of visual and written texts, in addition to expanding children's vicarious experiences through the use of a range of forms of texts.

An early years teacher talked about how, sometimes, video versions of popular books were an improvement on the written text:

> I think Jane Hissey, her sort of thing. Actually they make better videos I think than the books are. I find the books a bit static it's just like a whole load of cuddly toys dumped on the page and the videos are better . . . even more enjoyable.
>
> [Nursery teacher, TSX, p. 4]

This is an important consideration for teachers who are aiming to provide young children with enjoyable experiences of stories in order to then provide a springboard into literacy.

Teachers' views of the parents' stance on use of TV in school

Whilst it is clear that many teachers feel confident about the educational value of using schools' television in the classroom it was interesting to ask what they thought parents' views were. One nursery teacher felt that provided parents were kept informed then there was likely to be little opposition:

> I think they feel OK about it. You give them a newsletter and tell them what you're doing each half term *and* you will be watching the television to reinforce this particular aspect of their learning. I don't think that's a problem generally. If you're talking about the Literacy Hour then we're still educating the parents about what the Literacy Hour actually is, so who knows?
> [TSX, p. 4]

A teacher in a primary school felt the opposite:

> Parents probably don't approve of teachers using TV. The children come to school to learn. A whole new education of parents would be needed to show how TV can assist children's learning.
> [Primary teacher, TSW, p. 5]

I asked teachers whether they thought a video library would be a good idea as it could help raise the status of videos as an educational resource and provide a link between children's home and school experiences. All the teachers mentioned the prohibitive cost of such a venture, the logistical problems involved and the difficulties with videos not being returned. As one teacher put it, 'We have enough problems getting books back!' Theoretically however, all the I teachers spoke to felt that a video library could be beneficial:

> I suppose it might not be a bad idea. At least we could have videos for loan which had an educational purpose.
> [Primary headteacher, TSY, p. 4]

This headteacher felt that a school video library should contain art and craft videos, children's drama and other 'children's' films (e.g. *Babe*) with the proviso that these films were 'related to books that are part of the curriculum', information films and videos in community languages, in addition to 'videos for parents such as *Learning to Read* or the *How to Help your Child* type'. This headteacher was definite that 'every video would have an educational purpose'.

An early years teacher's list of video categories for the library was similar to those above although no mention was made of videos for parents. This teacher was uncertain about whether Disney films and cartoons should be included as she felt some, such as *Pocahontas*, presented a 'distorted view'. This teacher also felt schools' programmes such as *Come Outside* and *Words and Pictures* could be included and also that it would be helpful for parents if the films were graded for different ages, 'So parents would know that *Old Bear*, for example, would be suitable for the nursery' [Teacher, TSX, p. 5].

Another teacher was in favour of the idea of a video library but felt unable to suggest anything specific saying 'I don't know enough about them' [TSW, p. 5].

Television and OFSTED

Not all teachers were confident that the advent of government initiatives such as the Literacy Hour provided a favourable context for the use of televisual texts and many teachers were uncertain about OFSTED's views regarding the use of television and videos in school. One of the headteachers I interviewed was in no doubt that OFSTED would approve of schools using TV and videos to support children's literacy development but other teachers were less certain. One teacher, for example, felt that OFSTED would not criticize the use of television and videos for developing literacy provided: 'They see it as an "extension" or "part of" what we do' [Primary teacher, TSW, p. 5]. The teachers in my study were not unique in feeling a degree of uncertainty about the DfEE's and OFSTED's position on the use of television. Paul Kelley has reported that many teachers believed that OFSTED felt that the use of television was a 'poor teaching method' but, as Paul Kelley points out in his report, an OFSTED report on the use of television highlighted the benefits of using the medium:

> . . . broadcasts provided a stimulus which most of the teachers used effectively to support and enrich the curriculum. The quality of work in 80 per cent of these lessons was satisfactory or better.
> (OFSTED, 1993, quoted in Kelley, 1998)

OFSTED and the education policy makers have not actively criticized the use of television and video but have also not shown a commitment to the use of medium. The National Curriculum for Initial Teacher Training, for example, which was first introduced in 1997–98, does not stipulate that student teachers must be taught effective ways of using television and videos to support children's literacy development. A number of student teachers I spoke to felt that, although they had been required to review educational broadcasts, they would have found it useful to have had some input on how to use these broadcasts, and possibly commercially produced videos, with the age phase they were planning to work with. *The National Literacy Strategy Framework for Teaching* (DfEE, 1998) does not explicitly mention the use of videos or television until Year 6, Term One, during which teachers should plan work which includes the opportunity to:

> compare and evaluate a novel or play in print and the film /TV version, e.g. the treatment of the plot and characters, the differences in the two forms, e.g. seeing the setting, in losing the narrator.
> (DfEE, 1998, p. 50)

The research findings of Paul Kelley led to three key recommendations from the Independent Television Commission, one of which was:

> . . . educational television needs **the clear support of national institutions** such as the DfEE, OFSTED and NCET. These institutions should consider ways of encouraging greater and more effective use of educational television. (Original emphasis).
> (Kelley, 1998, p. 61)

Although nursery and primary teachers may feel relatively comfortable about utilizing educational broadcasts produced by Channel 4 or the BBC, there is less evidence in schools of primary teachers using commercially produced videos and television programmes to support children's literacy. This may be attributable to teachers' lack of both the training in the use of televisual texts and of the supportive back up provided by the teachers' notes and students' worksheets that accompany schools' broadcasts. This cannot be the whole story because commercial television is widely used by teachers in secondary schools (Kelley, 1998, p. 35). Charitable institutions, such as Film Education, publish materials and run INSET for primary and secondary teachers in an effort to develop the use of commercial films in the schools. During the National Year of Reading, which began in the autumn of 1998, Film Education ran workshops for children on aspects such as comparing screen adaptations with the original texts, exploration of characters and film adaptations of Roald Dahl's books. Films used included *Matilda*, *A Little Princess*, *Babe*, *Hercules*, *The Wind in the Willows* and *The Witches*. But what do teachers think about children's TV experiences, the quantity and value? Could primary teachers' willingness or reluctance to use commercial videos and TV programmes be related to the teachers' views about young children's out-of-school experiences of television? The following section explores this issue.

Teachers' views about children's home-viewing experiences

When conducting the research many of the teachers in the schools I visited freely volunteered their opinions about children and television. The majority simply felt that children watched far too much television at home:

> So you're doing research on children and television? I can tell you immediately
> that I think children watch far too much television, full stop.
> [Key Stage 1 teacher, inner city school]

Other teachers emphasized that it was not merely the quantity that was worrying but also the type of programmes and videos the children watched and the passive way in which the children watched television:

> Children in this school watch a lot of television, cartoons . . . I don't know. I've
> seen it happen in other people's homes. I've seen the children just sit in front
> of the television and just sit and I don't know what they are getting out of it, just
> endless cartoons. I *don't* know what they are getting out of it. . . . They watch
> too much.
> [Nursery teacher, inner city school, TSX, p. 1]

A headteacher held similar opinions, but also made the point that she thought the children were not selective about what they watched:

They come in from school and it goes on and there doesn't seem to be any dis-
crimination. What I say to the children here is, look at the programme and decide
which you really want to watch and watch it and then turn it off . . . Once you
slump in a chair you become seduced, it's a very seductive medium.
[Head of large suburban primary school, TSY, p. 1]

Headteachers' views are very important because they have an impact on classroom
practice throughout the school, as this reception teacher made clear when asked
whether she used any television with her class:

I can't. The headteacher thinks they see enough television at home and says that
they don't need to see any more at school.
[Reception class teacher]

Other teachers commented on the unsuitability of the videos watched by many of
the children:

Watching videos like *Exterminator* and *Aliens* decreases children's sensitivities;
it comes too soon in their experiences. They are going straight into really horrific
situations so anything that is as bland perhaps as say that situation in *Carrie's War*
when they are followed down the path, if this was their initial experience of something scary then they might be frightened but they've seen far worse than that.
I mean it comes into their conversations, it comes into their writing and if they
watched something particular last night they'll come in talking about it. But then
I suppose you come back to normality don't you? Straight away the teacher says
something, 'Well you must have gone to bed really late last night, now this is early
morning maths, come on, number bonds!'
[Primary teacher, inner city school, TSV, p. 4]

A headteacher expressed her uncertainty about passing judgment on what children
watch at home:

Our children watch loads of videos. From what they say they're always watching
them! A lot of kids are watching Indian movies, it's a link into their culture, in
India everyone watches them, the whole family. I find this one a hard one because
we could say the same about *East Enders*, it's part of some children's culture so
they should be able to watch it but then, so, where does it stop?
[Headteacher, TSY, p. 3]

Teachers' main concerns are that children watch too much poor quality television and inappropriate videos and that the children are a passive and unselective
audience. Some children may indeed fit this profile but as later chapters will show,
most children are clear about what they enjoy and they may be very active in their
viewing. Many parents and children claim that there are rules regarding both the
amount and type of television children watch: which would indicate a degree of
selection.

Why do teachers have this very negative view of children's television and video viewing habits? To begin with, teachers may feel that television plays a larger part in children's lives than it actually does because they hear the children talking in school about what they have seen at home on television; observe younger children, especially boys, engaging in dramatic role play based on television programmes (see Chapter 7) and see the television and video related toys and other merchandise children bring to school. Recent research into children's viewing patterns, however, has highlighted that 5 to 9-year-olds take part in a wide range of activities outside school, including reading and sport and although much of their leisure time is spent watching television, this has to be fitted in around other activities (Chambers et al., 1998, p. 11).

It would be unwise to underestimate the role played by articles and editorials in both the popular press and in specialist papers aimed directly at teachers (e.g. *The Times Educational Supplement, Guardian Education*) in raising or confirming anxiety about children's viewing habits and the consequences. For example, the apparent decline in young children's listening skills, particularly the ability to listen selectively, has been linked to difficulties in learning to read (Palmer, *TES*, 18 April 1997). Sally Ward's research findings were outlined by Palmer in the *Times Educational Supplement* under the title 'Turned on and switched off' and illustrated with a large photograph of a toddler clutching a television remote control with the caption 'Babies exposed to continuous television may be losing their ability to listen, seriously damaging their ability to learn' (Palmer, 1997). All-day television is cited as the root cause of the decline in children's listening skills and Sally Ward is quoted as claiming that:

> When television's on all the time parents don't interact with their children — they don't do those daily rituals with familiar language for the child to join in . . . they don't use nursery rhymes and tickling rhymes and so on. When the parent does speak the child can't hear properly because of the background noise — they learn not to attend to language as a major source of meaning.
> (Palmer, *TES* 18 April 1997)

Sue Palmer explicitly stated that the research '*confirms* teachers' suspicions' (my emphasis) and some teachers did in fact refer to Sally Ward's research to support their argument that television viewing had a negative effect on children's learning and was to blame for young children's inattentiveness, incapacity to concentrate during story time and inability to listen to instructions.

Similarly, *The Guardian* carried an article entitled 'Everybody say "Uh-oh" ' with a large photograph of a small child watching at very short range a television screen showing one of the Teletubbies. The article opened with:

> Children are spending more and more time watching television; two thirds have a TV in their bedroom. But why, and what effect is it having? . . . Parents and educationalists are given to moaning about children and television: it stops them reading; there's too much sex and violence; the Teletubbies are mindless gibberish. But they are not used to having their complaints taken seriously. So they will be surprised to find their worries shared at the highest level.
> (Coward, 4 March 1998)

A cursory reading of articles such as these are unlikely to encourage many teachers to reflect on their negative assumptions about the perceived relationship between children's television viewing and their literacy development. More careful reading of the articles would unearth thought-provoking statements such as:

> Media researchers have known for some time that children have an active, discriminating relationship with television.
> (Coward, 1998)

and,

> The problem grows more serious as successive generations are reared in a television culture . . . In a recent study, she [Sally Ward] employed a simple intervention technique: asking parents to turn the TV off for 20 minutes a day and talk to their children.
> (Palmer, 1997)

Interestingly, few teachers who quoted Sally Ward's research mentioned that it was the lack of parent–child interaction that was the key factor rather than 'wall-to-wall' television. That children are watching television for extensive periods rather than interacting with parents and other significant adults is possibly symptomatic of social changes. Sally Ward attributes the decline in young children's selective listening skills to a 'breakdown in the culture of parenting'. In this context what this means is that increasingly parents do not seem to know that it is important to talk to, listen to and play with babies and very young children. In *The Independent* a few months later, Heather Welford's article on young children's aggressive tendencies outlined the case of a 3-year-old boy who was diagnosed as having 'autistic tendencies' and quoted Sally Ward as saying:

> It turned out that the little boy had been with nannies, more or less from birth, who cared for him physically, but never really spoke to him. His mother was told she should read to her son. She read him bits from the *Wall Street Journal* — she just didn't know how to choose the right books, or how to use them. With help, though, she managed to change.
> (*The Independent*, 24 September 1998)

As there is no mention of television in this article the emphasis remains firmly on the need to interact appropriately with young children. Focusing on the ill-effects of all-day television and the improvements which result from parents switching off the television for a mere 20 minutes a day and talking to their children possibly places the emphasis in the wrong place. Could it be that it is not the 'wall-to-wall television' which causes difficulties but rather the lack of interaction? Without television there is no guarantee parents will talk to their children and, as later chapters show, television itself can provide the stimulus for much discussion and interaction.

Attention grabbing by-lines and emotive images of small children sitting alone in front of television sets, combined with inadequately reported research findings, do little to prompt teachers to critically examine their own assumptions and suspicions or to challenge 'common-sense' views. 'Too much television' simply provides a relatively uncontentious explanation for a range of problems children and teachers are experiencing within the classroom and also locates the blame outside school and so exonerates schools, the curriculum and teachers.

It is also important to bear in mind that many comments made about children's viewing habits are culturally and socially 'loaded'. As with the parents involved in the research by Gantz and Masland (1986), who felt that *other* mothers were more likely than themselves to use television as a 'babysitter', many teachers who are also parents feel that it is *other* parents who do not regulate their children's use of television. A teacher felt strongly about this issue and volunteered this information:

> I've got two children aged 4 and 7. When we get home they have a drink and then, if there is something they want to watch they might do, but only for a short while and then they go and play outside in the garden or in their room. When they go to their friends' houses for tea they often get fed up because all their friends do is watch television as soon as they get in.

The circumstances and value systems of families vary tremendously and there may be a whole range of reasons why television is used in particular ways in different families. For example, a classroom assistant who was involved in home visits to parents noticed that it was mainly Hindi films that were on the video which raises the possibility that in these homes the television was turned on by the adults, particularly the mothers, many of whom are involved in the care of young families, possibly socially isolated and not fluent English speakers, and therefore, enjoy watching videos in a language they understand. Parents phoning to participate in a live debate on radio focusing on the merits of the *Teletubbies* made a variety of comments that revealed a wide range of attitudes. A number of parents talked of television as a means of 'calming down' their small children whilst another parent declared that his daughter was not allowed to watch any television and instead the family visited museums and went on walks in the country and as a result she was a good reader (Phone-in debate, Radio Five Live, 26 May 1997).

It would be worth considering whether, in reality, the television is constantly turned on in the majority of children's homes and, if so, whether or not the children are simply sitting and staring at the screen. A classroom assistant commented on what she observed when carrying out home visits:

> I do home visits and I find it in many houses, the video is always on but the children aren't watching all the time, they go in and out. Often it is Hindi films on. [Bilingual classroom assistant, inner city school, TSZ, p. 1]

This comment is interesting as, whilst confirming that in many homes the television may be constantly on, it also highlights the fact that children may ignore the television and go and do other things. The children are not merely passively sitting in front of the television. The children are active, will come and go and they will watch what they want to watch and then move on to do other things.

Talking to teachers it soon became apparent that many of their negative views were based on 'suspicions' rather than hard evidence, a situation that could be overcome by teachers talking to children and parents in order to gain a more accurate picture of what children actually do when not in school. Cathy Pompe relates how one teacher, who was worried that her class spent all day watching television, carried out a survey of the children's out-of-school activities and was astonished at the range of activities in which her class were involved.

Literacy development and watching television and videos at home

The teachers I spoke to were particularly concerned about the quantity and quality of what children watch at home and many teachers were adamant that watching television and videos at home was detrimental to children's literacy development.

> You can always tell which children watch television because they find it hard to get into books and have little imagination and it shows in their stories.
> [Year 2 teacher]

This view is very reminiscent of those expressed by a teacher talking to Martin Large (1990) who pointed out several 'lazy readers' who found it difficult to 'get inside' what they read. This teacher claimed that the difficulty was linked with television viewing at home and stated that children who did not watch television at home tended to read regularly and did very well at school.

Another teacher I interviewed felt that the learning potential of television and videos was lost because parents and carers do not talk to the children about what they watch:

> I really hate the idea that the TV might be just bunged on, the children just sat in front of it, because I think that happens to an awful lot of the children when they *are* bunged in front of television sets and nobody really intervenes and says 'What did you watch?' and 'Why did you like that?'
> [Teacher TSX, p. 3]

Teachers found it very hard to name specific television programmes or videos that the children in their class currently enjoyed watching at home and those that did mentioned superhero/action programmes (e.g. *Extreme Ghostbusters*, *Batman*) or the generic category 'cartoons'. In view of this, it was not surprising that teachers also had great difficulty in naming a children's programme or video that they thought could help support a child's developing literacy. Some teachers of 3 and 4-year-olds mentioned programmes such as *Tots TV* and *Sesame Street* but teachers of older children were frequently at a loss when faced with the question.

A headteacher who was asked the same question talked about *Newsround*:

John Craven's *Newsround*. It's great for the children to hear news presented at child's level and to see other children reacting to that news. Particularly true for our EAL children who wouldn't hear discussion about the news in English.
[Primary headteacher, TSY, p. 2]

Teachers who were also parents of young children were more aware of current television programmes and videos but the majority of teachers without children, or those with older children, were clearly making assumptions about the quality of the programmes children watch. No teacher mentioned how television and videos had the potential to present a rich seam of stories to children at home, although they were conscious that watching a film, video or television programme was likely to have some influence on a child's reading. A primary headteacher said:

Absolutely, *Goosebumps*. If it's on TV they've got it. When we have a Book Fair the ones that go first are the ones that have been on TV. I've also read them books because there has been a new film because I wanted them to see it came from a book.
[Primary headteacher, TSY, p. 2]

In the schools involved in the study, teachers did not seem to take the initiative in relation to building on children's out-of-school viewing experiences. Few teachers talked to the children about what they had watched or what they themselves, as adults, like to watch. Although in talking to a group of Year 6 children it was clear that having experience of a teacher who *did* talk to children about television may lead them to believe that the teacher valued television as both an entertainment and learning medium:

NB: Do you think watching television helps your reading?
Shakir: Yeah . . .
NB: So if you said that to your teachers do you think they would agree?
Shakir: One teacher does! He talks to us in the playground in the mornings about programmes on television.

The relative lack of conversation with teachers on the subject of television leaves many children uncertain about their teachers' attitudes towards television and videos:

NB: What do you think teachers think about children watching television?
John: They think *computers* are good.
[Boy aged 5, TSH, p. 4]

A 5-year-old girl carefully considered the question:

NB: Do you think teachers think television is good?
Penny: Well, they might think television is good but we don't, we might not know, they might watch it at home and stuff.
NB: Do they think it's good for children?

Penny: Well, we watch *Words and Pictures* and stuff but I don't know if they think it's good.
[Girl aged 5, TSI, p. 6]

Some slightly older children answered the question by trying to make sense of what happens in school and the somewhat conflicting messages they received:

NB: Do you think teachers think that television is good for you?
Beatrice: No.
Anne: But we do watch it when it's wet, when it's wet lunchtime we go up after lunch.
NB: Do you ever watch it in the classroom?
Anne: No we watch it in the library.
NB: No, I mean do you ever watch it to, to help you with your reading and writing . . .
Anne: No, no, no, no . . .
Beatrice: No, no. Sometimes! You know when we were learning about transport . . .
Anne: Oh yeah, yes . . .
NB: Just occasionally? What do you think your teacher would say about children watching television at home?
Beatrice: No.
NB: What, just no?
Beatrice: Yes, just no.
[Girls aged 5 and 6, TSC, p. 4]

Summary

Primary and early years teachers are aware of how television and videos watched in school may support young children's literacy development and some teachers have moved beyond using programmes specifically produced for schools and utilize commercial videos. Although teachers have had no formal training in the use of televisual texts, either during their initial teacher education or as practising teachers, many are conscious of the importance of adult mediation of the experience and the need for children to talk about what they have seen. Teachers are less convinced about the value of children watching television at home, mainly because of their perceptions about the excessive amounts and poor quality of television that the children watch and the perceived lack of adult intervention. It was apparent that some of the perceptions were based on suspicions rather than a thorough knowledge of children's home-viewing experiences.

The next chapter moves into the home context and examines parents' views on the subject and children's perceptions of their parents' views.

Chapter 3

Children and Parents

The majority of young children's experience of viewing television and videos takes place in their own homes and, therefore, parents are likely to help shape young children's perceptions of the status, value and enjoyment potential of televisual texts. The first part of the chapter examines parents' response to the Parents' Questionnaire (Appendix B) and the face-to-face interviews. Exploring young children's perceptions of their parents' attitudes towards television and videos in the second part of this chapter provides an insight into how parents may influence young children's emerging views about the value and purposes of watching television. In exploring both sides of the child–parent partnership it is possible to gain a more comprehensive picture of how parents' views impact on and influence children's experiences and expectations of televisual and written texts and how this may influence the children's literacy development.

The chapter is based on face-to-face interviews with children ranging from 4 to 7 years old, face-to-face interviews with parents and an analysis of the responses to the Children's Questionnaire (Appendix A) and the Parents' Questionnaire (Appendix B).

Parents' views

Three key points regarding parents arose from the research findings and these concern parents' opinions about the general desirability of children watching television, the relationship between television viewing and literacy development and parents' involvement in their children's viewing.

Parents' general attitudes towards viewing television and videos

Most of the questionnaires were completed by mothers and the comments made by many of the mothers as they returned the questionnaires would suggest a certain level of anxiety about the family's viewing patterns, especially in the case of children who watched television and videos frequently:

> I'm embarrassed to give this back.
> (Parent of 5-year-old boy)

> I just let him watch what he wants just so that I can get on.
> (Parent of 4-year-old boy)

Part of this anxiety may stem from the fact that parents do not want to be criticized for using television as a 'babysitter'. Barrie Gunter and Jill McAleer (1997) cite the research of Gantz and Masland (1986) who found that mothers in America were of the opinion that it was commonplace for *other* mothers to use television as a 'babysitter' but unwilling to admit that they themselves used television in this way. However, the pattern of parents' involvement in their children's viewing, which will be discussed later in this chapter, and some of the parents' comments, would lend weight to the suggestion that many parents involved in this study may indeed use television as a 'childminder'. A mother of three small girls, for example, acknowledged the babysitting role that television played in her family's life:

> I do not encourage the use of videos and TV and see it only as a means of babysitting early on Saturday and Sunday mornings. It has no great benefit to the children but only to me, so we make little of it as an activity.
> (Mother of girls aged 2, 6 and 8 years)

Recent research would tend to confirm this pattern of use. The research findings of Chambers et al. (1998), for example, led them to conclude that:

> Parents view television as a babysitter. It pacifies their children and allows them to relax, while at the same time keeping them occupied and out of parents' way. Mums feel that children are entitled to relax after coming home from school.
> (Chambers et al., 1998, p. 23)

In contrast another mother involved in the study volunteered the information that she had no intention of using television in this way:

> ... but it's that baby sitter in the corner thing again, I wouldn't feel happy about them watching television for an hour and a half ...
> (Parent of two children aged 5 and 3)

The introduction to this book outlined some of the reasons for this censorious attitude towards an enjoyable activity that allows children to relax and keeps them occupied whilst their parents are busy. A major criticism of television viewing is that it is a 'mindless' activity, which encourages passivity in the watching child. Marie Winn argued that television is an 'insidious narcotic' and damaging to children's mental health and cognitive and social development (Winn, 1985, p. 11). This anxiety about the passivity of children watching television has a long history (e.g. Macoby, 1951; Singer and Singer, 1983, both cited in Gunter and McAleer 1997) and Large, 1980. Some parents involved in this study appeared to share this negative view of television. The mother of two children quoted above talked about how audiotapes rather than television featured strongly in her daughter's life. She went on to explain why she was happy for her children to listen to audiotapes 'morning, noon and night, in the house, [and] in the car' but did not feel equally happy about her children watching television or videos:

> Life is too short to be sedentary, children should be *doing* things . . . Because she really does *listen* to them [audiotapes], there's an active involvement. She won't be doing her Barbies when a tape is on. She'll ask questions, she's actively involved.
> (Mother of girl aged 5 and boy aged 3)

The extent to which children are passive viewers will be explored in later chapters but at this juncture it is important to point out that not all the parents expressed negative views about the value of television and videos. Some parents made generally positive comments such as 'Children learn a lot from videos', whilst others commented favourably on specific programmes: 'All children should watch *Sesame Street* before they go to school'.

It would seem, then, that some parents believe television viewing to be a useful means of amusing the children but see no intrinsic value in the activity, whilst other parents see television as being potentially educative. We move on now to examine parents' views about the possible relationship between television and video viewing and children's reading development.

Parents' opinions about the links between television viewing and literacy development

Parents who stated categorically that watching television was 'bad' for literacy development were in the minority (Q 22 of Parents' Questionnaire, Appendix B). Those that held this view tended to argue that watching television or videos prevents or discourages children from reading. Two of the questions in the Parents' Questionnaire (Q22 and Q27, Appendix B) were designed to elicit some information about parents' perceptions of the links between viewing television and videos and reading development and gain an idea of whether parents felt that schools, through a video library, should play a role in providing televisual texts and, if so, what types of videos should be available for loan. Not surprisingly, parents who were unconvinced about the value of viewing television generally argued that schools should not have video libraries. The reasons put forward tended to be based on the notion that reading is displaced by watching television: 'Access to videos in central London is not a problem. Encouraging children to read is!' (Parent of boys aged 7 and 1, girl aged 5)

While this parent seemed to argue that access to more videos would decrease children's interest in reading another parent was anxious that:

> Peer pressure may encourage them to want to watch more videos.
> (Parent of girl aged 6, boys aged 5 and 3)

The consequences for literacy development of this additional viewing are not spelt out but can be guessed at since the parent had stated earlier that watching television and videos are bad for children's reading.

The majority of parents thought that watching television and videos has no effect on reading or improves reading. Many parents tended to add the caveat 'but it depends on how much'. One parent summed up the views of many others when she wrote:

> It does depend on quantity and quality. Everything is fine in moderation!
> (Mother of boy aged 7 and girl aged 5)

When considering the views of the parents who held more positive views about the value of televisual texts a particularly pertinent point to emerge was that many parents were not only aware of and able to explain how watching a video, film or television programme had supported their own child's reading development, but also that the parents seemed to have a view of reading which encompassed more than merely saying the words on the page. Thus parents wrote or spoke about other aspects of reading such as understanding the plot and making comparisons and predictions. One comment focused on the children's understanding of the story:

> [The videos] helped her to understand the Rev. Awdry books (*Thomas the Tank Engine* etc.) as they are rather long-winded and complicated.
> (Mother of girls aged 5 and 2)

Other parents stated that the visual nature of television helped understand the written text:

> They are better able to picture characters and geography.
> (Mother of girls aged 8 and 6)

A number of parents commented on how videos and television programmes based on books provided a useful introduction to the written text:

> [Watching the video] helped her to get 'into' the book, discuss comparison, and different qualities, attention to detail and ability to predict.
> (Mother of girls aged 6 and 3)

> [Watching a video] helps because they were already interested in the story so they knew they'd enjoy the book.
> (Mother of girl aged 6, boys aged 5 and 3)

> The characters are already a 'real' part of her world.
> (Mother of girl aged 5, boy aged 2)

Other parents commented on the reading children had to do when watching television:

> Watching television helps his reading because he has to read things like captions.
> (Mother of boys aged 5 and 3)

The complexities of discerning a simple causal relationship between watching televisual texts and reading development was highlighted by one mother's reflections on her son's reading:

> *Parent*: Watching a video version of a book did not really help. Because he knew the story, he tended to skip bits when he read to me.
> *NB*: Do you think the video provided a 'way in' to books for him?
> *Parent*: Mmm. It's helped with his vocabulary . . . Watching videos has really helped him get an understanding of plot — when we're watching a detective programme he will know before anyone else does who committed the crime — he has a really good understanding of the different genres.
> [Mother of boy aged 9 and girl aged 7]

The comments made by this mother are particularly interesting in the light of the fact that she told me her son was dyslexic. Although watching videos did not result in word-perfect readings of the written text, it is clear that watching television has helped with other, very important aspects of his literacy development.

Schools and television and videos

The overwhelming majority of parents in the study do not seem to want schools to make more use of television than they already do, although most recognized that schools' television programmes may be a useful means of supporting children's reading development. The parents appeared to have faith in the judgment of their children's schools and teachers as the following comment testifies:

> I don't really know, I've never seen any school programmes. I think the teachers know what is best and they use just about the right amount, I think.
> (Parent of two children aged 5 and 2)

A few parents felt unhappy about the use of television in the classroom. A parent who had earlier expressed a fairly negative attitude towards television was emphatic about why schools should not make more use of television and videos:

> They[teachers] can achieve more with other methods and with class participation.
> (Mother of three girls aged 8, 6, and 2)

This view contrasts with that of another mother who observed that television was 'just another aspect of education'. The issue of balance was raised by another parent who was in favour of the use of television in schools:

> Educational TV/videos cannot be a bad alternative to the classroom's traditional role — *in moderation* (Respondent's own emphasis).
> (Parent of four girls aged 11, 10, 7 and 4, Q 26, Parents' Questionnaire)

A few parents were undecided about the issue. On the one hand they told me that the children learnt a lot from the schools' programmes but then went on to say:

I think they have TV time once a week. Maybe they could watch it more but they have so much else to do I don't think there would be any time.
(Mother of three girls aged 12, 5 and 3)

Generally, parents and teachers appear to be in broad agreement about the value of television in school (see Chapter 2), nor was there a wide disparity in the views of parents and teachers when it came to the issue of a school video library. The parents' views on the idea of school video libraries were revealing. Some parents felt that such a library might be a good idea but only if a limited range of videos was available, while the parents who viewed videos in a more positive light were more likely to feel that a school video library might be a good idea, but were clear about what these libraries should contain. One mother with four daughters aged from 4 to 11, emphasized that schools should only offer videos 'with an educational content'. 'Educational' videos for this parent included art and craft, children's drama, information and videos in another language. Her views are very much in line with those expressed by teachers (Chapter 2).

An analysis of the parents' responses showed that parents who were in favour of school video libraries had specific genres or types of videos in mind. Parents wanted art and craft videos, children's drama, information videos and videos in another language but were not keen on short cartoons, general interest films, and Disney cartoons and films or children's films. Not many parents identified which particular language videos they wanted, although those that did suggested French and Italian, with one parent responding, 'languages appropriate to the school'. As later chapters will show there can be a mismatch between what children enjoy watching on television and what their parents would prefer them to watch! Many children are very conscious of the purely didactic purpose of some videos and refuse to be drawn into the watching experience as this 4-year-old boy made clear:

NB: Do you ever watch videos in Spanish?
Ben: No.
NB: Would you like to watch videos in Spanish?
Ben: No.
NB: No? Why not?
Ben: Cause I don't like them.
NB: You don't like them?
Ben: I already know how to speak in Spanish.
NB: But you already know how to speak in English but you enjoy videos in English?
Ben: Yes.
NB: There might be some good videos in Spanish.
Ben: But . . . no . . . but my mum just got er one on French but I don't like.
NB: What's the one in French about?
Ben: Um they talk about dogs, everything more, I don't like.
NB: Is it a story or is it to teach you how to speak French?
Ben: Teach me how to speak French but I don't like that.
[Boy aged 4, speaks Spanish and English at home, TSQ, p. 7]

It is also interesting to reflect on how the types of videos favoured by parents would develop children's literacy (e.g. would information videos develop an understanding of this particular genre and lead children into reading non-fictional information texts?)

One parent, who felt that videos were educationally valuable, raised an important issue when explaining why she thought that school video libraries would be useful:

> Children learn a lot from videos, and it would give those children whose parents can't afford to buy videos the same opportunity as those who can.
> (Parent of boy aged 7 and girl aged 4)

The economic issue is an important one to consider as in schools with more affluent parents many parents, even those who felt videos could play an educational role, simply replied that schools should not have a video library as there was 'no need'. Some of the parents who responded lived in rural areas and sent their children to the village school. In rural areas, unlike inner city and suburban areas, there is not the same easy access to videos. Despite this, not all parents in the rural areas wanted a school video library which would suggest that they do not see it as the school's province to introduce children to a range of televisual texts, either because they feel it is part of the out-of-school culture or because they do not view videos as being educational.

The issue about out-of-school culture is raised in later chapters (especially Chapter 7) but at this point it is interesting to reflect on one mother's reason for not wanting a school video library:

> I like to choose and discuss appropriate videos with my children.
> (Mother of girls aged 6 and 3)

Although other parents probably also do so, she was the only parent to state explicitly that she and her children discussed what videos to watch. From my conversation with the older of the two girls it was clear that her mother also discussed books with her. Why is it that the mother was happy for her child to choose books from the school library but not videos? Could it be that she felt that children can benefit from reading any book but that the same could not be said of videos? Alternatively, she may have felt the teacher would be able to ensure the child chose an 'appropriate' book but was not so confident about teachers' ability to guide children's choices of videos. It may also be that whilst written texts, especially books, are seen to be what schools should be concerned with, there is a feeling that videos, however educationally valuable they may be, do not 'belong' in school. Another possibility is that this parent, who was very alive to the ways in which watching videos has supported her child's literacy development, nevertheless believes that there are practices concerned with developing literacy which are definable as 'school' practices' or 'teaching' and these are different to home-based practices and experiences which are not definable as 'teaching'.

As the later part of the chapter will show, children appear to be unaware that many of their parents may think that watching television and videos in moderation is not too detrimental to and, indeed, may actually help with their reading. There are a range of possible explanations for this, including parents' own ambivalence or uncertainty about the issue and the feeling amongst parents that children may watch too much television unless parents control and limit their viewing:

> The children are restricted to *Blue Peter* and *Newsround* and the occasional nature programme. Given a chance she [the daughter] would watch *Neighbours* etc.
> (Mother of boy aged 7 and girl aged 5)

Another explanation for some children's lack of awareness of their parents' views may lie in the pattern of parents' involvement in their child's viewing and it is to this that we now turn.

Parents' involvement in their child's viewing

An important finding was that it is not common for parents to watch television or videos with their children. Most children and parents reported that children either watched alone or with their siblings. Approximately 20 per cent of children watched television with their mother or father on a regular basis although, as will be discussed later, there was a noticeable difference in the proportion of girls and boys who viewed television with their parents.

As discussed earlier, many parents use television and videos as a 'babysitter' to differing degrees and it is therefore not surprising that many children do not watch television with an adult. Other parents believe that television and videos are of 'very little value'. Some parents' lack of involvement in their child's viewing was evidenced by the difficulties they had in identifying their child's current favourite programmes or being able to name programmes their child enjoyed when aged about 2 or 3. This prompts the question that if parents are not watching television with their children how is it possible for them to make judgments about what children may be gaining from the experience? Furthermore, would the children benefit from an adult's presence?

One of the mothers I interviewed talked about what she does when watching television with her two young children:

> . . . if children are passive and not engaging it's not very good. You *can* encourage children to be active. I ask questions like 'Have we got any books about that? Do you remember when we went on the river trip? What did *we* find?'
> (Mother of girl aged 5 and boy aged 2)

Questions such as these will certainly encourage the children to refer to their previous life experiences and help them relate to what they see on television. The questions asked are very similar to those that adults may ask a child when sharing a book. In both cases children are being encouraged to interpret texts by drawing on their personal experiences and in so doing create meanings which are personal to themselves. Research with young children has tended to highlight the value of adults and children talking about what they see on television and adults responding to and encouraging children to ask questions about what they are watching. Cathy Murphy (1983) found that very young children tended to talk more about programmes they had watched with someone else who, therefore, had a shared frame of reference. Children were able to discuss the programme without first having to explain what had happened. Cathy Murphy argued that an adult co-viewer increased the likelihood that the themes of the programmes watched would be extended and built on. The importance of a more 'knowledgeable other' to scaffold children's learning whilst watching television is not confined to nursery-aged children (see Davies, 1989). When watching television my own daughter asks as many questions now, if not more, than she did when she was 2 or 3. Many of these questions have an immediacy in the sense that they need to be asked and answered whilst watching the video or TV programme and enable children to, for example, seek clarification about a character's motives, maintain the thread of the story or 'check out' their emotional responses to a scene. In so doing they gain a deeper understanding of how responses to events in narratives may be influenced by culture and society. Patricia Marks Greenfield has cited research which has suggested that adults talking to young children about what they see on television can increase the benefits of and minimize the negative effects of certain television programmes (Marks Greenfield, 1984).

The importance of role play in children's literacy development is discussed in more detail in Chapter 6 but I would suggest here that if parents watch television with their children they will be more likely to recognize the origin of some of their children's play scripts and may even be able to help their child extend and develop them (see Chapter 6). A parent may be flummoxed by their child who, on being handed a tissue responds, 'Oh. Can you ever forgive me?' instead of the expected 'Thank you'. If, however, they had watched a video of *The Lion, the Witch and the Wardrobe* with their child they would have immediately recognized Mr. Tumnus the Faun and possibly been able to respond as Lucy does on the video. In similar vein, Neil Kitson has argued that teachers and other adults should interact with children engaged in socio-dramatic fantasy play in ways that will 'challenge them and deepen their experience' (Kitson, 1997, p. 32) but has also asserted that it is important that:

> . . . the play and action must be that of the children. Their ideas must be used. The
> words spoken must be their words expressing their thoughts.
> (Kitson, 1997, p. 35)

I would suggest that if the dramatic role play is based on a televisual script, parents who have watched the programme or video with their child, answered their questions and been aware of the child's response to the programme, will be well placed to support and extend the child in the way Kitson proposes.

This notion of high quality learning and talk occurring when children and adults are talking about a shared experience is not a new one (see Wells, 1987). What is being suggested here is that shared viewing of television programmes or videos can stimulate high quality conversations between parents and children. It is not always possible for parents to watch with their child but, as Cathy Murphy has pointed out, children can then be encouraged to be explicit when talking to an interested adult who has not seen the programme (Murphy, 1983).

Viewing patterns of mothers and their children

One of the most outstanding findings was that parents tended to be very conscientious about returning their questionnaires when these related to their daughters, with a return rate of approximately 50 per cent. When it came to boys a disappointingly low proportion of parents (approximately 10 per cent) returned the questionnaire. There are a number of possible reasons for this very different response rate. Firstly, it is possible that some of the parents were unwilling to share information about their child's viewing habits, especially if they felt they may reflect badly on the child or themselves as parents, although this may not explain the gender-based difference.

A second reason may be related to who watches television and videos with children. Three times as many boys than girls reported that they watched television alone (i.e. without a sibling or adult). When it came to watching with siblings, similar proportions of girls and boys watched in the company of their sisters and/or brothers. That more boys than girls in the sample watched television alone was not linked to a disproportionate number of the boys in the study being an only child. There has been little research into how parental involvement in young children's viewing may be influenced by the child's and parent's gender. This study has merely thrown up the possibility of a gender-based link and more research in the area would be valuable before making generalizations. In terms of this study, however, I would suggest that one outcome may be that parents of boys may be less knowledgeable about the details of what their sons are watching which could result in a lower response rate to questionnaires.

Bearing in mind the fact that more research on parent–child viewing behaviours is needed, it is nonetheless useful to try to offer a possible explanation for the pattern observed within this study and to consider the implications of the viewing patterns of the families involved in the sample. The first question that arises is, why are parents, and in particular mothers, more likely to watch television with their daughters than with their sons? It is possible that the answer may lie in the content of television programmes and videos that boys seem to enjoy. This study has found that boys' favourite videos and television programmes tend to feature boys, men or male protagonists but, more significantly, boys in the sample, particularly the over 5s, tended to talk about watching more cartoons, particularly action cartoons, than any other sort of programme. The ITC report *Cartoon Crazy* noted that mothers tend not to watch cartoons with their children (Chambers et al., 1998, p. 25). Conversely, it is feasible that girls' viewing choices may closely reflect their mother's preferences in a similar way and for the same reasons that girls and women may enjoy the same type of book and tend to focus on the same issues. One result of this could be that the mothers of daughters may be happy to spend at least some time watching television with their daughters but are less likely to be drawn to watch the programmes or videos their sons may particularly enjoy. The different viewing preferences of girls and boys and the implications of these viewing preferences for the literacy development of girls and boys is examined in greater detail in Chapter 7.

Children's ideas about what parents think about television

The extent to which children's experiences of the televisual medium and their expectations of what they will need to do as readers and watchers of television and videos is influenced by the children's perceptions of their parents' value systems, is explored in this section. Children and parents may not talk explicitly about issues surrounding television but, from a very young age, children will have experienced the outcomes of their parents' attitudes through the ways in which their parents may monitor, regulate or talk about their viewing of television and videos. Children may begin to draw conclusions from their parents' comments and behaviour, about their parents' values and attitudes and it is to these conclusions or emerging ideas that we now turn.

Children's ideas about parents' attitudes towards children watching television and videos

The majority of the children interviewed had formed a clear picture about whether or not their parents and other adults approved of children watching television and videos. In addition, it was clear that some of the children had begun to develop an understanding of what type of television programmes and videos their parents valued.

Most of the children believed that their parents did not think that watching television or videos was 'good for them'. Many of the children appeared not to have been given a reason for their parents' views whilst others were unclear about the reasons. In response to the question, 'What do you think grown ups think about children watching television and videos?' an overwhelming majority of the children provided answers that suggested parents would prefer their children to watch much less television and fewer videos. The following responses were typical:

James: She thinks you shouldn't watch so much. She says, 'Don't watch so much'.
NB: Why does she say that? Has she told you why she thinks you watch too much television?
James: No.
NB: Can you guess why she says you watch too much?
James: No.
[Boy aged 5, TSJ, p. 4]

A girl of the same aged noted :

> *Penny*: Well, my mummy thinks you shouldn't watch things that much.
> *NB*: Does she say why?
> *Penny*: No.
> *NB*: So do you know why she says that?
> *Penny*: Er . . . um, no.
> [Girl aged 5, TSI, p. 5]

Two other children compared the restrictions their parents placed on television viewing during the course of a week:

> *India*: We're not even allowed to watch, um, telly um, in the week except on Friday and weekends.
> *Sasha*: In the week you're not allowed to?
> *India*: Except Fridays and weekends.
> *NB*: What about you?
> *Sasha*: Well, I suppose I'm allowed to watch it in the week, yeah . . . I am. But not very often. Anytime I'm not allowed to watch it often.
> [Girls aged 5 and 6 TSF, p. 4]

The questionnaire included the same question that children were asked during face-to-face interviews, 'What do you think grown ups think about children watching television and videos?'. Children's written responses tended to confirm the view that most children were convinced that parents disapproved of television and videos. Children's answers to this question ranged from simple statements to slightly more complex explanations. Many children wrote variations of 'They don't think it is good' (Boy age 6). In other children's responses the adults' voices could be clearly heard:

> 'Not very impressed'
> (Girl age 6)

One 6-year-old wrote 'They are cross about me watching TV because they think it is rubbish. They are happy about me watching videos', whilst another 6-year-old wrote that her parents thought she should watch 'Not too much.'

For many of the older children the rules imposed by their parents seemed to be a potential source of conflict and resentment. A 5-year-old explained the reason for her compliance:

> *NB*: Would you like to watch more television than you're allowed to?
> *Beatrice*: No, because my mum would just shout at me and I don't like it.
> *NB*: Yeah, but if she didn't shout at you and said, 'Yeah, that's fine . . .'
> *Beatrice*: Yeah.
> *NB*: Yes what? You would like to watch more then?
> *Beatrice*: Yes.
> [Girl aged 5, TSC, p. 4]

Other children however, appeared to have more success in their negotiations with parents as this 5-year-old attested:

> I have to ask [whether I can watch TV] and if she says 'No,' then we say, 'Oh, we'll be very good. Pleee-ease?' And then finally she gives up and says 'Okay'.
> [Girl aged 5, TSD, p. 4]

The various comments made by the children were interesting for three reasons. Firstly, it is apparent that these young children have a clear knowledge of their parents' views about television and the restrictions that result. Secondly, the children also seem to know the degree of flexibility that exists regarding the rules about watching television. Thirdly, it would appear that children may be aware that rules parents impose relating to television and video may not merely reflect their beliefs about the 'worth' of television and videos, but rather that this was an area in which parents felt able to exert control. The 5-year-old's promise that 'we'll be very good' suggests that access to television was perhaps related to behaviour, a treat that could be withheld if children misbehaved. The fact that many parents do not give children adequate reasons for their rules would also lend support to this view.

It was much less common for children to report that their parents were indifferent about the amount of time they spent watching videos or television. Some children commented that 'My mum doesn't mind' or 'They think it's OK'. A small minority of children felt that parents were quite happy for them to watch television or videos. One 4-year-old boy told me 'Mummy doesn't mind 'cos I like it'. [TSJ, p. 4]

It was possible for children to interpret the question 'What do you think grown ups think about children watching television?' in a number of different ways. One 5-year-old, for example, replied to this question in the following manner:

> *Mark*: Good.
> *NB*: Why do they think it's good for you?
> *Mark*: So you know why, so you can hear the sound what's on telly.
> [Boy aged 5, TSN, p. 2]

This child's reply bears scrutiny. Although it may appear that the child is simply telling us that adults think watching television is valuable it is also possible that the child has interpreted the question to mean do adults think it's good to *watch* television, i.e. concentrate and focus on it rather than talk, play or wander out of the room? The final comments make more sense if the child has interpreted the question in this way. There is no similar evidence that other children involved in the research interpreted this question in the same way as Mark, although there were varied interpretations of other questions the children were asked.

A 7-year-old girl stated that her parents '. . . think it's all right because when you want to, when you write stories then you know what to write, they think it's all right.' [TSK, p. 2]. Amongst school-aged children, positive responses such as these were very rare. Interestingly, most of the more positive responses were made by children aged 5 and younger. It was also apparent that within families children may have different perceptions of their parents' views depending upon their age. In one family, for example, a 6-year-old girl stated that her parents thought that watching television was 'a bad thing because sometimes your eyes go square' whilst her 4-year-old brother was confident that his parents 'think it's a good thing'.

One reason why younger children may feel that parents are happy for them to watch television or videos may be because viewing had not become an area of conflict with these very young children as they were less conscious of the viewing habits of their peers and, consequently, less likely to challenge any rules their parents may have enforced about the amount or type of programmes or videos watched. A further clue to the more harmonious state of affairs regarding television-watching amongst parents and their younger children may be found in the research findings of Rosemarie Truglio and her colleagues in America, which tended to suggest that parents were more relaxed about the amount of time children aged 3 to 5 spent watching television programmes or videos specifically aimed at children because they not only believed children's television aimed at the younger age group was innocuous but, furthermore, that it possibly exerted a positive influence on their young children. (Truglio et al., 1996, p. 488)

Parents' inconsistency did not provide children with very clear ideas about the value of viewing TV and videos:

Louise: Well my mum, it depends whether she's in a good mood. If she's in a bad mood then she thinks it isn't and if she's in a good mood then she thinks a little bit is and too much isn't. And she thinks films are better than cartoons.
[Girl, aged 6, TSA]

Children's ideas about the reasons for parents' negative atittudes towards television and videos

Some children appeared to be fairly clear that one reason for their parents' limiting their television viewing was that it interfered with the smooth running of the daily routines (e.g. getting dressed and ready for school). In such cases parents were seen to be more willing to allow their children to watch television during the evening, weekends and holidays.

Loiuse: Well, she [Mummy] doesn't really like it but if there's time in the morning and we've got all ready for school then she lets us watch a video and then on the weekends when we wake up she lets us and at the summer holidays, but not the weekdays.
[Girl aged 5, TSA, p. 4]

Another child, aged 5, explained what she and her 9-year-old sister do over the weekend:

Elizabeth: We wake up very early in the morning.
NB: Is that when you generally watch television?
Elizabeth: Yeah. We always want to watch television in the morning so we always wake up very early and wake up the whole household and it's like six o'clock in the morning, or five, and we watch television until seven and then we get out of bed.
[Girl aged 5, TSE, p. 5]

Sometimes parents have given only vague explanations as this 5-year-old made clear when asked whether he was allowed to watch television:

NB: What do they say to you?
Shaun: They don't normally let us [himself and his younger sister aged 2] watch it . . .
NB: Have they said why?
Shaun: Mmmm, because we've got too other, too many other things to do and they said it's bad for you.
NB: Why is it bad for you?
Shaun: Well . . .
NB: Have they said why it's bad for you?
Shaun: No.
[Boy aged 5, TSF, p. 3]

In some families the parents appear to hold conflicting views. The mother of a 6-year-old girl and a 2-year-old boy, for example, commented in positive terms about the value of television and video and reported that the older child watched live television every day and videos four to five times a week. When the 6-year-old was asked about parental attitudes to television she wrote, 'No. I think my Dad feels that it is silly' (TSG, p. 4). Although a number of other children also made a point of commenting that their fathers were not keen to encourage television watching, analysis of the children's viewing habits would suggest that where parental conflict exists it is the mother's views that determine what actually happens. This pattern has also been noted by Lull (1990) and Sanger, (1997).

Another child seemed to be unclear about her parents' motives for limiting the amount of television they were allowed to watch but suspected that it may be related to a conflict of interests:

Melissa: They think it's bad for children because they say we have to go upstairs because they want to watch cricket.
[Girl aged 5, TSM, p. 3]

In another interview with two 6-year-olds, one child's observations seem to suggest that the potential conflicts are more likely to centre around television programmes, as parents are not averse to watching some of the videos their children enjoy watching:

> Well, they [parents] keep on being bossy. Give me the remote control and then change it to boxing. They like me and my sister watching videos 'cos they keep on looking and then it gets interesting for them.
> [Girl aged 5, TSM, p. 6]

A number of children stated that their parents had told them that watching television is bad for the eyes and many had been told that excessive television or video viewing could result in square eyes. Bearing in mind the young age of the children being interviewed it is perhaps not very surprising that a sizeable number of the children appeared to have accepted this explanation.

> *Alice*:   They think it's bad for your eyes because my sister's got glasses already, she's short-sighted.
> *NB*:   So, they think it's bad for your eyes? You also said no, so why did *you* think grown ups think it's not good for you?
> *Rachael*:   Well, it's because Mummy thinks you get, that you *really* will, that you'll get square eyes.
> [Two girls aged 5 and 6, TSD, p. 4]

Children's interpretations of the restrictions parents impose

In addition to imposing rules about the amount of time children could spend watching videos and television and about when during the day or the week children were allowed to watch television, the children in the research sample also commented that parents sometimes restricted what they were allowed to watch. Children were prevented, or strongly discouraged, from watching certain programmes, most frequently cartoons and programmes deemed to be too 'babyish' by parents.

> *NB*:   Do they [parents] think some programmes are better than others or some videos better than others?
> *Alice*:   My mummy does. And she thinks films are better than cartoons.
> *NB*:   Do you think that?
> [Child shrugged her shoulders.]
> *NB*:   Why do you think grown ups think that films are better than cartoons?
> *Alice*:   Because, because they're. . . . cartoons are really meant for kids.
> *Sophie*:   I think cartoons are um, more of, kind of like for babies.
> *Alice*:   *Tom and Jerry*'s a cartoon.
> *Sophie*:   Yeah and they kind of don't speak or don't speak properly and they can only speak in baby voices and grown ups and big children don't think they're very good.
> [Two girls aged 5, TSG, p. 42]

Another child reported that her mother appeared to feel that cartoons were unsuitable as they were either 'babyish' or frightening:

NB: What do grown ups think about children watching television?
Anne: My mummy doesn't like it.
Beatrice: My mum, because we often watch cartoons and she says they're like
           babyish and really scary and she says they're too scary for us and she
           turns the television off.
[Girls aged 5 and 6, TSC, p. 3]

Some of the children's comments provided an insight into how parents may exert a fairly subtle but effective means of control over their children's choices of programme or video. A 5-year-old who talked in a very animated fashion about the *Teletubbies* then went on to say:

Alice: In the weekend I always used to watch *Tetetubbies* but now I don't.
NB: Why don't you watch *Teletubbies* anymore?
Alice: Because it's too babyish for me now. [Long pause] Because they're babyish.
           They're actually meant for 2-year-olds.
NB: You reckon?
Alice: They are because my mummy says so.
[Girl aged 5, TSG, p. 3]

Suggesting a programme was 'for babies' was a successful strategy employed by other parents. In common with the majority of 5-year-olds, this little girl chose to forgo watching a much-loved programme rather than risk being categorized as a baby.

   Parents not only discourage or ban the watching of specific programmes and videos but may also actively encourage the viewing of programmes of their own choosing. Barrie Gunter and Jill McAleer (1997) cite research by Dorr et al. (1989) which revealed that in America parents also encouraged their children to watch certain programmes on the basis that the parents perceived the content of these programmes to be valuable. In my study many children were conscious that television programmes such as *Blue Peter* and *Newsround* were favoured by their parents. The encouragement tends to take place in two main ways. Firstly, parents may permit their children to watch only a limited number of specified programmes as was the case for this 6-year-old:

NB: Do you watch television when you go home from school or not really?
Sophie: No, not really . . . unless it's *Blue Peter*. But unless it's, it's the holidays
           I'm not allowed to watch it in the morning.
[Girl aged 5, TSG, p. 3]

Or, secondly, parents may allow their children to watch only pre-recorded programmes and then videotape programmes the parents themselves perceive as worthwhile, programmes such as *Newsround* and *Blue Peter*.

   Parental regulation of the amount, timing and type of television watched by children has previously been noted by other researchers (e.g. Comstock, 1989, Sarlo, et al., 1988 and St. Peters et al., 1991 cited in Truglio et al., 1996, Robinson, 1997).

Recent research in Great Britain showed that parents, specifically mothers, of children aged from 5 to 9-years-old felt 'toons' such as *Tom and Jerry* and *Rugrats* were innocuous but were less happy about their young children watching 'action' cartoons such as *Batman and Robin*, *Spiderman*, *Men in Black* and *Street Sharks* as they felt these 'action' cartoons were 'too adult' for their under 5s and too violent for their slightly older children. (Chambers, et al., 1998, p. 39). Most viewers of these 'action' cartoons are boys aged 5 to 7 (Chambers et al., 1998), and it is interesting to note that in the UK, parents are currently expressing anxiety about very young children being exposed to 'adult' content and are not happy about their slightly older children watching 'action' cartoons on the grounds of excessive violence and aggression and, in the United States of America, parents are expressing exactly the same concerns (Truglio et al., 1996). As the children's comments reveal however, many parents express negative views about 'toons' and seek to control their child's viewing of any sort of cartoon.

The children's responses to questionnaires and interviews suggest that parents who closely monitor and regulate the kind of television programme and videos their children watched seem to place a high value on magazine-type and children's current affairs programmes such as *Blue Peter* and *Newsround*. This group of parents also tend to video nature programmes and children's films for their children. The reasons for the emphasis on the more educational programmes was not lost on some children who were able to confidently and succinctly explain that their parents did not think watching television was particularly valuable:

> *Lizzie*: [Because] they think television makes you not be clever.
> [Girl aged 5, TSB, p. 2]

Children who were only allowed to watch a very limited range of programmes tended to categorize these programmes as their 'favourites', but it is likely that this is because they did not have a broad spectrum of programmes or videos from which to choose.

Children who watched a wide range of children's television programmes and videos and possibly also watched some family television programmes (e.g. *Neighbours*, *The Bill*, *You've Been Framed*) seemed to feel that their parents allowed them to watch television and videos because it was seen as a source of entertainment and fun.

> *NB*: What does Mummy think about you watching television?
> *Matt*: She says it's OK.
> *NB*: So Mummy doesn't mind you watching it?
> *Matt*: No, 'cos I like it.
> [Boy aged 4, TSJ, p. 4]

An older boy, aged 6, felt that his parents' views could be best expressed by 'Let them enjoy the film' [Children's Questionnaire, no. 6].

The range of TV programmes parents recorded for their children and their reasons for so doing suggested to these children that television and videos could be a source of fun rather than a source of information. Furthermore, this group of parents were also willing to record their *children's* favourite programmes. Amongst this group of children the following sorts of comment were not unusual:

NB: Does a grown-up ever record a programme for you?
Adam: Yeah. My mum recorded *Junior*, *TV Cop*, *The Lost World* and *Jurassic Park*.
Parveen: Yeah.
Adam: She like records *Jumanji* [a cartoon series].
Parveen: And *Beethoven*.
Adam: And wrestling.
NB: Wrestling? You like that do you?
Adam: Yeah.
Parveen: And football and sometimes *Rugrats* [earlier in the interview she had named *Rugrats* as her favourite programme]
[Girl aged 6, boy aged 7, TSL, p. 2]

Children's views about whether parents think watching television and videos is a worthwhile activity

Despite the young age of the children involved in the research, a number mentioned that parents wanted them to 'do their homework' rather than watch television. One 6-year-old was very positive about the reason why her father disapproved of her watching television but also insisted that his concerns were unfounded:

Hannah: No! ... My Dad, he always says don't watch a bit more TV, you're meant to be doing your homework.
NB: He says that to you?
Hannah: But I *do* do my homework.
NB: And is that, then, only reason he doesn't want you to watch TV, because he thinks it will stop you doing your homework?
Hannah: Yes.
[Girl aged 6, TSE, p. 1]

The majority of the responses from school-aged children revealed their belief that parents preferred their children to read rather than watch television. One 7-year-old boy stated unequivocally that:

Adam: They [grown ups] think you should read books and not watch TV.
NB: Mmm?
Adam: They think I'd like to read a book.
NB: They think you'd ...
Adam: Like to read a book.
NB: So, what do you mean, they think you *should* read a book ...
Adam: Yeah.
[Boy aged 7, TSL, p. 6]

Children's awareness of the paradoxes between parental attitudes and parental behaviour

Many of the children were unable to provide reasons for their parents' views and this may be attributed to the fact that parents seem not to adequately explain their reasons for their apparent antipathy towards television and videos, especially in view of the fact that adults spend a fair amount of time watching the small screen and seem to enjoy it!

> My mum and Dad like watching it.
> [Boy aged 5, TSM, p. 3]

> *Anne*: She don't like it [children watching television].
> *NB*: Does she say why?
> *Anne*: Because it's too babyish for us . . . but my Daddy watches it!
> [Girl aged 6, TSC, p. 3]

And finally, the views of two 5-year-olds:

> *NB*: Do you know why your grown ups think that television isn't very good for you?
> *India*: I know, and it's not very good for adults too. My dad watch telly for midnight, my dad has watched telly until midnight, two times!
> *NB*: Do you think he watches too much?
> *India*: [laughs] Ten actually.
> *NB*: So why do, what I'm really asking you is why do grown ups think that television is bad for children?
> *Sasha*: Well it's bad for them too.
> *India*: Yeah, and they watch it even more than we do so . . .
> *NB*: Why are they allowed to watch it and you're not?
> *India*: I don't know.
> *Sasha*: We're younger and . . .
> *India*: They're silly and . . .
> [Both children laugh]
> [Girls aged 5, TSF, p. 4]

Summary

Asking children about adults' views was revealing in that it suggested that many parents do not explain or discuss their stance about television and videos and, consequently, the children have to draw their own conclusions. These are interpreted from incidental comments made by parents, or from the rules parents impose regarding watching the small screen, or from the parents' behaviour (e.g. whether or not they videotape programmes for their children, whether they buy videos and so on). Children found it relatively easy to give a simple answer to the question about parental views about television but, as the extracts illustrate, they found it much harder to give explanations for their parents' attitudes. This difficulty was probably due to the complex issues surrounding the place of television and videos in families' lives. It is undoubtedly the case that parents' values are transmitted to the children through a variety of means, some more explicit than others, but it is also true that these very young children are still trying to determine the relevant weighting of the various signals (e.g. does the fact that they are not allowed to watch live television during the week say more about their parents' views on the place of TV and videos than the fact that they can watch videos for two hours on weekend mornings?)

On the whole, while children feel that parents have very negative views about the value of television and video viewing for children, many parents hold the view that television viewing either has no effect or a positive effect on children's literacy development. Few parents were firmly of the opinion that videos and television were seriously detrimental to young children's literacy development and those that were felt this was because viewing television displaces reading.

Only a minority of parents watched television with their children on a regular basis. This may result in the loss of many learning opportunities as children's questions about what they are watching may remain unanswered and parents are not so well placed to extend children's socio-dramatic play. The responses to the questionnaires suggested the possibility of a gender-based difference in mother's viewing patterns — mothers being more likely to watch television with their daughters than their sons. The possible reasons for, and implications of, this are examined in more depth in Chapter 7.

The next chapter explores children's own views in more depth with a special focus on children's views on the relative merits of, and the relationship that exists between books, television and videos.

Chapter 4

Children's Perspectives

In talking to the young children involved in the research it was apparent that they were actively constructing their understanding of the purposes and position of television, videos and books in their lives and their communities. It was also evident that many of these children were not simply accepting the views of their parents. At the relatively young ages of 5, 6 and 7 many children not only had very decided opinions of their own but were also capable of supporting their views.

The process of children beginning to formulate their viewpoints

The following three extracts are illustrative of different positions young children may adopt as they endeavour to make sense of and critically evaluate their parents' values in order to eventually develop their opinions of their own. Many children, mainly, but not exclusively the younger children, seemed to closely identify with their parents' values and appeared to accept their parents' views:

Lizzie: Because they think television makes you not be clever.
NB: Is that what they say to you?
Lizzie: Yes.
NB: Do *you* think that?
[Lizzie nods]
NB: What sorts of things *do* make you clever?
Catherine: Doing like lots of work, times tables . . . reading books.
NB: So why does reading books make you clever? What do you have to do when you read a book?
Lizzie: You have to know all the words, how to write and learn.
[Girls aged 5, TSB, p. 2]

Gradually, partly as a result of wider experiences outside the home, contact with peers and attendance at school, it is clear that the children may begin to critically explore the validity of their parents' views. It was possible to have a glimpse of the process as children are seen to be discussing their different experiences and grappling with their emerging ideas and attempting to clarify their views:

NB: Do you think it [watching television] is bad for you?
Sasha: No.
NB: Do you think it is good for you?

Sasha and India:	[Simultaneously] Yes!
NB:	Okay, so why is it good for you?
India:	I don't know, I just think it's good.
Sasha:	Because it's having fun.
NB:	Because it's fun . . .
India:	Yeah, well, it isn't good because it makes your eyes squarey.
NB:	Does it really make your eyes squarey?
India:	No.
NB:	But you're convinced that it's good for you are you, Sasha?
Sasha:	Mmm. Because it's very fun and it makes me laugh some of the pro . . . programmes.

[Two girls aged five, TSF, p. 4]

A number of children in the research sample had moved still further and were able to confidently assert their own view, despite the fact that it may have been in direct conflict with that expressed by their parents. One such 6-year-old succinctly outlined how her views differed from that of her parents:

NB:	Do they [parents] think television's good for you?
Lauren:	Um, they don't think it's very good for me but it *is* because it helps me read.

[Girl aged 6, TSE, p. 2]

It was also apparent that although the majority of the children had never been asked to articulate their views about whether they thought television and videos were 'good for them' it would seem that the children had reflected on the issue and begun to formulate arguments to support their personal viewpoints:

NB:	It [television] helps you read? That's interesting . . .
Lauren:	And videos because some of them have, um, like hard words in them that I don't know and if I watch the video then I know what the word is.
NB:	That's a good idea. Did *you* think of that idea?
Lauren:	Yes.
NB:	So, do you ever say to your mum, 'If I watch the video it will help me read'?
Lauren:	[Laughs] No!
NB:	Why? What do you think she would say?
Lauren:	My mum would say, 'Don't be silly.'
NB:	So, do you think that grown ups don't listen to children then?
Lauren:	Sometimes my mummy does and sometimes she doesn't. When she's in a hurry she doesn't and when she isn't she does.

[Girl aged 6, TSE, pp. 2–3]

Children's attitudes towards reading, video and television

In order to educe the children's attitudes towards books and reading and watching television and videos the conversations with the children were informal and free ranging. In an effort to avoid 'leading' questions I opened the interviews with a brief statement in which I explained that I wanted to find out what children of their age liked to watch on television and what they liked to read. My first question, 'What do you want to tell me about first, videos, books or television?', was designed to be a fairly open-ended one, while also serving to establish some parameters for the discussion. The question also allowed the children to take control of the direction of the ensuing conversation.

A significant feature of all the interviews with the children was the children's eagerness to share their thoughts and ideas about books, videos and television programmes. Only a very few children did not make significant contributions to the informal discussions. A number of factors may have contributed to the children's willingness to talk. Firstly, I was a visitor to the children's schools who was not introduced as a teacher but simply as 'someone who wants to talk to you'. Secondly, it rapidly became apparent to the children that rather than asking them questions that tested their knowledge, I was asking them questions only they knew the answers to. Furthermore, the children were encouraged to talk about and reflect upon their out-of-school experiences. The presence of the tape recorder also encouraged the children to talk as they were all keen to listen to part of the interview at the end of the session. The children frequently ignored me as they debated a point or took delight in reliving a shared experience (e.g. discussing a favourite book or video).

One question, however, did appear to unnerve some of the children involved and these particular children initially showed some ambivalence in their responses. When I asked whether they preferred television or books I felt that they suspected there was a 'right' answer to the question and they were clearly not sure whether to give their honest opinion or whether to say what they felt they should:

> *NB*: What do you like better, watching television or videos or reading?
> [Both girls laugh a little, exchange glances and do not answer]
> *NB*: Be honest, say whatever you think. Some children say they like books better and some children say they like television better.
> *Alice*: I like television.
> *Sophie*: Probably books.
> [Girls aged 5, TSG, p. 4]

Another child, who was clear that her parents were not impressed by television expressed her ambivalence in the following way:

> *Catherine*: Well, I know I like books more than videos but I like videos . . .
> [Girl aged 5, TSB, p. 3]

The question about the relative merits of videos, television and reading also resulted in a great deal of discussion and occasional squabbles between the children being interviewed:

> *Harriet*: I think they're both the same.
> *Krishen*: I think books, I think books . . .

Harriet: NO! They're both the same.
Krishen: No, books.
Harriet: NO! They're the same.
NB: That's all right, you think they're the same and Krishen thinks books
             are better, that's fine, people have different ideas, that's why I'm asking
             this question to find out what people think . . .
[Girl and boy both aged 7, TSK, p. 3]

There are likely to be a range of explanations for the children's response to this particular question. One explanation could reside in the fact that, in spite of my attempts to ensure the children felt I was genuinely interested in their views and opinions and not testing them, it was an inescapable fact that most of the interviews with the children occurred within the school environment. The relevance of this is clear in view of the fact that the majority of the children believed that the adults in their lives do not appear to value the activity of watching television. The 'right' answer, therefore, is likely to be that books are preferable to television. Furthermore, many of those interviewed were new initiates into the schooling system who were, as yet, uncertain about when the classroom rules about providing the 'right' answer could be suspended. Moreover, some children were uncertain about my status, was I really merely an interested adult who had time to talk with them or was I a teacher? Gordon Wells and others have provided ample examples of how young children learn to play safe and not risk providing potentially unacceptable answers to teachers' questions (Wells, 1987). These three factors were likely to shape the children's response to this and some of the other questions, as young children are aware of the differences that exist between home and school in terms of values and expectations, and for those children involved in the study who perceived a mismatch between the values of their homes and those of the school, attempting to guess what might be the 'right' answer to an unfamiliar question was a daunting prospect. Importantly too, for the vast majority of the children, the question was a key one in that it was a source of explicit or potential conflict at home as the previous chapter shows. This conflict partly arises from the belief that television displaces other activities, in particular reading (see research cited in Gunter and McAleer, 1997) but also, as the previous chapter highlighted, children are clear that their parents do not seem to think that their are any real benefits in watching television and videos.

Reading: children's experiences, preferences and opinions

There was no discernible pattern to what the children chose to talk about first. Keen readers did not necessarily choose to talk about books first and avid television or video viewers sometimes opted to talk about their favourite book.

The following extracts and accompanying brief analyses are intended to provide a context for the children's views about television and videos, and, very interestingly, their conception of the role of television and videos in supporting children learning to read.

Attitudes towards reading and books

When asked about what they liked to read, the children's answers were interesting, not because they provided many surprises regarding children's favourites, but rather because the children's responses revealed a great deal about their attitudes towards reading.

NB:	What's your favourite book?
Lizzie:	I don't have one.
NB:	Do you like reading?
Lizzie:	Yes.
NB:	So, what sorts of things are you reading at school?
Lizzie:	My one at school is *The Sunflower* and my one at home is Roald Dahl.
NB:	Which one?
Catherine:	I got Roald Dahl
Lizzie:	It's got lots of stories.
NB:	Is that the *Treasury*? It's got lots of extracts, parts from different books?
Lizzie:	Yes, and it's big.

[Girl aged 6, TSB, p. 2]

What struck me was that the child appeared to have an expectation that one would read different books at home and at school and felt it important that I know what she was reading in both contexts. A number of other children revealed that there were differences between what they chose to read, or were given to read at school and what they chose to read at home:

NB:	What book are you reading at the moment?
Beatrice:	At the moment? At home or at school?
NB:	Do you read a different one?
[Both children look at each other and laugh]	
Beatrice:	Yes.
NB:	Why?
Beatrice:	Because . . . I don't know.
NB:	Don't you like the school's books?
Beatrice:	Yeah, I like the school books but one of my books is at home and one is for school.
NB:	So what are you reading at school and at home?
Beatrice:	I'm reading at home right now, *Angelina Goes Ice Skating* and at school I'm on the Blue Books and I'm reading . . . erm . . . um . . . um . . . um . . . oh, I don't really know.
NB:	Can you remember the last book you read?
Beatrice:	The last bit . . . the whole page?
NB:	No, the last book, the name of it.
Beatrice:	Erm . . . *Briony Goes . . . at the Gardening Centre* or something.
NB:	Shall I just say you are reading blue books?
Beatrice:	Mmm.
Annie:	I'm reading thick books.

NB: Thick books?
Annie: I get to choose them because they're thick.
Beatrice: She's reading thick books
NB: But what book?
Annie: *The Tinderbox*.
NB: Is that at home and at school?
Annie: That's for my homework.
NB: So what do you like reading at home?
Annie: Um . . . baby books.
[Girls aged 6 and 5, TSC, p. 2]

As with the previous child, both children made it clear that there were books for school and books for home. The children either refrained from, or were unable to articulate, their reasons for this pattern of reading but claimed not to actively dislike the books from school. Other comments made by Beatrice would suggest, however, that here was a child who was not particularly interested in the school books she read. She could not, for example, remember the titles of her current book nor the book she had read previously. Her query as to whether I wanted her to 'remember' the 'last bit . . . the whole page?' may have been triggered by a mishearing or misinterpretation of my question but Beatrice's inability to tell me very much about the book, not even the title, suggests that this particular child was probably not reading these 'Blue Books' with a high level of interest and engagement. Children who have enjoyed a book will talk about 'what happened at the end' and will not be concerned with word-perfect recitations of the final page. The rather depressing attitude towards school books was also reflected in the manner in which the two children spoke about 'thick books' rather than the content. The final comment also hinted at the possibility that what Annie currently needed and enjoyed was the affirming experience of reading books that did not present too much of a challenge rather than struggling with 'thick books'. Without further discussion with Annie it is impossible to state with any degree of certainty what she meant by 'baby books' and it is feasible that Annie was referring to short, relatively easy to read chapter books, picture books, or books she had enjoyed as a slightly younger child. However, it became clearer later in the conversation that Annie's current focus was on the length and 'thickness' of the book rather than the content alone or the presence or absence of pictures (TSC, p. 4) Two other 5-year-olds appeared to have a very similar approach to choosing books but were able to provide a clearer explanation of their reading preferences:

NB: What book have you got in your reading folder?
Sasha: Um, I can't remember.
NB: Is your mummy or daddy or someone else reading you something at home?
Sasha: Well, at home I'm reading *Pippi Longstocking* and my Daddy is reading me, um, *The Wizard of Oz*, they're the adventures of the Tin Man and the Scarecrow.
[Brief diversion as other child talks about *Wizard of Oz*]

NB: When you say you are reading it at home, do you read different books at home than you do at school?

Sasha: Yes.

NB: Why?

Sasha [Pulls face and doesn't reply]

NB: Do you not like the school books then?

Sasha: No.

India: Well I like the school books better than um, home books because home books are like normal books and school books are like easier. I like school books a bit better.

NB: So when you say easier, what are they about? Are they not story books?

India: Like they've got easy words and they've got little words like 'and' *Beauty and the Beast* they've got hard words.

NB: And haven't you got any books like that at home, or not as many?

India: Yes.

Sasha: Well at school reading, um, um, my books aren't easy so I don't enjoy it. I try and choose easy ones because I'm on the choosing level, not like India.

NB: Right, so, you don't like reading the difficult books you are told to read?

Sasha: No.

[Girls aged 5, TSF, p. 1]

Many children, however, conveyed their excitement about reading and their enjoyment of books. A 4-year-old boy talked enthusiastically about his favourite books:

NB: Do you like Thomas books?

Jack: Yeah. Three or four I read, every night.

NB: Every night?

Jack: Yeah.

NB: Do you have a favourite Thomas book?

Jack: Yeah, when Percy falls in the mud and they get dirty.

NB: When Percy falls in the mud did you say?

Jack: Er, I mean coal. Sometimes I get all muddled up 'cos they . . . er . . . all black.

[Boy aged 4, TSI, p. 2]

Reading at home and at school

A conversation with a 6-year-old confirmed that, for some children, reading at home is an enjoyable activity which is sometimes shared with other family members:

Elizabeth: Um, my favourite book is *Horrible Science*.

NB: *Horrible Science*?

Elizabeth: And it tells you how to make Frankenstein, what bits you need of the body and how to do it. It's called *Blood, Bones and Body Bits*.

NB: Does your sister like *Horrible Science*?

Elizabeth: Yeah, we share together.
NB: You both read it?
Elizabeth: Yeah, but I'm reading it by myself.
[Girl aged 6, older sister aged 9, TSE, pp. 1–2]

Other children also talked enthusiastically about reading to themselves and of being read to by parents or older siblings:

Sophie: At home well, my favourite book is because, I have my favourite book because and it's a *Year Full of Stories* and every day of the year it has every day of the year in and so, and every night we read the story, nearly every night.
NB: Do you have to read the right one for the day of the year?
Sophie: Well, if it's really short and we go to bed a bit earlier we probably read another short one.
NB: When you say *we* read it, do you read it or does somebody read it to you?
Sophie: My mummy or Jessie [older sister] reads it to me.
NB: What about you? Does somebody read to you at home?
Alice: First I do some reading from my reading book and then Mummy reads to me.
NB: So is Mummy reading you *Charlie and the Chocolate Factory*?
Alice: Yes, *Charlie* by Roald Dahl.
[Two girls aged 5, TSG, p. 3]

Two 5-year-old boys talked with great vivacity about their home-based experiences of reading. The boys' enjoyment of the books was very evident in Gary's delight in sharing his growing knowledge of poetry and in John's anticipation of the promised story at bedtime:

NB: Do you like reading?
John: Yeah.
Gary: Yeah.
John: I got a big fairytale book, it's got *Sleeping Beauty*, *Little Red Riding Hood*, erm . . .
Gary: I got a poem book!
John: I don't know all the others.
NB: Can you read them?
Gary: My mum gonna, they're bedtime stories.
NB: Does mum read them to you?
John: Yeah, at bedtime, but she ain't read one yet, she's going to read me one today before I go to bed.
Gary: I got a poem book and I know one.
NB: Mmm.
Gary: I like the light. I like the dark [laughs]
NB: Is that from your poetry book?
Gary: Yeah.
[Boys aged 5, TSJ, p. 3]

The fact that reading at home is not a pleasurable experience for some children can not be ignored:

> *Dileep*: I don't like reading books because my mum gets tired when I read it and she keeps saying 'I have to do it. I have to do it' and I don't like doing it.
> [Boy aged 6, TSM, p. 3]

It would be unwise to draw conclusions from young children's initial statements about reading since further discussion with the children often revealed that children's interest in books and their attitudes towards reading were sometimes fairly complex. For example, on the basis of what Sasha had initially said about attempting to choose 'easy' books (TSF, p. 6) it was somewhat surprising to find that when asked to name her favourite book she had some difficulty:

> *Sasha*: At school or at home?
> *NB*: Um, anywhere.
> *Sasha*: Well, that's hard. Well, *all* of my books are favourites.
> *NB*: All of them? OK, if I said to you we are going on holiday tomorrow and you can take a few books with you what would you choose?
> *Sasha*: Erm, all my chapter books and then it would take me a long time to read them.
> *NB*: So chapter books like *Pippi Longstocking*?
> *Sasha*: Yes.
> [Girl, aged 5, TSF, p. 6]

Sasha was apparently, at the time of the interview, not relishing the challenge presented by the 'hard' books she was expected to read at school. It would seem, however, that she enjoyed the activity of reading *per se* as she chose books for her imaginary holiday that would take her a long time to read. Reading between the lines, it is also possible that Sasha's taste in books was not catered for in school, hence the comment that she didn't like the 'school books' but felt that all *her* own books were favourites.

Two reception-aged boys also seemed to be very definite that they did not like books but as the conversation wore on it was clear that they not only enjoyed reading certain books but also they became quite animated when they collaborated in the retelling the story of a book they had both read:

> *Michael*: I don't like books.
> *NB*: Can you tell me why you don't like books?
> *Michael*: I don't really usually like books.
> *NB*: Mmm. Are there any sort of books that you *do* like?
> *Michael*: Yup. The sort of like school books.
> *NB*: When you say school books what do you mean, school books?
> *Michael*: When we get school books to take home.
> *NB*: You mean the *Biff and Chip* books, those sorts of books?
> *Michael*: No . . .

John:	No, we get them 'ere with numbers and stories, they're yellow aren't they, we choose them and then we bring them back, we gotta read them at home.
Michael:	Yeah, when we read the *Biff and Chip* books and then . . .
NB:	Yeah . . .
Michael:	I read straight through *The Wobbly Tooth*.
NB:	Excellent . . .
Michael:	'Cos, 'cos when . . .
John:	I did as well
NB:	So is that one of your favourites then?
John:	It's good, *The Wobbly Tooth* wasn't it?
Michael:	It was good when he was pushing, um, the swing for Biff, when Biff jumped off, the swing hit back and it hit his chin . . .
John:	Yeah . . .
Michael:	And one of the tooths, um it, he didn't actually know that it had gone like that [indicates how a tooth may be knocked into a mouth] and it, and it actually, actually knocked one of his tooths down and it actually went down into his, um, tummy.
John:	Yeah.
NB:	Did he swallow it?
Michael:	Yeah, by mistake.
NB:	Oh no! Poor thing.
Michael:	Mmmm.[Pause] One time my brother did that, he did.

[Two boys aged 5, TSH, pp. 2–3]

These two 5-year-olds appeared to have a much more ambivalent and fluid attitude towards reading than did Sasha. Their position changed during the course of the conversation until, towards the end of the interchange, they were taking great delight in retelling the story and checking their understanding with each other. It is possible that these two reception class children, as relatively inexperienced readers, were still in the very early stages of forming their attitudes towards reading. Observing the two boys talking there was a sense that similar experiences may contribute to these particular children's growing awareness of the possibility of discussing a mutually familiar text. Furthermore, whilst relishing the 'best bits', the children were learning about the social nature of reading and how this shapes one's understanding of the text. Each child in the extract above, for example, would have learnt that it was possible for another reader to share their view about what was the 'best bit'. Furthermore, John's perception of the likelihood of the event may also have been shaped by Michael's comment about his brother's tooth. The conversation between the two boys is likely to have played a role in developing their growing understanding of the use of dramatic devices in writing. In this particular instance the drama did not reside in, for example, the humour of the incident or the improbability of the episode, but rather the slightly frightening fact that the key event fell well within the realms of possibility, as Michael had testified.

Returning to the boys' initial position as regards reading, it is possible that the comments were influenced by issues related to gender. This is an aspect explored in more depth in Chapter 7.

Children's ideas about the relationship between television, videos and reading

Do videos and television programmes have any effect on reading?

Not surprisingly, some of the children interviewed had not formulated any ideas about the possible links between videos and television and reading whereas others, whilst having definite opinions, were unable to explain the reasons for these opinions. In many cases this may have simply been due to a lack of sufficient experience as in the case of Anne:

> *NB*: How about you? Do you think watching television and videos helps you read?
> *Anne*: Yes!
> *NB*: Why?
> *Anne*: Don't know.
> *NB*: If you think really hard, can you think of a way in which watching television or videos has helped you read? Have you ever read a book that's quite difficult and maybe seen the video first or . . . ?
> *Anne*: I have seen *Cinderella* and I've read the book but I haven't done another one, I've only read *Cinderella* and got the tape.
> *NB*: The audio tape or video?
> *Anne*: Video
> [Girl aged 6, TSC, p. 4]

A 5-year-old was strongly of the opinion that watching a video based on a book did not make it easier to read the book:

> *NB*: Do you think watching the video helped you read the book — made it easier to read the book?
> *Catherine*: It goes too fast.
> *NB*: What, the video goes too fast?
> *Catherine*: Yes.
> [Girl aged 5, TSB, p. 1]

Catherine was unable to explain why she felt the video was 'too fast' but her comment is interesting in the light of what she had told me earlier in the conversation.

Catherine had previously told me that her favourite video was Disney's cartoon version of *101 Dalmatians*. She went on to state that 'I got all of the things, the video, the cassette tape and the book'. The book was 'a little one' and it is therefore possible that she was able to read along with the cassette tape but this was not possible when watching the video because the video contains a wealth of detail and the pace of action is fast, allowing little time for reflection.

Other children were more willing or able to articulate their clearly thought-out ideas:

NB: Do you think watching television helps you with your reading? Do you
               think it would make you into a better reader?

Sasha: Yes.

NB: Can you say why?

Sasha: Because it tells you like words, like difficult, it sounds out like di-ffi-cult,
               then if you recognize it in a book you can just say it and it makes your
               reading better.

[Girl, aged 5, TSF, p. 5]

Sasha was not alone in possessing clear notions about the role of television and videos in supporting children's reading and writing. The clarity of Sasha's views is fascinating in view of her limited experience of watching videos and television. It is necessary to note at this point that Sasha's mother reported that she herself never videotaped programmes for Sasha, who also never watched live television programmes and 'rarely' watched videos. Sasha herself reported that she and her younger brother possessed 'Thomas' videos, a French video and *The Secret Garden*'. A longer extract of the conversation with Sasha and India provides further insight into the two girls' perceptions of the link between reading and screen-based texts. It is worth noting that India's screen-based experiences are somewhat different to those of Sasha. India claimed to 'have got loads' of videos including *Bugs Bunny*, *Scooby Doo*, *Dennis the Menace* and *The Wizard of Oz*. India also talked about how her 'whole family likes watching *Coronation Street*' after which she and her 7-year-old brother go to bed. The two girls differed in terms of their reading attainment at school, a point that Sasha highlighted when she informed me that when it came to selecting school reading books she was 'on the choosing level, not like India'.

NB: Right. So still talking about how television is good for your reading, you
               said it helps you with the words, does it help you with anything else?

Sasha: Yeah. It helps you with your writing sort of, because it . . . it sometimes . . .

India: I know what it does. It helps you with your talking like . . .

Sasha: It . . .

India: It helps you with your talking like if you come to England and you're
               American and you say 'Hey, that's cool' [*said in American accent*] and
               then you watch telly and it's this sort of accent and then they'll talk like
               us.

NB: Right, mmmm.

Sasha: Yeah. But with writing it sounds out the words, but just like the reading,
               so you know how to spell the words.

NB: So it helps you read the words' cos it sounds them out, it helps you with
               your writing because it helps you spell them, anything else?

India: I think one more thing.

NB: Yes, go on.

India: It helps you with your . . . spelling.

NB: Right, OK.

[*Brief detour in conversation*]

NB: Have you ever read a book that's actually quite difficult but you'd also
               seen the video?

Sasha: No.

NB: You've never done that? So you haven't read anything like *Matilda* or *Charlie and the Chocolate Factory*?

Sasha: No, I don't even know those two stories.

NB: What about you?

India: Yes, I've tried to read *The Secret Garden*, about a thousand times.

NB: But you haven't got the video have you?

India: No.

NB: Do you think if you had the video it might help you read the book?

India: Well, not exactly. Because videos have kind of different words and it's er, sort of a bit different because it's got colours and um, it, it doesn't really say the words and you might not get it in order because um, they might say it in a different time because they're doing actions too.

NB: Right. So it's not exactly the same as the book so it won't necessarily help that much?

Sasha: I think it would really, because like it tells you the words, the difficult words like. . . . um. . . . so because like they help you because they tell you the words. That's why I think television programmes are quite good.

[Two girls, aged 5, TSF, p. 5]

The two children covered a number of issues in this brief interchange. At various points both children focused on a particular surface feature of written texts, graphophonics, the relation between the written symbols and the sounds they represent. Sasha is very clear that videos 'help you spell' and read because videos 'sound out' the words. This is useful for her as she is confident about her phonological knowledge, she is able to identify the sounds that words are composed of and transform the sounds she hears into the written symbols or graphemes conventionally used to represent these sounds. India initially agreed that watching videos and television helps with spelling but then later argued that watching a video of *The Secret Garden* would not help her read the book.

The divergence in the children's views may be attributable to their different experiences of watching television and videos. Possibly India's greater experience of watching videos and television programmes has resulted in her being more aware of the limited extent to which videos are simply reproductions of books (e.g. in terms of the language used). Sasha may not have a well-developed understanding of exactly how television texts may differ from books, although earlier in the conversation she made comments that suggested that she had some idea that videos and books were not identical:

NB: You said that your videos are not the kind of ones you can have a book of but you mentioned *Thomas the Tank Engine* videos . . .

Sasha: I know, but there are lots and lots of stories and we've got *Thomas* books but not the actual video sort of thing.

NB: Oh right, so they're not exactly the same is that what you are saying?

Sasha: Yes.

[Girl aged 5, TSF, p. 3]

India is clear that familiarity with the video will not necessarily help her read the words of the pages of the book. Her standpoint was different from Sasha's and her reasoning was intriguing. India explained that 'videos have kind of different words' and a video 'doesn't really say the words and you might not get it in order because um, they might say it in a different time because they're doing actions too'. India is right in many ways, screenplays of books may deviate from the original text, particularly in terms of the dialogue, the order in which key events happen, and, very importantly, on video the narrative is usually carried by the visual images and dialogue. The point she made about 'doing actions' is very pertinent. Laurene Krasny Brown, a researcher into children's responses to stories in different media stated that films 'visualize more of the story's active verbs' (cited in Messeneger Davies, 1989, p. 72). The consequence of this is that inexperienced readers cannot rely on their verbal memory to help them read passages in books which are rich in action and which they have seen on a video. Viewers may have a strong mental image of the action but little idea about what words may be used to describe what they have seen.

The fact that Sasha was a considerably more confident and fluent reader than India may have meant that India was looking for a degree of 'scaffolding', or support of a specific nature, which she was aware that videos did not provide and which Sasha, perhaps, did not require any more. It is interesting to note how Sasha mentions videos helping with 'difficult' words whereas India, the less accomplished reader, makes no such distinctions.

A 5-year-old boy, who was an even less experienced and fluent reader than India, appeared to concur with Sasha regarding the usefulness of videos and television:

NB: You know when you were reading the *Tots TV* books, do you think that um, watching television helped you read the book?
Michael: Yeah.
NB: Do you know how it helped you read the book?
Michael: Um . . . [long pause]
NB: How did it help you read the book?
Michael: Um, because they say the same words in the book.
[Boy aged 5, TSH, p. 2]

It is probable, however, that the *Tots TV* books did indeed have the same words as the programme, particularly in terms of the dialogue. These books, unlike *The Secret Garden*, are also short and the language and plot is simple. Furthemore, being illustrated, the *Tots TV* books do not include long sections of descriptive or contextualizing text which are difficult for inexperienced readers to make sense of without access to cueing systems such as clear pictures and secure knowledge of the probable storyline. The pictures will generally provide clues, too, about the characters' actions and thus help children make predictions about the text. Perhaps if India had attempted to read picture books which were very close to the video in terms of plot and dialogue, she may have felt that videos could support her reading.

Reviewing the responses of all the children involved in the study, it was interesting to note that beginner readers who felt that videos and television helped them read tended to support their argument by referring to short videos and short, simple books with clear pictures such as the *Noddy* books published by the BBC, *Teletubbies* books and illustrated books related to short cartoons. Amongst beginner readers the most common view was that videos 'help me read the words'.

David:	Yeah, I got about five videos about Batman.
NB:	Five videos of Batman! My goodness. Have you got any books about Batman?
David:	Yes.
NB:	Are they story books?
David:	Yeah.
NB:	What are the stories?
David:	First it's Batman getting Mr Freeze and then it's Batman getting Mr, um, [indistinct]
NB:	Are these books you can read yourself?
David:	Yeah.
NB:	Do they have lots of pictures in them?
David:	Yeah

[Boy aged 4, TSP, p. 2]

The more fluent or experienced readers acknowledged that videos may be particularly helpful with reading 'difficult' words:

Natasha:	And I've read *Matilda*.
NB:	You've read *Matilda*, all of it?
Natasha:	I saw the video first and then read the book.
NB:	Do you think that seeing the video helped you read the book or do you think that it didn't make any difference?
Natasha:	It helps you read the book 'cos it gives you more words, 'Cos if you're like, say, in the middle of it you can't read a word you can just remember what word it said.
NB:	Mmmm, what you think back to when you watched the video?
Natasha:	Yeah.

[Girl aged 6, TSE, p. 4]

Confident readers also tended to mention how videos help with the 'big shapes' of the text:

Penny:	Well, we've got books and we've got the videos and they're the same and we read um, we've got the video of *Sleeping Beauty* and we've got the video of it. And sometimes I like, I read them myself and no one helps and sometimes someone else reads them to me.
NB:	How can you read the book on your own?
Penny:	I'm, well I'm, er, well I'm just a really good reader really and I was starting, and I was on the last book of my reading books and now I'm on Year 2 books.

NB: Do you think that watching the video helped you read those books? Watching *Sleeping Beauty* helped you read the book?

Penny: Yeah.

NB: Can you think about how it helped you?

Penny: Well, they're both, they got the same thing.

NB: The same thing, what do you mean 'the same thing'?

Penny: Well, they both, like they both prick their finger and that and the prince wakes her. And, um, I think it helps me 'cos the video tells the story as well and I think . . . I . . . I . . . remember it and then when I want to read *Sleeping Beauty* I can read it by myself and also I know quite a lot of words and I can spell lots of things.

[Girl aged 5, TS1, p. 3]

A fluent reader aged 6 had the following view:

Figure 4.1   *Example of writing about* Harriet the Spy

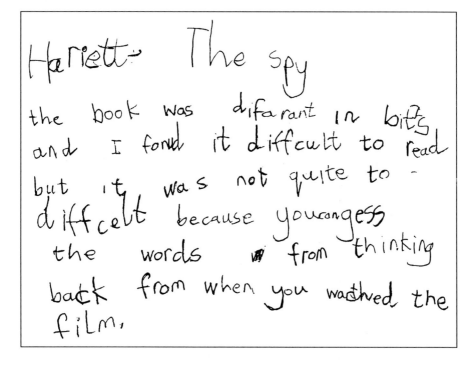

Fifteen months later, when this child was asked whether videos could help one learn to read her response was less definite:

Rehana: I don't think they help you learn to read because you can't see the words . . . no, actually I think it *does* help you because it helps you when people say the word. Like say they said 'and', when you read the thing 'and' if you can't read you remember when one of them is saying

> 'and' on the video and you think it could be 'and' so I'll just see and
> you could sound it out and you could be extra sure.
>
> NB: How else do they help maybe?
>
> *Rehana*:   Well you can guess what the words might be because you'll know the
> story.
>
> [Girl aged 7]

Here we have a fluent reader attempting to analyse what strategies are employed whilst reading. She mentions more than one cueing system, predicting and guessing supported by drawing on knowledge of the text, albeit initially the screen-based text. Her comment about 'sounding out' to be 'extra sure' highlights how fluent readers orchestrate the various cueing systems and check by cross-referencing. Bearing in mind what has been written earlier in this section about videos supporting children's reading of dialogue it is interesting to note how this fluent reader initially focuses on the spoken words on videos: 'it helps you when people *say* the word' [my emphasis].

Older children, when asked whether or not watching a TV programme or video based on a book then made it easier to read the book, made very similar comments to those made by younger children. Some of the older children mentioned the usefulness of hearing the words:

> NB: Why do you think it would help you read the book if you've seen the
> video?
>
> *Khalid*:   Because you heard the words already so . . . you heard the words
> already . . . it's a good idea.
>
> [Boy aged 11, TSU, p. 6]

When discussing the role videos may play in helping their younger siblings learn to read the older children acknowledged the usefulness of the visual images:

> NB: How do you feel it would help if they saw the video first?
>
> *Michael*:   That'd be good.
>
> *Khalid*:   That'd be easy then and then they could read the book.
>
> *Michael*:   But they could do something else, instead of watching videos they
> could watch erm, listen to a cassette and they could follow it.
>
> NB: Do you think cassettes would be as good as videos or better?
>
> *Khalid*:   I think videos are better 'cause you can *see* the story, you can see all
> the stuff that they are doing.
>
> [Boys aged 11, TSU, p. 5]

From the comments made by these Year 6 children, it would seem that children's views on the utility of videos for reading development remain fairly stable through the primary years of education. I would suggest, however, that what is seen by the children to be useful is related more to their reading ability than to their chronological age. As children become more confident, fluent and experienced readers videos and television can continue to play a supportive role but the emphasis shifts from support with individual words and 'sounding out words' and knowledge of the 'big shapes' to some of the more complex aspects of language:

NB: How about you now? Now that you're a really good reader do you think watching videos and television helps you?

Rehana: Yes, I think it does. Because say they said an expression like 'Don't let the cat out of the bag' and I didn't understand it and it was on video it would be a bit easier to understand because they have, um, they have action and you sort of understand it better, because it's got the action. But [in books] it's still a bit harder because when you um, you don't actually have people saying it, *you're* reading it and it's a bit harder it's just easier because if you read 'cat out of the bag' and you've already seen it on television you thought back and thought, oh, I know what that meant because of the actions.

NB: So in the book if it said 'She let the cat out of the bag' . . .

Rehana: I thought, I might have thought it meant a bag and don't let the cat out of the bag.

NB: You might have taken it literally?

Rehana: Yeah, but when it's actually shown on television when they're saying that you think actually it can't be, because they haven't got a picture of a cat coming out of the bag.

NB: So now that you're a really good reader is that how watching videos helps you? Does it help you with the words or anything?

Rehana: No, but if you're littler it helps you sound out the words, no not littler, people who can't read very well.

[Girl aged 7]

When reflecting upon how videos and television may help her now, as a fluent reader, this child focused on how videos and television may help to identify idiomatic phrases and clarify their meaning. Confident about her ability to read individual words, this child is concerned with getting to grips with the meanings of specific phrases which are not accessible through knowledge of the individual words.

Blurb on books

Not all children agreed that videos were particularly useful in learning to read. Two children in a Year 1 class discussed the importance of the blurb on books and how this was lacking in the case of videos:

NB: Now this is about what you as *children* think. Do you think that watching television or videos helps you at school or with your reading or . . .

Alice: I think books help us 'cause if we remember our words for when we're reading it will help us.

Sophie: I think books can as well because they can give you the infor . . . information of the story and that kind of thing like they don't say, they don't just tell the story.

Alice: They give you information on the back of the book about the story.

Sophie: Yeah and about the story.

NB: Do you mean background information?

Sophie: Yes and well on videos it's just straight on the with story really, instead of giving you infor . . . information.
NB: That's a very good idea, a very good thought there because that's what grown ups sometimes say, that it is just too easy with videos, you just watch the story and you don't read all the other interesting information.
Alice: Yeah, because the information on the backs of the books like give you the simple parts of the books, not every single word like 'and', 'the', 'the' . . .
NB: Well, they give you the main points of the story don't they?
Sophie: Yeah and they give you what kind of books you might like and TV kinda like don't. They just show you the video, you know when you open that there maybe some videos that [you] can see [advertised] but they don't give you information like and like books do. With books. . . .
Alice: So you can get the books.
[Two girls aged 5, TSG, pp. 4–5]

Only one of these two children was a fluent reader, but both children were able to identify what was missing from a video. The fact that inside video cases there may be pictures of 'other videos that you can see' was not enough. Both these children were aware of the existence and purpose of the blurb on books and felt that this was lacking in the case of videos. The covers for most children's videos do, in fact, provide an outline of the story but there is certainly a lack of detailed information about the author and the book on which the video may be based. Furthermore, no suggestions are offered about other videos or books the children may enjoy. Helen Bromley (1996) has written about her work with slightly older children, part of which involved asking the children to read the video case of Disney's *Beauty and the Beast*. She outlines how the children were able to read the words and were able to analyse why certain styles of script were used, the reason for including certain pieces of information (e.g. the fact that the film was an 'Oscar-winning classic') and also the role the pictures played in providing clues about the characters involved and also providing some inkling of the drama about to unfold. Helen Bromley argues that the children were 'reading texts from a variety of genres'; and draws on the work of Margaret Meek (1991) in asserting that children need to be encouraged to develop their ability to be 'critically literate' when reading texts composed of words and or images. Alice and Sophie make a valid point regarding the importance of the blurb on books but, as Helen Bromley's work suggests, as we approach the twenty-first century and in view of the technological developments, it is perhaps timely to review what counts as literate behaviour and children need to be encouraged to recognize the diversity of texts which can be read.

Children's preferences: books or videos

When the children were asked whether, in general, they preferred books or videos and television the responses suggest that the amount of television and videos children watched was not a good predictor of children's preferences. Some children who watched very little TV and very few videos made comments such as:

Alice: I like television.

NB: You like television better? Can you say why? What's nicer about television?

Alice: You don't have to read it and the pictures aren't completely frozen like in a book.

NB: So you like the movement? What about you, what do you prefer?

Sophie: Probably books.

NB: So why do you like books?

Sophie: Because, not because they're frozen but it's because if you want the sound to go really low down and you can still hear it but if you, but like on television you can't get it right . . . um, . . . the right. . . . so say if I wanted it the middle I couldn't really hear, I couldn't really hear it in the middle but with stories you can because a person, well *you* are reading it.

[Girls aged 5, TSG, p. 4]

A child who watched moderate amounts of videos and TV (e.g. up to three times a week) opted for books saying:

Elizabeth: I think I'd choose books because books is more interesting, they teach you more things, there could be very funny ones, there could be picture ones that you might like, there could be things with tapes you might like and I think I'd just go for books.

[Girl aged 6, TSE, p. 5]

Another child, also a moderate viewer, opted for television:

NB: You'd choose television. Why?

Natasha: 'Cos it's sort of, like in the *Teletubbies* they always say 'Heho!' at something funny and um, if like in a serious book it's not so funny.

NB: What about a funny book though?

Natasha: But then, if you, but then a funny book is like, if you want to look at it, if you want to read it all and the next night you forget well it's easier like in television, it's easier because in television like if it's quite a short one and with more activities, then it's easier to have the video in one whole day.

NB: That's true, I'd not thought of that.

[Girl aged 5, TSE, p. 5]

Some children who watched live television virtually every day and who owned and watched a number of videos preferred books:

Krishen: I think books are better because they are more important because they, they, your reading gets better and if there's a test at school, yeah, at school, and there's some questions at least you can read it and get it right.

[Boy aged 7, TSK, p. 3]

A younger girl appeared to be drawn to non-fiction and humorous books:

Lauren: Because some of them are more true than videos and they're really good
          to read, they're really fun and funny.
[Girl aged 6, TSE, p. 3]

Other regular TV and video viewers preferred videos and television; two 5-year-old
boys were clear about their preferences:

Michael: Videos are better.
NB: Why?
Michael: Because you can watch them and they're good.
NB: What about you, John?
John: Videos are better because they're more sort of talky. And they saying
          things that they mean to say.
[Boys aged 5, TSH, p. 2]

Two older children explained the reasons for their preferences:

Parveen: Videos are better than books.
Adam: Yeah.
NB: Why?
Adam: 'Cause videos are . . .
Parveen: 'Cause when you're tired your hands get tired you get . . .
Adam: 'Cause if you read a book, yeah, and you lose it, yeah, you don't have
          a video of it and you like this book, then you can't read it any more
          'cause you lost it, then if you have a video you can watch it all the time
          . . . you can't lose a video . . . Like if you like the book and it's lost
          then you can't read it, that's why I like a video 'cause you can watch it
          every time.
[Boy aged 7, girl aged 7, TSL, p. 4]

Many children felt that they did not have an overall preference and simply replied
that books and videos 'were the same'. Other children felt that the context or their
mood would determine their preference:

Keir: Videos are better for when I'm having snugs [a cuddle] and books are
          better for when I'm going to bed.
[Boy aged 4]

In the light of the research findings discussed in Chapters 2 and 3 it is interesting to
note that all the children in the study stated that they enjoyed watching TV and
videos. However, when asked to make a choice between books and videos and TV
it was apparent that children's preferences were influenced by a range of factors
and not *all* the children preferred videos and TV. Children chose books because, in
comparison with videos and TV, they were deemed to be funnier, more true-to-life,
more interesting, more informative and, for one 7-year-old, important for improving
reading. Furthermore, some children, such as Sophie, preferred books because they
felt they were more in control of the experience. The children who preferred videos
and TV mentioned enjoying the action or 'the movement', being able to hear the

characters talk and the fact that, unlike many books, complete videos can be viewed within a day. Other children preferred videos because they do not need to be held, while another child felt videos were less likely than books to be mislaid.

There were, however, two discernible trends in the children's responses. The first pattern to emerge was that the boys in the sample tended to express a preference for videos and TV while the girls' preferences were more evenly balanced between the small screen and books.

The second pattern to emerge was that, in general, children's preferences seemed to be linked more to their reading confidence than to the amount of television or videos they watched. Confident readers tended to express a preference for books and less confident readers were more likely to opt for videos and television. The sample size and the lack of a rigorous quantitative analysis of children's reading ability and levels of confidence means that it is not possible to draw firm conclusions. Recent research however, conducted by the NFER, would suggest that there is a positive correlation between achievement and frequency of reading for fun or pleasure (Brooks et al., 19, p. 31). What is not clear is whether a causal relationship exists between video and television viewing patterns and children's reading attainment. Barrie Gunter and Jill McLeer and have discussed how research findings over the past 30 years, which have tended to be used as evidence that television viewing results in lower attainment levels and poorer reading skills, could be interpreted somewhat differently. Whilst acknowledging that television viewing may hinder the development of reading, Barrie Gunter and Jill McAleer offer an alternative in suggesting that children with reading problems are more likely to turn to television for amusement than are confident readers (Gunter and McAleer, 1997).

It could be that the tendency for boys in the sample to prefer television and videos to books was linked to their reading ability and perception of reading as an enjoyable pastime. Analysing the available data pertaining to the reading attainment of the children in the study, it would be fair to state that more girls than boys in the sample were confident, fluent readers. This pattern is in line with other research findings which have recently highlighted differences that exist between girls and boys in terms of a range of aspects of reading, including attitudes towards reading, reading for accuracy and reading attainment (HMI, 1996; Brooks et al., 1997; DES, 1991; Osmont and Davis, 1987; QCA, 1998). It is beyond the remit of this book to discuss critically the growing body of research centred around this issue, but the implications of boys' underperformance in reading and their possible preference for screen-based entertainment is clearly an issue that merits further research. Gender issues are discussed in later chapters, as it is apparent that it is not merely that boys may prefer TV and videos to books, but that this may impact negatively on their reading development (Chapter 7).

Children's opinions about videos based on books

In addition to asking children about their overall preferences, the children were also invited to talk about their opinions about videos based on books. Many of the young children in the study were able to articulate their ideas about the relative merits of a specific book and the related video or television programme. Charlotte, by outlining the slight differences in the story as shown on video and that in her book, was able to explain why she preferred the book:

Charlotte:	Well. . . . [thinks for 25 seconds] I've seen the book of *Sleeping Beauty* and I saw . . . I mean I've seen the video of *Sleeping Beauty* and then I saw the book and thought the book was better.
NB:	Why did you think the book was better?
Charlotte:	Well, I don't really actually know why I thought the book was better.
NB:	Did you maybe like the pictures better, or was it that the story was slightly different or. . . .
Charlotte:	Yeah. Yeah, slightly different because in the video right, she only sleeps for about one night and, um, in the book it's a hundred years and I think it's more exciting a hundred years 'cause she didn't grow up.

[Girl aged 6, TSA, p. 3]

Lauren explained why she preferred the video version of *Charlie and the Chocolate Factory* despite having read the book first and there being a degree of dissimilarity between the video and the book:

NB:	Have you seen the video of *Charlie and the Chocolate Factory*?
Lauren:	Yes.
NB:	What did you think of it, did you like it?
Lauren:	Yes.
NB:	Have you read the book? Or has Mummy read it to you?
Lauren:	No, Daddy reads it to me.
NB:	Did you enjoy the video more or did you enjoy the book more?
Lauren:	The video.
NB:	Why did you enjoy the video?
Lauren:	Because it's quicker and you don't have to turn the pages.
NB:	That's a good reason! Is the video a bit different to the book in any way?
Lauren:	The Oompa Loompas were different because they had long stretched hair on the book, on the picture . . . and their voices are really, really funny, squeaky.

[Girl aged 6, TSE, p. 1]

Older children may be conscious of the reasons why a particular video may be confusing and unintelligible to a younger child and furthermore how reading the book first may help minimize possible misunderstandings:

NB:	Have you seen the video of *The BFG*?
Shakir:	Yeah, I saw a cartoon version.
NB:	Did you think it was good?
Shakir:	Yeah.

NB: Have you read the book?

Shakir: I read the book but I think if little children saw the BFG they might not understand it.

NB: Why?

Shakir: Even though I read the book that's why I understood it but when I saw the film I didn't understand it quite well.

NB: Why do you say that?

Shakir: 'Cause they had complicated bits from . . . first there's that BFG, BFG is a giant and he takes that little boy[sic] and then suddenly he's walking through the streets and then he comes to this place where's there's more giants and I don't know how he got there.

NB: But in the book it's made clear is it?

Shakir: Yeah.

[Boy aged 11, TST, p. 5]

How videos may influence children's reading choices

When novels such as *Pride and Prejudice* or *Far From the Madding Crowd* are dramatized on television there is a noticeable increase in the sales of the book and the number of borrowings from libraries. As a daily traveller on London Underground it is impossible not to notice how the number of passengers reading a particular novel increases when it has been dramatized for television. From talking to class teachers, children's librarians and booksellers it would appear that children respond similarly. Research in the past has also noted how children have been motivated to read books which have been dramatized for TV or the cinema (Potter, 1982). Many children's books also currently bear the legend 'Now a new TV drama series' on the cover which not only serves to draw children's attention to the book of the film, video or TV series but is also an explicit acknowledgment of the existence of links between different types of texts, in this case written and televisual texts.

A number of children reported how they wanted an adult to read a particular book to them after having watched a video or television series they had enjoyed:

NB: What's your favourite book?

Paul: Um, *Farthing Wood*.

NB: Has it got lots of pictures in it?

Paul: Yes.

NB: Do you read it yourself or does someone read it to you?

Paul: Mummy.

NB: Do you ever watch *Farthing Wood* on television?

Paul: Yes.

NB: Which do you like better, the television series or the book?

Paul: The book, 'cause I like the reading.

NB: Are you having a go at reading it yourself then?

Paul: Yeah.

[Boy aged 4, TSP, p. 2]

A 6-year-old girl explained why her father was reading *Matilda* to her:

> *NB*:   Have your parents ever read you a book that is too difficult for you to read on your own?
> *Lauren*:   Yes. My daddy has read me *Matilda*.
> *NB*:   Right, did you enjoy it?
> *Lauren*:   Yes. And that's really hard . . .
> *NB*:   That is hard.
> *Lauren*:   'Cause sometimes it has 'constant' or 'something' or 'difficulty'.
> *NB*:   Have you seen the video of *Matilda*?
> *Lauren*:   Yes.
> *NB*:   Did you see the video before Daddy started reading you the book?
> *Lauren*:   I saw the video before.
> *NB*:   You saw the video first?
> *Lauren*:   I saw the film, the video and then the book.
> *NB*:   So why did you want Daddy to read you the book?
> *Lauren*:   'Cause I'd seen the video and thought it was good.
> [Girl aged 6, TSE, p. 4]

There were instances of children talking about how a video had captured their interest but the book on which it was based was far beyond their capability or level of understanding. Charlotte, for example, talked about how seeing a play and a televised recording of a stage show had stimulated her desire to read a book when she was older:

> *Charlotte*:   Well, I've seen a video and always wanted to read the book but it's too long.
> *NB*:   What's that?
> *Charlotte*:   *Les Miserables*. I seen the play and decided it was nice so Daddy recorded it for me on television and then I wanted to read the book but it's far too long, the book is about this thick [indicates with hands] so when I'm older I'm going to start reading it.

Not all children feel sufficiently enthusiastic or confident enough about reading to attempt to read the challenging books on which many enjoyable children's videos and TV series texts have been based: A 5-year-old, without having read the book, had decided that the video of *Matilda* was 'better' than the book:

> *Clarissa*:   Because books are always long and boring. Because when you read books sometimes you always have to say, 'Mum, what does this say?' and it's difficult to do but I just break it in half.
> *NB*:   What, the word?
> *Clarissa*:   Yeah.
> [Girl aged 5, TSM, p. 3]

Three 11-year-olds discussed why they might not want to read a specific book after having enjoyed the video. Again, the book in question was Roald Dahl's *Matilda*:

NB:	Tell me about *Matilda*.
Michael:	I rented it on Saturday . . . it was good.
NB:	So you enjoyed the film, would you read the book?
Michael:	No. 'Cos in the film yeah, it's got more graphics that you can *see* the stuff like floating up in the air, in the book you only got it in your mind.
Amina:	It's quite hard to imagine it in your mind, imagine it and everything *and* read at the same time.
Khalid:	In the book it was a bit more boring than in the film.
NB:	So you don't like imagining things just in your mind?
Khalid:	[Shakes his head]
Michael:	It's quite hard.
Amina:	I like imagining things and then seeing the video, it's your own imagination how it looks.
Michael:	I like seeing it, I just like seeing.
NB:	What about if you were to watch something — you've read the book and then you were to watch the video and for some reason it was different, like you were saying the *101 Dalmatians* was different and sometimes the characters are a bit different. Do you find that annoying or do you think that's OK, that's the book and that's the video and it doesn't really matter?
Amina:	It doesn't matter if they like make it more exciting, but if it was like the same as the book . . .
Khalid and Michael:	[At same time] It would be boring.
Amina:	. . . it might be boring.

[Girl and two boys aged 11, TSU, pp. 6–7]

Two younger girls discussed the reasons for their differing viewpoints:

NB:	. . . What about you, have you read the book of *The Lion, the Witch and the Wardrobe*?
Louise:	Mmmm n-o-o-o. I've got the whole versions of it.
NB:	Would you like to read the books yourself or have someone read them to you?
Louise:	Not really
NB:	Why wouldn't you like any one to read you the book?
Loiuse:	Well, I would but . . . I know the video so it'd be a bit boring.
NB:	Do you agree with that? That if you've seen the video the books are boring?
Charlotte:	Um, no, 'cos the books are different 'cos it takes longer.
NB:	Mmmmm.
Charlotte:	And also, well, um, it's got more parts in it because you could have lots of books and the video's just one part of it.
NB:	Mmm. And sometimes the videos are very different aren't they?
Charlotte:	Yes, because videos are faster than reading.

[Girls aged 6, TSA, p. 2]

One child commented on the advantages and disadvantages of reading a book based on a video or vice versa. (Figure 4.2)

Figure 4.2   Child's view about advantages and disadvantages of watching the video before reading the book

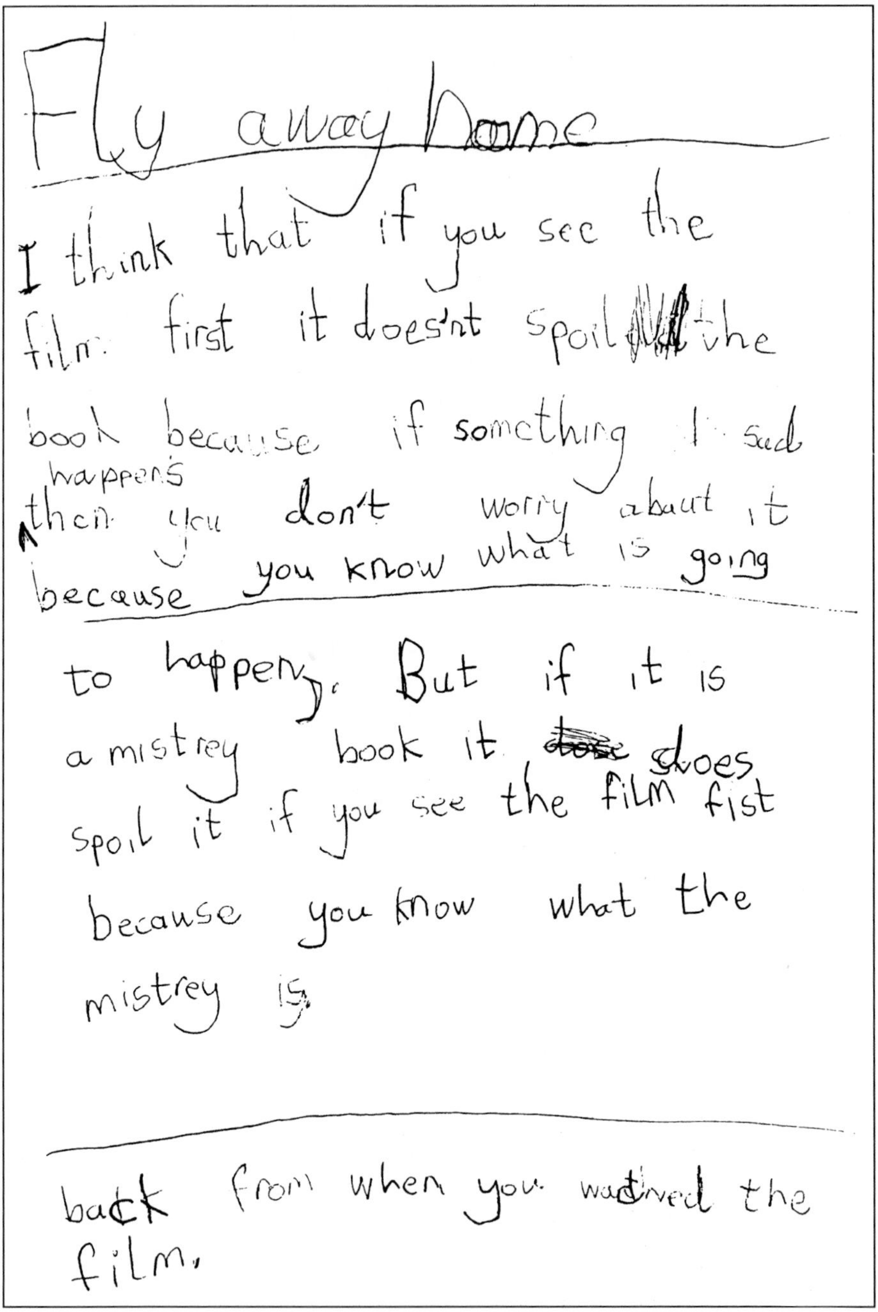

Fly away Home

I think that if you see the film first it does'nt spoil all the book because if something is sad happens then you don't worry about it because you know what is going to happen. But if it is a mistrey book it does does spoil it if you see the film fist because you know what the mistrey is.

back from when you wadived the film.

Not surprisingly, children who enjoyed reading, or who had enjoyable experiences of being read to at home, were more likely to contemplate reading the book linked to a film video or TV series. Furthermore, those children who had had the experience of watching a dramatized version of a book and then had the book read to them, or read it themselves, were less likely to feel that reading the book after seeing the film or video would be 'boring', possibly because they were more conscious of the fact that differences are likely to exist between the screen version and the book itself.

Children watching videos in different languages

A few of the children were able to draw on their personal experiences and talk about how videos helped them to read languages used in their families. Beatrice, who described herself as Swedish, talked about how a particular video supported her reading:

NB:	Do you think videos help you with your reading?
Beatrice:	Yes.
NB:	Can you tell me how?
Beatrice:	Well, because *Pippi Longstocking* is in Swedish and I, it helps me learn some Swedish words, learn some Swedish and like I have book that's Swedish and I don't understand it, and I don't know how to say it, so I watch *Pippi Longstocking* 'cos I might want to know how to read it.

[Girl aged 5, TSC, pp. 3–4]

This extract illustrates how Beatrice is conscious of how familiarity with the video supports her understanding and develops her vocabulary. I suggest that this familiarity would enable her to draw on her developing phonological knowledge of Swedish and on contextual, syntactic and semantic cues when reading the book.

Videos and writing

A few children spontaneously discussed their ideas about how videos and TV may help develop children's writing.

NB:	Do you think that watching television makes you a better reader?
Elizabeth:	No, um . . .
Natasha:	Sometimes . . . You get more ideas for, for writing and if you want to read, write a story. You get more ideas from television.
Elizabeth:	And if like on *Blue Peter* you are doing a project about Queen Elizabeth the . . .
Natasha:	That's what they did yesterday.
Elizabeth:	Um, then you get more ideas, 'cause there's more in there 'cause they talked about *Blue Peter*, um, not *Blue Peter*, Queen Elizabeth.

[Girls aged 6, TSE, p. 4]

Television was seen as providing useful facts which children felt they could use to improve their writing of information texts. The following chapter explores in more depth how videos, television and books can enhance children's writing.

Summary

It was inspiring to discover that despite their age and relative inexperience of reading and writing the children involved in the study were able to articulate clearly their ideas about the impact videos and television may have on their reading and writing development.

The majority of the children tended to focus on either the more reductive 'skills' of reading (e.g. being able to read specific words, and 'sounding out' words) or mentioned how familiarity with the story is useful. With regard to books which have been dramatized for television or video, or books which are based on televisual texts, the children themselves highlighted four main ways in which television and videos may support their reading: offering help with graphophonic cues; increasing children's ability to make predictions about the words in the written text; providing children with an overall knowledge of the story; providing help with comprehending unfamiliar uses or combinations of words or phrases (e.g. idioms). Some children also talked about being motivated to read the books on which television series or videos had been based. Relatively few children spontaneously talked about how watching television and videos can help with their writing and those children who reflected on this aspect of literacy focused on how television and videos may provide help with the spelling of words or providing children with information which would help in writing non-fiction texts. It would also appear that children's choices about whether to read or watch TV are informed and shaped by a complex web of factors, not least the children's confidence, enjoyment of reading and their expectations of the texts and themselves.

The following two chapters explore in more depth how videos and television can support children's literacy development.

Chapter 5

Reading Different Texts

The previous two chapters have outlined parents' and children's attitudes towards, and opinions about, video, television and books. The children's comments made clear that it is not possible to make sweeping statements about the effects of children's television and video-viewing habits on their reading development and preferences. The conversations with the young children in the study hint at the complexity of the issues and suggest that children's preferences and opinions are mediated by a range of factors. Frequency of viewing is merely one of a range of influences. Throughout the previous chapter it has been possible to gain a sense of young children's views on the commonly-held assumption that increased viewing of TV automatically has a detrimental effect on reading. It would appear that many of the young children I interviewed believe that television and videos can prove to be a supportive element in their development as readers and, to a lesser extent, as writers.

The young children involved in the study demonstrated an impressive ability to not only analyse what is involved in reading written texts, but also to reflect on how televisual experiences have supported their reading and writing development. This chapter takes the children's ideas further. The utilization of a case study approach, in which a child's literacy development has been tracked and analysed over a period of five years, provides an opportunity to explore how videos and television played an important role in the literacy development of one child between the ages of 2 and 7-years-old. The aim of the next two chapters is not to provide evidence on which to base generalizations but rather to provide a degree of qualitative detail which is missing in quantitative studies of the relationship between television and video viewing, reading and writing.

It is difficult to examine children's reading and writing development as mutually exclusive processes, as understandings and competencies a child gains in and from reading may influence her writing development and vice versa. In order to highlight some key issues, however, the following two chapters explore reading and writing separately but with the underlying knowledge that ideally the development should be explored simultaneously. This chapter, which focuses on reading, includes an examination of the range of possible ways experience of videos, television and books may influence children's reading development. This chapter highlights what may be happening when children watch television and videos and explores how this may be different at different times and in different contexts; what is of concern to a 3-year-old may not be of interest to a 7-year-old and, similarly, as suggested in the previous chapter, the ways in which children's experiences of books, television and videos interact may vary, depending upon the child's interests, the context and also the child's experience of reading and watching television and videos.

Transition from televisual texts to written texts

Videos supporting reading of written texts

Many children involved in the study acknowledged that experience of a text on television could help in the reading of the related written text (see Chapter 5). The earliest instance of television explicitly supporting and shaping Rehana's reading occurred when she was almost 3 years old. As she sat on the stairs at home she began to read one of the stories from her *Sesame Street* magazine to her favourite doll:

> It's a gift. Telly Monster getting ready for Christmas. There is lots of pr . . . presents under him tree. [Anxious voice] I'd like to open them said Telly Monster but will it be all right? [Deep, gruff voice] Sure, you enjoy it, said Harry. . . . Um, ... Jack in the box jump up see? [Shows her doll the picture] Ping! I told you, said Telly Monster. I must go home said Telly Monster pulling on his coat. [Turned to last story in comic] Ernie and Bert getting ready for Christmas Day. I don't know this one. [Made no attempt to read it]
> [Rehana aged 2.11]

Earlier in the day I had read her the story 'It's a Gift' once and, whilst I had probably read it with a degree of expression, listening to Rehana read to her doll it was clear that the voices and manner she adopted were not based on my rendering of the story but rather on her knowledge of the two main characters, a knowledge which had been built up during the previous few months during which she watched *Sesame Street* five times a week. In addition, it is likely that her recall of the story was supported by the fact that the characters' behaviour and dialogue was in line with her expectations. Her familiarity with the characters and their likely responses enabled her to focus on other aspects of the story and, for example, to notice and then use the language of stories. The phrase 'pulling on his coat' was what was written but was not a phrase she tended to use in everyday life. It was interesting to note how her final sentence brought the story to a satisfactory end. During this reading event it would appear that she was concerned with reading a text she felt she knew as, after having looked at the illustrations for the final story in the magazine, identified the main characters and decided on the probable focus of the story, she then made the comment 'I don't know this one' and did not attempt to read or create her own story although she was quite happy to do so on other occasions.

Two months later there was a vivid example of how her previous experiences of a book and the related video supported her reading of a written text. I had read *The Tale of Mrs Tiggy-Winkle* by Beatrix Potter to her on a number of occasions and she had also watched the video fairly frequently, when she decided to take over the reading of the book.

She began with a conventional opening for a story, 'Once upon a time' and went on to use phrases from the written text but her intonation and cadences were clearly derived from the video e.g. 'What's this? That's not mine'. She ended her reading of the book by saying 'But oh my goodness how tiny Mrs Tiggy-Winkle had grown and she was running, running, running up the hill'. The last scene on the video is that of Mrs Tiggy-Winkle bidding Lucy goodbye and simply disappearing over the brow of the hill. In the book the penultimate paragraph begins, 'She was running, running, running up the hill' and the final paragraph begins 'And how small she had grown'. Rehana's version of the end of the story is significant in that it provides a very clear example of how she was combining the televisual and written texts to synthesize a meaningful text of her own. It was apparent that experience of both the video and of the book had enabled her to read *Mrs Tiggy-Winkle*. On occasions, her familiarity with the written text was sufficient to enable her to continue her reading whilst on other occasions she drew on her experience of the video to help her read the book. It is likely, for example, that when she could not recall the written text her familiarity with the structure of this particular story meant that she was aware of the specific point in the story she had reached and was able to draw on the strong visual images on the video in order to retain the sense, if not the precise words, of the section of text. Thus she read: 'She could see something white on the hills' instead of the printed text, 'And a great way up the hill-side she thought she saw some white things spread upon the grass'.

A month later she read Beatrix Potter's *Jemima Puddle-Duck*. Her version of the story consisted of the bare bones of the story but, as with her reading of *Mrs Tiggy-Winkle*, it was apparent that her reading of the written text was influenced by her experiences of both the book and the video. She used certain 'bookish' phrases such as 'She set off . . .' coupled with dialogue very similar to that on the video. Towards the end, for example, she chose the friendlier and more sympathetic: 'Let's go home', rather than the somewhat emotionally detached, 'Jemima Puddle-Duck was escorted home in tears on account of those eggs'. It is only possible to speculate on the reasons underlying some of her choices. Did she, for example, prefer the more sympathetic ending on the video because she empathized with Jemima Puddle-Duck, or could she simply not recall the written text? In the context of exploring how videos can support reading it could be argued that the reasons for her choices are less important than the fact that watching the video and reading the book had provided her with the possibility of choice. From an early age, she was learning that different interpretations are possible and acceptable. Helen Bromley's research has led her to conclude that children feel that books and videos are complementary, mutually supportive and, furthermore, as a 6-year-old told her, offer a 'new way of seeing' (Bromley, 1996, p. 80).

The notion of alternative interpretations is very important to those who believe that reading involves more than merely decoding the marks on a page. Margaret Meek (1988), for example, has argued that 'the signs of genuine reading development are hard to detect as they appear and bear little relation to what is measured by reading tests' and goes on to state that one of the important steps readers take is 'a growing tolerance of ambiguity, the notion that things are not quite what they seem' (Meek, 1988, p. 30). Jerome Bruner writes about 'stories of literary merit' as being about the 'real world' but which 'render that world strange, rescue it from obviousness, fill it with gaps that call upon the reader, in Barthes's sense to become a writer, a composer of a virtual text in response to the actual' (Bruner, 1986, p. 24). A child's interpretation of a written text, or how she fills the 'gaps', will be mediated by her own life experiences, expectations she may have of the text itself, and by her past experiences of other texts, both written and televisual.

Six weeks after her first reading of *Jemima Puddle-Duck*, Rehana watched the video version of *The Tale of Jeremy Fisher*. During the course of a week she watched the video approximately five times but subsequently did not watch the video again until after she had received and read a copy of the book, a fortnight later. The book had never been read to her and she had not had the opportunity to browse through the book before we settled down to read it. As I assumed she would perceive the text to be unfamiliar, I had been expecting to read the book to her and was some-what surprised when she chose to take over the reading of the book from the start:

For ease of reading a new line is started for each new page of the book.

Once upon a time there was a frog called Jeremy Fisher. He lived in a little house.

One day he say 'I go fishing' he say to himself.

[*At Rehana's request I read the next page*]
He dig in the garden for some worms.

He hopped into, next to a stream for his supper.

He saw a most delightful pond.

He fishing.

He fishing.

He sat on his fishing box.

He ate. . . . what's that? [I told her] . . . a butterfly sandwich.

A rat came and bit him.

A fish came. . . . where fish?
[Rather anxious tone of voice]

[Turned next five pages rapidly as she searched for the big fish]
He swallowed him.

And spat him out.

[Hurriedly turned the next 3 pages]
And him friends come for tea.

[Rehana aged 3.3]

Her version of the story was fairly close to the original in terms of sequence and it is apparent that on occasions she was supported by the pictures. Closer analysis of the reading event would strongly suggest that, although the pictures provided some cues, familiarity with the video played a central role in enabling Rehana's first attempt at reading the book. The video had clearly given her an overall sense of the direction of the story and the sequence of the key events. This is evident, for example, when looking at the picture early in the book which shows Jeremy Fisher carrying a jug and two plates, she confidently stated that 'He say "I go fishing" . . .' It is only much later that there is clear picture of Jeremy Fisher fishing, but being unfamiliar with the book the pictures on subsequent pages could not have provided any cues. The reasons she chose to state he was going fishing so early in the story are probably two fold. Firstly, near the start of the video Jeremy Fisher looks out of the window and then goes inside his house saying, 'Be good fishing today I shouldn't wonder'. Immediately before the fishing trip, Jeremy Fisher collects his macintosh, galoshes and sandwiches from the hall and the scene on the video is remarkably similar to a picture early in the book, even to the snail crawling up the wall. Her anticipation of the appearance of the fish ('A fish came . . . where fish?'), is further evidence that she knew what happened in the story. Furthermore, she knew which pages were likely to carry those parts of the story she found unnerving on the video (e.g. when Jeremy Fisher struggles ashore after his meeting with the trout) and chose to skip over them. Her use of an unfamiliar form of words also illustrates how Rehana's reading of the book was influenced by the video. On the video both *The Tale of Mrs Tiggy-Winkle* and *The Tale of Jeremy Fisher* are told and, in order to provide continuity, Mr Jeremy Fisher relates his story to Mrs Tiggy-Winkle. Mrs Tiggy-Winkle is prone to provide emphasis to her statements by the use of 'most' before adjectives (e.g. 'a most elegant and gentlemanly frog' and 'most terribly particular') Rehana's description of the pond as 'most delightful', echoes Mrs Tiggy-Winkle's speech patterns. The use of the phrase also begins to capture the essence of the manner in which Beatrix Potter's characters express themselves, a knowledge she would also have derived from her previous experiences of other Beatrix Potter books and videos.

It was very obvious that watching the video had provided Rehana with the confidence to choose to take the lead in reading an unfamiliar book. A reasonable degree of familiarity with the screen text helped her to make the transition from the screen text to the written text in the book with a high level of success.

It was not only short videos that played a supportive role in Rehana's reading development. Watching feature-length Disney cartoons of well-known fairy stories also had a positive impact on her reading. At the age of 3 and a half Rehana had seen the Disney video of *Cinderella* on numerous occasions and I had read her the Disney Ladybird version of *Cinderella* a few times. At this point she decided to read me the Ladybird book:

Rehana: [Looking at cover] By Janet and Allet Allberg. Who *is* this by?
Me: It doesn't say who it's by.
Rehana: Shall I just say what I usually want to?
Me: Yes, say what you want to.

Rehana:	*Cinderella* by Janet and Alder Bolberg.
	Fairy Tales by Annette and Allan Allberg. I don't want to let you see the pictures.
Me:	Oh all right then.
Rehana:	You can close your eyes if you like and just listen to the words.
	[Turns to first page of the story] One day. Cinderella. Cinderella lived in a fairy castle. She didn't like her step sisters or her step mother but she liked the three mice and Bruno the dog.
	One day them gone off on a party them did. . . . I don't know where it is. One day . . . I'm, I will be a teacher. One day . . . you're a little girl. I'll start again, shall I start again? Snow White, oh sorry, it's not called Snow White. Shall I just pretend it's Snow White?
Me:	I'll get confused then.
Rehana:	Why?
Me:	Because you told me you were reading me *Cinderella*.
Rehana:	*Cinderella*. A fairy tale 'bout Cinderella. . . . *Beauty and the Beast*
	Cinderella doesn't like her step sisters or her step mother but she loved Bruno and the mice.
	Mustn't look at the pictures . . .
	One day them come to a party and one day . . . and one day a prin . . . there was a letter to a ball in the house. . . .
	'Huh! *You* go . . .' That means *I* can go too,' said Cinderella but the horrid stepmother said,
	'Huh! *You* dancing with a prince are you if, if you be kindness, um?' Cinderella cried and her moth-her step mother scolded her for being so slow.
	A coach arrived and they climbed in chattering and chuckling.
	Poor Cinderella went out in the garden and a lady stand in front of her and said, 'I'm your fairy godmother. You *will* go the ball,' she said, 'If you fetch a pumpkin I will magic it' and mice and Bruno the dog helped them to, her to bring a pumpkin to the fairy godmother.
	And she changed it into a coach
	and then she turned Cinderella into a lovely ball gown and
	then she stepped inside it and she was off!
	And she did, she did, even her stepsisters didn't know who she was. Soon Cinderella 'got about the time,
	she rushed down the palace stairs,
	jumped in the coach and rushed off to a palace and
	and she was there in no time and she was home just in time.
	Next morning . . . a prince . . .
	was, said, there was, 'Well, it doesn't fit you'.
	Cinderella came down, just you, I thought you said there was no other people in this house?
	No, no, no, she only a servant and and it broke in half and it fitted perfectly on Cinderella and she went to a proper ball and she asked where [indistinct] and the prince pick it up for her and they lived happily ever after.
[Rehana, age 3.6]	

Although it is fairly difficult to follow the story from reading the transcript, it is very apparent that Rehana had a clear sense of this particular story, the sequence of events and the characters involved. She worked hard at creating a very good approximation of the written text through integrating her knowledge of the story, the characters and the dialogue, much of which she had gained from watching the video, with her recall of the written text aided by cues provided by the pictures in the book. Certain phrases from the written text were recalled with complete accuracy (e.g. her stepmother 'scolded her for being so slow' and 'she['s] only a servant'). Her very expressive reading was enhanced by the use of certain phrases, intonations and the voices of the characters which were drawn directly from the video. Familiarity with the video also provided her with the opportunity to experiment with ways of verbally communicating complex emotions. For example, the phrase 'Huh! *You* dancing with a prince are you if, if you be kindness, um?', is an approximation of part of the screen text and the sarcastic tone in which Rehana said the words was apt, as was Cinderella's response. Rehana's attempts to extend the written text at this particular juncture in the story is also significant in light of the fact that a few weeks earlier she had asked numerous questions about why Cinderella's step-sisters and step-mother always looked so cross and wanted explanations for their unkind behaviour. It is also interesting to note that it was at this emotionally charged point in the narrative that Rehana slipped into 'video mode' in that she initially omitted to clarify who said what. Watching the video it is very obvious who is speaking. She very quickly returned to 'reading mode' and consistently made clear who was speaking.

It is conceivable that she may have read the story as effectively without having watched the video but, given her inexperience as a reader, I would contend that familiarity with the video provided her with a higher level of confidence about reading the book than may otherwise have resulted from the relatively limited experience she had had of the book at that time.

Much has already been written about how very young children may be supported in their reading of 'known' books because they are able to predict the text and make informed guesses about what will happen next and I am suggesting that children may be similarly supported through viewing a dramatization of the book. The previous examples provide evidence of how a very young child was supported by having seen videos of the books she was attempting to read. It would seem that knowledge of the 'big shapes' of a particular narrative helps drive the reading as the child's predictions about possible events and even the probable language patterns empowers the young reader. There is evidence that words that would normally not feature in books for very young children become meaningful when used in context on video. Videos may thus also not only play a part in broadening children's spoken vocabulary but also extend children's reading vocabulary.

As Rehana became a more experienced reader it was still possible to see how dramatized versions of books that she had watched on video continued to play an important role in her reading development. On the video of C.S. Lewis's *The Lion, the Witch and the Wardrobe* (1950), for example, the importance of the prophecy of Cair Paravel is explained and when Rehana, aged 5, chose to read aloud her favourite part of the story she had no problems reading the following paragraph:

> 'Because of another prophecy,' said Mr Beaver, '. . . Down at Cair Paravel there are four thrones and it's a saying in Narnia time out of mind that when two Sons of Adam and two Daughters of Eve sit in those four thrones, then it will be the end not only of the White Witch's reign but of her life . . .'
> (p. 77)

Lyrical phrases such as 'time out of mind' are likely to prove difficult for a young child to read, not because of the individual words but because the arrangement of the words within the phrase are unexpected and unfamiliar. Many of the words and the pattern of the language in this extract lie beyond the scope of most books written for 5-year-olds and it would be unlikely for a young child to have heard such language as part of every day life. Whilst reading *Heidi*, at the age of 6, Rehana stumbled over more prosaic but equally unfamiliar sentence structures. Rehana's reading of *The Lion, the Witch and Wardrobe* was supported by her knowledge of the story, reading the words in context and her recall of the dialogue from the video, but she had no such supporting framework to fall back on when reading *Heidi*.

It is also the case that unfamiliarity with names can hinder a reader's fluency and enjoyment of a book, as many adult readers of books such as *A Suitable Boy* or *Anna Karenina* will testify. At various points in time it has been apparent that Rehana has found names problematic. Whilst reading Joanna Rowling's *Harry Potter and the Chamber of Secrets* she observed that 'It's difficult to read what Hagrid says, isn't it?'. Thus, the way in which authors denote accents and unfamiliar dialects can similarly impede the fluency of one's reading. These difficulties have clearly been minimized when she has seen televised dramatizations and been able to hear both the names and the unfamiliar language forms.

Audiotapes may help with difficulties surrounding names, but are unlikely to provide much support with understanding unfamiliar language. Watching a video, however, enables children to hear unfamiliar words or phrases being spoken whilst also being able to *see* the context in which they are said and the addition of strong visual cues is likely to promote understanding. The probable outcome is that as the words are more meaningful to the children, they are likely to find them easier to read.

The value of the visual cues provided by televisual texts

One of the key differences between videos and books is that videos offer powerful visual cues which help children explore ideas or events which would be too complex or abstract if merely written or spoken about. Videos can help support children's understanding of a story as situations or characters do not have to be conjured up in the mind's eye and, instead, young viewers are able to see the story unfolding before their eyes. The visual power of videos is exemplified by instances such as the child, who was relatively unmoved by being read the account of the fight between Prince Caspian, a hag and a werewolf, but was very frightened by the vision of the green-faced, long-nailed hag when confronted with the same event on video. The child explained that the video frightened her 'Because in the book it doesn't make such a scary picture in my mind'.

It ought not be reduced to a choice between books and videos (e.g. Wilce, TES, April 1996). A child may use books and videos in tandem to deepen and further their understanding. A prime example of this dual use of book and video is provided by a 5-year-old watching a video of and being read *The Lion, the Witch and the Wardrobe*. When read a phrase such as 'But the Witch suddenly turned on him with such a terrible expression on her face', she was uncertain about the precise expression the words were describing and therefore found it difficult to understand the significance of the statement. On numerous occasions similar phrases in the book of *The Lion, the Witch and the Wardrobe* prompted the question 'Like what Mummy? Show me'. This request was frequently followed by 'Why did s/he look like that?' Babies and young children are very skilled at decoding facial expressions in order to understand a situation but descriptions of expressions such as 'working and twitching with passion' and '. . . neither angry nor afraid, but a little sad' (p. 140) are difficult for a young child to understand and virtually impossible for the adult reader to reproduce to order! The fact that it is possible to see such expressions when watching a video helps the child make sense of the event. The child may still ask 'Why?' but will not need to ask 'Like what?'. Furthermore, the next time the child reads the words in the book she will have a mental image to refer to which may facilitate her understanding of the events, the relationships and the overall plot.

It has been argued that children's imaginations are not developed and stimulated by television and videos precisely because children are presented with ready-made images (Large, 1990; Singer, 1980; Winn, 1985). In contrast, so the argument runs, when children read they have to create their own images. Marie Winn quotes Bruno Bettelheim's observation, 'Television captures the imagination but does not liberate it. A good book at once stimulates and frees the mind' (Winn, 1985, p. 59). Maire Messenger Davies however, draws on Laurene Brown's research in America to support her contention that children may be 'stimulated by television's own special techniques into producing more unusual and original work' (Messenger Davies, 1989, p. 74) Laurene Brown found that 9 and 10-year-old children who had seen a film version of a story were more likely to grasp the main point of a particular story than were children of the same age who only heard the story. The 'viewers', furthermore, were also able to represent the character's emotions because they had seen close-up shots of the characters' faces which the 'listeners' obviously did not. Marie Messenger Davies goes on to state that imaginative responses to stories are partly dependent upon understanding the motivations and emotions of the characters (Messenger Davies, 1989, pp. 74–5).

Elliot Eisner has cogently argued that different forms of representation make different contributions to our understanding and 'we use different forms to say different things' (Eisner, 1996, p. 19). Gunther Kress utilizes the concept of synaesthesia in emphasizing the importance of acknowledging that there are 'best ways' to represent meanings and, whilst written language may be the most appropriate medium for expressing and communicating certain meanings, it is also the case that other meanings may be best expressed through pictures, smells, colour, texture etc. Encouraging children to move between the different forms of representation and communication would 'circumvent the limitations of each' (Kress, 1997). In the context of this study the views of Eisner and Kress are significant as they lend support to my theory that the visual images, and sometimes also the sound effects or background music on videos, can make difficult or abstract ideas explicit and consequently more accessible to younger children.

Adults who have read to children are likely to be conscious that certain ideas cannot be easily communicated to young children by words alone. From observing and talking to children it is clear that, in many instances, the combination of language with visual images on video or television has proved to be the most effective form of initially representing these difficult ideas. Once the child has grasped the concept through this means, she may be able to deal with the concept in a more abstract way, through language alone. Rehana's developing understanding of Edmund's internal conflict is a prime example of this process. Edmund experiences a degree of inner conflict when journeying to meet the White Witch in Narnia which is shown clearly on the screen through the device of two overlapping images of Edmund. One image of Edmund raises doubts about his own actions and the good intentions of the White Witch whilst the superimposed image chooses to ignore the 'inner voice'. Although the idea that Edmund was having second thoughts and beginning to question his own actions is raised in the book the clues are spread over a couple of chapters. When reading these chapters to my 5-year-old daughter she was oblivious to Edmund's inner turmoil and was more concerned with the overall direction of the story — what was going to happen to Edmund, what was the Witch going to do, would Peter, Susan and Lucy and the beavers be captured? Experienced adult readers will have had similar responses when reading a book for the first time: interest in the story often overrides one's ability and willingness to consider the finer points. However, when the book is reread or a dramatization of the book is seen, new understandings and interpretations are possible. In this instance, the dual images of Edmund on the video prompted a wide range of questions which helped Rehana clarify Edmund's plight. Interestingly, it was very clear that her comprehension of Edmund's internal conflict influenced her response to specific incidents in the next book in the series. On reading *Prince Caspian* for the first time, she felt it entirely appropriate that Edmund should have a high degree of faith in his younger sister in view of the fact that his judgment had proved unsound in the previous book when 'he hadn't believed her'. Through watching the video Rehana had been introduced to the concept of an 'inner voice' which she was then able to build on in her understanding of other narratives (e.g. Disney's *Pinocchio*). Two years later she was able to transfer her knowledge about ways in which 'inner voices' may be represented in screen texts to help her understanding of written texts. The book, *The Demon Headmaster* (Cross, 1982) includes the following:

> Her hands, clasped on top of the dressing table, began to shake slightly, but the face that looked back at her out of the mirror was amused.
> *See? You're afraid yourself, and you don't know why.*
> (*The Demon Headmaster*, p. 59)

On reading this potentially confusing chunk of text she commented that the reflection was 'not really talking, it's really Dinah thinking'. Thus, not only had watching a video encouraged her to reflect on a character's motives, which the book for a number of reasons had failed to do, but it had also introduced her to a complex concept and one or two devices utilized by book authors and screen writers in order to indicate to the reader what is happening.

Visual cues can also make other types of abstract ideas more accessible and enable children to reflect on some of the deeper meanings within a narrative. Whilst watching *The Silver Chair* Rehana was fascinated by the scene where Aslan appears to die. After having watched the scene a few times she said, 'Why do they have to put the thorn in Aslan's paw? Oh! I know why. His blood formed and went into the boy [Caspian] and made him come alive again'. As a result of being able to see the image of Aslan's blood flowing into the river and reviving Caspian, Rehana was able to ponder about the possible meanings of the scene.

Sometimes watching a video and reading the book forces children to reconsider their interpretations and this can be a cognitively unsettling experience. For example, as we read *The Willows in Winter*, Rehana frequently commented on differences and similarities with the video. A major event she tried to make sense of was Ratty's sight of the 'Beyond'. On video, as Ratty is thrown from Toad's aeroplane, he hurtles towards earth and as he does so hazy scenes swim before his eyes which appear to be underwater scenes with indistinct images. In the book, Ratty catches sight of the world beyond the Wild Wood with its cars, trains, roads and people. On both video and in the book it is clear that the sight of 'Beyond' seriously unnerved Ratty and Rehana tried to understand what the 'Beyond' actually was and why seeing it had had such a profound effect on Ratty. Whilst watching as the blurred images swam across the screen she asked 'Is he going to die?', perhaps because the images were not dissimilar to the near-death scenes she had watched on other videos (e.g. Mole falling into the river during his first boat trip with Ratty in *Wind in the Willows* and Jeremy Fisher's disastrous meeting with the trout). When Ratty was rescued by his friends she said, 'He was dying wasn't he and that's why he saw those — the Beyond'. Reading the book, however, caused confusion: 'I thought he saw underwater things 'cos he was drown — dying. They — we didn't see cars and things on the video did we? Why would seeing cars and things make Ratty . . . why is that the Beyond? I don't understand'. The interpretation of the visual images shown on videos do not always map easily onto the written text but, when there is such a mismatch, the dual experience of watching and reading may encourage children to revisit their original theory and refine it further.

Complex narrative structures

Many authors writing for newly fluent readers have attempted to ease the transition from picture book to chapter book by simplifying storylines and language, minimizing the characterization and side-stepping significant issues. Young experienced readers who have become accustomed to considering important issues through reading high quality picture books are disappointed to find this element absent in books written for the newly confident reader. Many of the resultant books are mildly diverting and possibly humorous, but they are ultimately unsatisfying because they fail to engage the young reader at a deep level. A possible dilemma arises because children who are developing fluency may be hindered by both the more superficial aspects of the reading process (e.g. ability to read the words, understanding of punctuation etc.) and their ability to follow a complex plot. There is a wealth of research evidence that supports the view that reading to children is a positive factor in children's reading development (e.g. Dombey, 1983; Holdaway, 1979; Meek, 1991; Wells, 1981). Children continue to enjoy having books read to them throughout their childhood and, by reading children the books that they would be unable to read alone, they are able to concentrate on meaning-making, rather than other aspects of the reading process. Teachers and parents need to be sensitive to the fact that young children are frequently aware of their own needs. The fairly fluent reader who said, 'I think you'll have to read this to me, the story's a bit complicated' was not saying that the words were 'difficult' or that other surface features of the text itself were complicated but rather that she needed to concentrate on the story itself. There remains a need to continue to read to children as they become more confident, independent, fluent readers.

Many newly fluent readers have begun to develop a relatively sophisticated response to literature. These readers are happy to lose themselves in books, enjoy identifying with fictional characters, are able to extend their personal experiences through reading, relish the new and varied language forms they are introduced to through books and may be beginning to realize that messages and meanings in books sometimes lie beyond the text itself. These young readers need literature that is going to fire their imaginations and confirm the expectation that reading fiction is satisfying in a range of ways.

As children become more fluent they begin to move on to books which have fewer illustrations and are frequently longer than the average picture book. The step from picture books to chapter-type books is a big one. Fewer illustrations mean that picture cues are no longer available to support the child's reading and understanding. The meaning is contained within, and sometimes beyond, the words. Children have to attend to the language much more closely than before in order to follow the story and to create mental images of the setting and the characters. Furthermore, the child may have to retain the threads of the story as it weaves its way through a number of chapters. Added complications occur when successive chapters deal with events that are happening simultaneously in the story. Inexperienced readers encountering phrases such as 'Edmund meanwhile had been having a most disappointing time', (*The Lion, the Witch and the Wardrobe*, Chapter 11), have to learn that this signals the need to put part of the narrative 'on hold' and find out what else has been happening. Flashbacks may prove even more difficult to cope with and, once more, inexperienced readers have to learn to recognize clues embedded within the text that indicate a backward step in time. Rehana, whilst reading J.K. Rowling's *Harry Potter and the Chamber of Secrets*, was checking that she had 'read' the signs correctly when she said, 'I think they've gone back in time because it's about

Professor Dumbledore when he was young'. Stories within a story appear and the sub-plots may seem to diverge and then converge before the final resolution.

Releasing the child from reading challenging texts enables her to concentrate on following the twists and turns in a story, to develop her understanding of narrative forms and conventions and to reflect on the characters' motivations and intentions. By reading the text a more experienced reader can free a child to reflect on the written text. An alternative route could be through the agency of television and videos. Videos and television programmes have a role to play in helping children learn about complex narrative structures and develop a relatively sophisticated understanding of the relationships between characters in a story and what motivates them. Young children watching videos and television can be introduced to complex narratives long before they are able to read them for themselves, as children can concentrate on making sense of the characters and the story as a whole. Younger children may find that many books written for more experienced readers could be fulfilling if they could be rendered more accessible to the less experienced reader and it is here that videos have a role. Charlotte, the 6-year-old quoted in the previous chapter, who wanted to read *Les Miserables* is a case in point. Similarly, videos have played an important part in both broadening Rehana's repertoire of known books and extending her reading. Between the ages of 3 and 5 she was read a wide variety of books including *The Lion, the Witch and the Wardrobe*, *Prince Caspian*, *The Borrowers*, the *Mary Poppins* series, *A Little Princess*, *The Sheep Pig*, *Alice in Wonderland* and *Pollyanna*. Requests for many of these books were prompted by seeing videos, films or TV serializations (e.g. the *Mary Poppins* books, *Alice in Wonderland*, *The Sheep Pig*, *A Little Princess*, *Bedknobs and Broomsticks*, *The Borrowers*, the *Famous Five on a Treasure Island*, *The Silver Chair*). Some of the other books were read for the first time before the video was seen (e.g. *The Lion, the Witch and the Wardrobe*, *Prince Caspian*) but watching the video heightened her involvement in the books and resulted in the books being reread.

Re-viewings and reviewings

Charlotte:	Well, she thinks um, videos I haven't watched very much are good for me. She doesn't think it's good watching videos over and over again.
NB:	Why is that then?
Charlotte:	Well, it's because she says it's boring.
NB:	Would she mind you reading the same book over and over again?
Charlotte:	No, she wouldn't mind that.
NB:	I wonder why grown ups don't mind you reading the same book but they do mind you watching the same video. Funny really isn't it?
Charlotte:	Because mummy thinks good, um, that books are good for you.
NB:	Even if you read the same one over and over again?
Charlotte:	[laughs] Yeah. Yeah.

[Girl aged 6, TSA, p. 4]

Observing how my young daughter has watched videos over the course of the past five years one feature has remained fairly constant. From the time that she first started to watch television, aged 2 years and 9 months, she has frequently watched a specific video repeatedly and exclusively for a period of days and even weeks before suddenly losing interest in it and moving onto watching a wider range of videos. This cycle has been repeated on numerous occasions. It is an interesting phenomenon for a number of reasons. Firstly, in talking to other parents it is apparent that this is a pattern repeated in many households although, for obvious reasons, children with siblings are less likely to be allowed repeated viewings of their current favourite:

> *NB*:　　So, what's you favourite television programme or video?
> *Alice*:　Mary Poppins
> *NB*:　　That's a video isn't it? Do you watch it often?
> *Alice*:　I can't, my brother wont let me.
> *NB*:　　Oh, that's a bit mean.
> *Alice*:　He makes me watch baby *Thomas the Tank Engine* videos. But luckily now we've started that I choose a video one day and he chooses a video one day.
> *Sophie*:　I like watching *Matilda* . . . me and my sister always watched it because me and my sister loved watching *Matilda* but when I ask my sister to watch it she says no because we were always watching it most of the time last time.
>
> [Girls aged 5, TSG, p. 1]

Secondly, the pattern is very reminiscent of some children's insistence that they are read the same book over and over again. Thirdly, this viewing pattern may not be confined to children. Muriel Robinson writes of how her own repeated re-watchings of her video recording of the drama series *Tutti Frutti* led her to consider 'how children make sense of narrative in the different discourses they encounter' (Robinson, 1997, p. 1).

From what the children have said, it would appear that there may be some similarities between the supportive role played by videos and repeated readings of favourite books. Repeated readings of favourite books by adults to children helps children gain a knowledge of the story itself, the 'tune on the page' (Barrs et al., 1991), the language of that particular book, in addition to understandings about the physical acts of reading (e.g. page turning, where particular texts start etc.). Watching videos also provides a familiarity with a text, initially the televisual text, which then enables children to make the transition to the written texts. Children have talked about how videos help them 'know the story', 'know what happens' and videos 'tell you the words'. It would be unwise to draw too close a parallel between what children learn from having a book read to them and watching a video of a book, not least because as children became more fluent readers, it is unlikely that they will request or experience repeated reading of texts they are able to read themselves. The supportive role of videos depends upon the juxtaposition of the video and the child's reading development. Video versions of novels may support those readers who are beginning to tackle these longer texts but will not appear to offer much in the way of immediate practical support to beginner readers. On the other hand, videos of shorter texts with high levels of dialogue are more supportive to inexperienced readers as are videos of shorter, heavily illustrated texts.

Many of the 'lessons' children learn from repeated sharings of a book (e.g. about the role of pictures in picture books, the conventions about written text) cannot be replicated by watching a video but what children can learn from videos is important, not least because it can help them approach the reading of written texts with confidence and enjoyment. It is also the case that repeated viewings offer the child the opportunity to gain a clearer understanding of the narrative itself, to explore the story from a different stance, to attempt to gain a deeper understanding of the characters' motivations and, possibly, to compare how the dramatization and the written text compare.

As with books, not all videos bear constant revisiting. At a time when Rehana was avidly and repeatedly watching recorded episodes of the BBC dramatization of Dick King-Smith's *The Queen's Nose* and *Harmony's Return* she watched a video of *Brambley Hedge* and when asked whether she would like to watch again observed:

> I don't always like to watch the video again straight away because if you leave it
> for a few days you forget some of the, um details and it's like it's fresh.
> (Rehana aged 6.2)

She never returned to this particular video, possibly because she did not find it cognitively or emotionally challenging or intriguing. Reflecting on which videos Rehana has watched repeatedly it would be true to say that they have had a strong emotional appeal (e.g. *Mary Poppins*, a videoed episode of *Sesame Street* in which Telly goes into hospital), or they have presented a cognitive challenge in that, for example, the narrative has been complex and the character's motivations and intentions not immediately obvious, or subject to change during the course of the narrative (e.g. the *Narnia Chronicles, The Little Princess, The Secret Garden*), or they have provided an opportunity to observe the social interaction of a character in a range of situations (e.g. *The Borrowers, The Queen's Nose*). The other category of videos that she enjoyed watching on numerous occasions were those I would describe as humorous and heavily intertextual. This last category includes *The Muppet Christmas Carol*, Disney's *Aladdin* and *Muppet Treasure Island*. And those familiar with these videos will know that they are littered with references to other texts and, especially in the case of the *Muppet* videos, present a range of problems to be solved which start with an ambiguity about the type of narrative itself. How is it possible, for example, to have a tour party of rats being shown around *Treasure Island* with the tour leader saying 'And this is where they filmed *Muppet Treasure Island*' whilst in the background the search for the treasure is at its peak? Some of the videos obviously fall into more than one category and, as with repeated readings of books, Rehana's focus of interest changed through time. Her viewing of all of these videos was characterized by her asking numerous questions and, especially between the ages of 2 and 6, by active participation in the action and the dialogue.

Issues relating to the impact of videos on children's reading

Auditing books and videos

Reading a book and watching a video which is an interpretation of the story helps children begin to develop an understanding of different viewpoints and how a story can mean different things to different people. Young children are not uncritical viewers, they are alert to, and can comment on, the characterization and changes or omissions in the plot or language used.

If a book was read to Rehana after she had seen the video version her comments would suggest that she was auditing the book for changes and omissions: 'That happened on the video . . . they didn't do that on the video'. Sometimes she would make judgments about the book or video. As we finished reading *The Little Princess*, already having seen the video, Rehana's view was: 'I like the video better than the book, it's not so sad'.

When reading *The Prime Minister's Brain*, whilst simultaneously watching the BBC serialization on television, she made the following comment, 'It's not true that is it? It's not like on the video 'cause that doesn't happen does it?' I was intrigued by her use of the word 'true' as I wondered whether she thought that the video was 'true' in the sense of being true to life or whether she was defining the video version as the original and therefore the 'true' version. When I asked her, she replied that she knew the story was not 'real' but she had meant that the book and the video were not 'exactly the same story', demonstrating that she was sensitive to the differences between televisual and written texts but was also checking the modality of the narrative. This is important in the light of a later discussion we had about what constitutes a 'soap' (see Chapter 6).

Language

Children may be so finely tuned to the language that relatively minor changes are noted as in the case when Pole says 'I'm getting too old for magic' the watching 5-year-old interposes, 'No, to *believe* in magic it says in the book'. Not all changes in language were seen to be negative. Two years later I was reading *The Demon Headmaster* to Rehana as she had enjoyed the TV series. She was struck by the rather archaic language used in the book and asked me to explain why one of the central characters insisted on using phrases such as 'blue bananas' when emphasizing a point. She commented that 'It sounds silly' and whenever we came across similar phrases in the book she complained about the incongruity of the character's speech. She also went on to say that 'On the television he doesn't say things like that. I think the television version is better'. This brief interchange suggests that not only was she sensitive to unusual forms of language but was also able to judge whether the language used was appropriate to the context and in keeping with the overall manner in which the author wrote. Clearly, this opportunity to reflect on the appropriateness of language used by authors and screenwriters depended upon having the chance to compare the screen and the written texts.

Another incident occurred which highlighted how experience of videos may influence a child's response to a written text and help them access what would otherwise have been a very difficult genre. At the age of 7 Rehana was attempting to solve a puzzle presented in *The Footprint Files*, (an Usborne Puzzle Adventure Kit). The solution to the mystery depended upon solving a series of problems, all of which relied heavily on reading for meaning, an understanding of syntax and a willingness to tackle 'old-fashioned' scripts and phraseology. When presented with one of the problems Rehana was at a loss where to start and she began singing, 'If you need to know an answer, look it up!' This refrain was repeated throughout episodes of a BBC *Look and Read* series which required the characters to decode a poem or rhyme each week to find the clues (e.g. 'The first is in bark but not in bite with one thousand before'). Rehana had clearly made the link between the two types of texts and later articulated this saying, 'It's a bit like *Look and Read*'. The sequential nature of solving language based problems was common to both the televisual text and her puzzle kit and experience of the televisual text provided her with ideas about how to approach an unfamiliar form of written text.

Visual images

Children also do not accept uncritically the visual images presented on the screen. Rehana was struck by the 'grumpiness' of the two children in the BBC version of *The Silver Chair* as this was at odds with her own mental picture of the children from having read the book. Similarly, the mental image she had created of Dr Cornelius in *Prince Caspian* did not accord with that shown on the video and she stated emphatically that 'it doesn't look like him. He's not dressed right'. The video of Roald Dahl's *The* BFG was not greatly enjoyed, despite the fact that she loved the book and listened avidly to her audiotape of the book. The main reason for her disappointment with the film was attributed to the visual images: 'I don't like this little girl — she looks like a boy and I don't like her voice, do you?' Whilst on seeing a black and red aubergine shaped vegetable being identified as a snozzcumber she was very quick to state 'I didn't think a snozzcumber was like that — I thought it'd be green with knobbly bits on it'.

She was similarly very disappointed with the screen version of *Charlie and the Chocolate Factory*. Roald Dahl's writing had conjured up some extremely vivid images in her mind which the film did not replicate: 'This isn't how I imagined the Chocolate Room, I'm really disappointed, are you? I thought it would have glass walls and all chocolate everywhere . . . I thought the boat would be a lovely pink sweet, not like this'.

Characterizations and motivations

When reading *Prince Caspian* for the first time, 5-year-old Rehana drew parallels between Lucy's experiences with her siblings in the previous book in the *Narnia* series and her experiences in *Prince Caspian* when she sees Aslan for the first time. She commented that, 'You would think that they would listen to her after last time, when they were wrong' and was very quick to ask why the video did not show clearly that Edmund was the first to trust Lucy.

Two years later, at the age of seven, whilst reading her *The Prime Minister's Brain*, she spontaneously observed 'I like the characters better on the video because there's no one really horrid — none of the children is really'.

When reading the book *The Willows in Winter*, Rehana had little sympathy for Portly because he is the cause of Mole's troubles as Mole sets out in a blizzard to 'rescue' Rat and Otter. Whilst reading the book she repeated on a number of occasions, 'I *HATE* Portly'. But the portrayal of Portly on the video prompted a very different response, 'Oh, poor Portly'. In my view the video lacks the emotional depth of the book and the producers of the video clearly decided against devices such as 'asides' to deepen one's understandings of characters (e.g. at the start of book Mole is fed up with the company of his nephew and this is made apparent in the book and notions about frustrations arising because of his sense of duty are explored). Rehana responded very sympathetically to Mole's feelings in the book. On the video there is only a slight indication of Mole's irritation, but this is explained by Mole saying 'I wish it were Spring and things started happening', implying Mole is bored rather than in search of solitude. This creates a very different, less complex picture of Mole. When watching this scene on video Rehana made no comment but looked at me quizzically. The next day she talked about the video before watching it again:

> I don't think the video is so detailed [as the book] but it's still good. I don't think it has such a good start, like they don't play chess in the book do they? And Portly doesn't get tucked . . . well, we don't know. Also in the video he doesn't start crying and go and hide in the corner . . . It's good though. If I hadn't read the book I would have thought it was OK . . . the rest of the video is really . . .

It is interesting to note that at this point she had only read the initial chapter of the book and the 'rest' was an unknown quantity!

There have been numerous examples of Rehana's expectations of characters' behaviour and responses not being met by books and videos. What is important, however, is that over the years she has displayed a fairly even-handed approach in terms of her preferences, and sometimes, despite having read the book first, she has preferred the screen portrayal of a character, whilst on other occasions she has preferred the image created by the book.

Condensing books for videos or television

Videos frequently condense the story so that that which requires a page of text or even a chapter to describe occurs in a few seconds or minutes on the screen. The rapid contextualizing and explanation of events or characters' responses also supports a child's understanding. Videos are frequently a selection of the key events in the story which can result in clarifying complex storylines and so aid a child's ability to follow the plot. It is also true however, that condensing a story can make it more difficult for a child to follow a storyline and to work out characters' intentions and causes and effects. In these instances a more experienced companion is required to fill in the gaps. Arguably, a film or video version of a book that abridges the story to the extent that comprehension is endangered is of limited value. Rehana made the following comment following her reading of certain *Famous Five* books that she had decided to read after having seen the series on TV: 'I prefer the books because they tell you more and you can understand better what's happening than on television'. This was a very valid comment, as the series frequently condensed whole books into 25 minutes or, occasionally 50 minutes of screen time.

The ability to evaluate different texts critically is an important aspect of literacy, as is the ability to discern what is of central importance to a plot, or important for characterization, and what is superfluous.

Impact of videos on child's enjoyment of books

Videos and films clearly played a considerable part in making certain books accessible to a young child. Seeing a film or video version of a book does not necessarily lessen the impact of the book, indeed it could be argued that it heightens children's enjoyment of a book, as they are able to predict and anticipate particularly important scenes and events.

When she was 5 I asked Rehana whether watching a video before reading the book would spoil the book (see Figure 4.2). Two years later she was still of the same opinion:

> No. It will make me enjoy the book more because I'll know what happens — like — er — if something terrible happens like Toad has a crash with his aeroplane — like usually happens — then I'll know what happens and I won't get into a panic when you read me the story.

Books written for the older, more experienced reader may be off-putting to younger or less experienced readers for a range of reasons including the size of the typeface, the absence of pictures, the complexity of the story, and the length. Some of these problems can be dealt with. *The Chronicles of Narnia*, for example, have been published in an unabridged form but with a larger typeface than is the norm for a paperback novel. When my 5-year-old daughter found *The Silver Chair* in this format in the local library she happily settled down to read it. Some features of novels for older children cannot be so easily dealt with. The length, for example, can become a major obstacle to a child who is reading relatively slowly and has yet to develop reading stamina. Videos can help children over this and other hurdles and launch them into these books.

Watching challenging, long videos also supports children's reading development in that watching a story in episodes is similar to reading a chapter book. The child must remember what has happened previously and be able to incorporate the new part of the story into previous parts so as to create a meaningful, seamless narrative.

As Rehana becomes a more fluent reader and is reading longer and longer texts in the form of novels I find it increasingly less possible to discuss the various twists and turns of the plots and the motivations of the characters etc. and, when she asks for clarification about something in the book, it is very difficult to provide a satisfactory answer as I may not be *au fait* with the context (i.e. the story and the characters). Videos and television, in contrast, continue to be a shared experience and therefore continue to offer opportunities for Rehana and I to construct, share, evaluate, refine and question the meanings we create from the text.

Reading the screen

Apart from interpreting the story, children may read text on the screen. As Rehana's understanding of the medium of television and videos has developed so has interest in aspects of the productions, such as the cast lists, the screenplay writers and reading other information that appears on screen. Rehana was 5 years old when she first saw *Fly Away Home*. She had read the book soon afterwards but then almost a year later she watched the video. When watching the video she said, 'Does it start with the car crash?' It does, but I had forgotten it did! She remembered other key instances (e.g. the gosling falling into the toilet) and anticipated them. She forgot or needed reassurance that 'All of them [the goslings] do fly don't they? None of them get left behind do they?' Interestingly, she was also very concerned that Igor (the goose that couldn't fly well and who was transported in the plane) flew back in Spring and was not left behind. We only know he does from reading the text at the end of the film. When Rehana first watched the film she was not particularly concerned with reading text on the screen and I suspect she would have remembered this better had she seen a powerful image of Igor returning rather than having to read the words, if in fact she read the words. Now, she would not miss this key point of information as she insists on reading the credits from start to finish. This interest in the cast list and credits has led to a great deal of learning about the medium and authorship and adaptations.

Whilst watching *The Queen's Nose* on video the following interchange occurred:

Rehana: Is *The Queen's Nose* by *Dick-King Smith*? (she had been reading the titles and screenplay details etc.)
Me: Yes, why?
Rehana: It's very unusual for him. This one and *George Speaks*.
Me: Mmm — why do you think that?
Rehana: Um, I don't, um I don't know really.
Me: You're right, they are unusual when you think about who the most important characters in his books usually are, like Babe . . .
Rehana: Animals! Mmm.
[Rehana, aged 7.1]

Whilst watching *The Phoenix and the Carpet* she not only noticed who had written the screenplay but also commented on the adaptation:

Oh look, Helen Cresswell, didn't she do that other one, the . . . *The Psammead*? . . . She . . . it's good 'cos she's done it like the book, nearly.'
[Rehana, aged 7.3]

A few weeks later she asked whether Helen Cresswell had also adapted the *Narnia* series and when I was not able to tell her she then began to read the credits written on the video box — not only for *The Lion, the Witch and the Wardrobe*, but also for some of her other favourites such as *Pollyanna*. She was interested to discover that Helen Cresswell was involved in the BBC serial of *The Demon Headmaster*:

Rehana: She's done *The Demon Headmaster* and . . . and *The Psammead* and hasn't she done *The Legend of the Lost Keys*?
Me: I don't think so. She hasn't *written The Demon Headmaster* though has she?
Rehana: No, she's done the thingy, you know the script thing.
[Rehana 7.3]

A couple of months later we had another conversation about Helen Cresswell:

Rehana: 'Helen's, Helen Cresswell's done the screenplay for this. Does that mean she wrote the story?
Me: No, she read the book, well, the books and then thought about how she would adapt it for television.
Rehana: Oh, so she told the children what to say and how to say it.

This interchange was interesting because when, at her request, I had read Rehana the first two books in *The Demon Headmaster* series, she had noticed some of the differences between the television series and the books and two months earlier we had discussed the fact that Helen Cresswell had written the screenplay but not the books. Rehana was clearly still needing to sort out the roles played by the author of the book and the screenplay writer in the creation of a television serial based on a book.

At around the age of 7 Rehana became aware of the fact that Teletext could provide information about programmes that was perhaps lacking in the TV listings in the newspaper. When deciding whether a particular programme would be of interest to her, she noted that in the paper it was described as a repeat of a series. Her knowledge of television series such as *The Demon Headmaster* and *Harry's Mad* led her to ask whether it was the 'first one of the series'. We looked at Teletext for further information:

Rehana: *The Biz.* Sasha has a crisis at Caro's party. What's a 'crisis'?
Me: A disaster probably, something going wrong.
Rehana: I don't think it is the first episode.
Me: Why?
Rehana: Because they would say something like 'The three sisters go to wherever'.
Me: Why?
Rehana: Well, otherwise we wouldn't know who they are talking about . . . so they know. People watching are going to say I don't know who Sasha is or . . . Caro, is it? They need to tell us.
[Rehana 7.6]

Whilst reading books which are part of a series she has commented, sometimes with some irritation, that in the first chapter the characters always seem to be re-introduced. Conversely, when watching a television series, having missed the first series, she has noticed how it is sometimes taken for granted that the viewer will be familiar with the characters and the setting and she has had to work hard at filling in the gaps and looking for clues.

Rehana had a clear understanding by this age that it is important to ensure that all readers of a text, be it screen or written, are in possession of certain information in order to provide a context necessary for shared understandings. The absence of contextualizing information is a probable sign that assumptions have been made about the viewers' previous knowledge of the text. This lesson has been learnt without formal instruction, but through her broad experience of books and televisual texts and, as the following chapter demonstrates, had an impact on her storytelling and writing.

Books into videos

By the age of 7, Rehana had a growing understanding of the process by which books can become videos and vice versa. When watching videos she would ask whether it was based on a book and, if so, who had written it. When watching *The Muppet Christmas Carol* and *Muppet Treasure Island* she was not only intrigued to discover that Charles Dickens had written the original *Christmas Carol* saying, 'Matilda says Darles Chickens, I mean Charles Dickens doesn't she?' (a reference to a scene in the film version of *Matilda*) but she also wanted to know how close to the originals the *Muppet* versions were. I would suggest that this sort of curiosity is likely to motivate children to read books they may not otherwise consider reading.

Whilst musing one evening on what books Rehana would like to see as videos, we had the following conversation:

> *Rehana*: I think *the Mennyms* would make a really good video — all they'd have to do is have people dressed up like rag dolls.
> *Me*: And maybe have masks for their button eyes . . .
> *Rehana*: Yeah, and for Soobie [who is blue]. Vlad would also be a good video *AND* the Fiend books, they've got good stories. I think *The Mennyms*'d be really good though.
> *Me*: Yeah, but the books aren't very popular.
> *Rehana*: But they soon would be if there was a video.
> [Rehana aged 6.11]

The final comment showed very clearly that this child understood how watching videos could lead into reading books.

The next chapter explores how experience of televisual texts may support young children's storying and writing.

Chapter 6

Storytelling and the Moves into Writing

Having outlined a range of ways in which watching videos and television could be seen to play an important role in a young child's reading development, we move on to look at the development of writing through the 'bridging activity' of storytelling. In the case of Rehana, storytelling in a wide range of forms, seemed to be an activity that provided an important connection between reading and writing.

Between the ages of 3 and 7 she explored characterization, motivation, plot, and other key issues through dramatic role play, acting out stories, the telling of made-up stories using puppets, retelling stories from books and video, and telling made-up stories whilst simultaneously developing her expertise in writing. Reflecting on the transcripts of her oral stories and puppet shows, the videos of some of her dramatic role play and other relevant contemporaneous notes about these events, it is apparent that these were very rich learning experiences in relation to literacy.

For the sake of clarity the chapter is organized in such a way that dramatic play is discussed first, followed by storytelling with puppets and oral storytelling. Examples of how this dramatic role play and oral storytelling influenced her writing development are referred to throughout the chapter. This organization ought not to suggest that children follow a linear path in developing their writing. Although at the age of 3 Rehana did not write stories, at the age of 7, in addition to writing stories, she continued to engage in dramatic role play and told stories orally and with puppets, or through the medium of dolls. I would suggest that children do not automatically discard a particular form of storytelling and replace it with a new form, rather they accumulate a range of different ways of analysing and telling stories and are able to select the most appropriate means to achieve their purposes. Unfortunately, for many children, as they progress through school, an over-emphasis on certain forms of 'telling', in particular writing, can result in other forms of 'telling' being devalued or ignored.

Dramatic play, storytelling and writing

Pellegrini and Galda have provided a fascinating overview of research examining the links between what is described as symbolic play or dramatic play and literacy development (Pellegrini and Galda, 1993) and have concluded that the research suggests that symbolic play can play a part in supporting children's reading and writing. Reading development is supported through the negotiation of meanings, which requires the use of metalanguage. The ability to talk about and use language to reflect on language has been shown to be a significant predictor of reading ability at the age of 5 — whilst 3-year-old children's use of symbolic transformation was a significant predictor of writing at age 5 (Galda, 1989, Pellegrini, 1991 quoted in Pellegrini and Galda, 1993). If writing is conceptualized in Vygotskian terms as an example of 'first-order symbolization', then it follows that children need to understand that something can represent something else. A child involved in symbolic or dramatic play is actively involved in the process of symbolization, objects may be used to represent other things and the child may transform herself into someone else (e.g. a slipper can be a car for a teddy, a child is transformed into a witch). This experience is important for writing development as it leads on to children being able to understand that writing involves the use of symbols. The black marks on the page do not bear a clear relationship to the object or idea they symbolize (e.g. the written word 'teddy' does not look or sound like the object it symbolizes).

According to Pellegrini and Galda, dramatic play in itself has a minimal effect on children's understanding of story but what does help children with story comprehension is that when engaged in dramatic or symbolic play with others, children frequently have to take a metastance towards play in that they have to explain what is happening, what things stand for and to negotiate different viewpoints.

> Reading and writing seem to start off as different things, with the former having roots in the oral language and conflict characteristics of peer play, while the latter has its roots in interrelated symbolic processes of peer play.
> (Pellegrini and Galda, 1993, p. 172)

The variety of labels used to describe different forms of children's play can lead to confusion on the part of the reader. Smilansky (1990), for example, makes a clear distinction between socio-dramatic play and dramatic play and states that socio-dramatic play is distinguishable from dramatic play in that socio-dramatic play involves the cooperation of at least two children and involves interaction and communication between the participants, whilst Pellegrini and Galda use the terms symbolic or dramatic play. For simplicity, in this chapter the term dramatic play encompasses both socio-dramatic play with others and solitary role play.

Wells Rowe has highlighted how the views about reading underpinning the research reviewed by Pellegrini and Galda has implications for the research findings (Wells Rowe, 1998). Children's comprehension of stories was measured through the use of multiple-choice questions or analysis of retellings of the story. However, if reading is seen to involve more than simply reconstructing the author's message then the findings of these studies need to be treated with caution in relation to providing insights into how dramatic play can develop children's comprehension of a story. In the previous chapter a view of reading was put forward in which it is clear that the reader is not a passive recipient of the 'author's message' but rather an active participant in the creation of the message. Furthermore, individuals decide what counts as an important aspect of the narrative and these aspects will be foregrounded in any retelling. Children's and adults' decisions about what is particularly significant in a story will depend upon a range of factors such as their age, their previous experiences of a range of narratives, their emotional development and current concerns and interest, a point highlighted by a study of memory in the 1930s (Bartlett, 1932 cited in Fox, 1993, p. 68). Such a model of reading and recall of stories makes it difficult to measure children's understanding using multiple-choice questions or judgments of the 'accuracy' of the retelling. It would seem, as Deborah Wells Rowe puts it, that the research design offered the opportunity to:

> ... explore the researchers' hypotheses and perspectives about the connections between literacy and story-related play ... [but] have also effectively limited the possibility of understanding the *children's* own ways of making this connection and their purposes in doing so.
> (Wells Rowe, 1998, p. 15)

Neelands has claimed that drama provides the opportunity for young children to experience, represent, interrogate, create and experiment with the range of possible meanings contained within a story. (Neelands, 1984, p. 25) It is for these reasons that I chose to focus on *child*-initiated dramatic play and storytelling.

Drawing on the work of James Britton, it is possible to further clarify how various forms of storytelling can support children's development as writers of fiction. In addition to distinguishing three functions of language (transactional, expressive and poetic) Britton put forward the idea that when using language we are placed in either the role of spectator or of participant (Britton, 1970). As a participant we use transactional language to report, inform and persuade. In spectator mode we are free to reflect, evaluate and reshape our understanding of how the world works. When engaged in dramatic role play or storytelling involving puppets, I would argue that children are in the role of 'spectator'. They are free to set out and follow their own agenda, explore their own concerns, make predictions about how characters may react, how the story may progress but are also free to make changes and adaptations in their search for meaning.

There are discernible links between children's dramatic play, their storytelling and the development of their narrative competences. Both dramatic play and storytelling activities involve the children in symbolic play. In the case of storytelling, Carol Fox has described the stories of the children in her study as 'forms of verbal symbolic play' and outlined how the children invented worlds and characters and used magic, fear and suspense (Fox, C., 1993, p. 25). Margaret Meek, in arguing the case for reading stories aloud to children, quotes Vygotsky: 'The creation of an imaginary situation is not a fortuitous fact in a child's life but is rather the first manifestation of the child's emancipation from situational constraints'. (Vygotsky quoted in Meek, 1991, pp. 112–13). This 'emancipation' enables children to explore other possibilities, create alternative scenarios, investigate different viewpoints and experiment with ways of telling. Later in this chapter I will discuss how some videos and television programmes may also encourage children to explore other worlds.

Although writing has a great deal to do with 'spatial' arrangements: the words in a line, the text on the page, pages in the book etc., narrative and writing come together because of the temporal aspect of writing. Children's earliest experiences of narrative are likely to have been through the medium of speech, narratives are not spatial, they are not concerned with the use of space but are concerned with ordering events in time: writing, too, is about ordering things in time. When writing a story, for example, we write and read a succession of sentences and paragraphs and in so doing the narrative unfolds. When telling a story orally we are conscious of the order of the events and action and tell them in sequence. Children expect that by the end of the storybook they will have got to the end of the story, stories start at the beginning of the book and end at the end. I would argue that children who are developing their narrative competencies, which includes their abilities to organize events and tell stories with clear beginnings and endings, are well on the way to being able to write stories. Of course, children need to know the conventions for written communication in the language and culture they are operating within, but they also need to have a firm foundation in the form of experience of experimenting with ways of telling what you want to say, i.e. a sense of how things are best communicated to others, since knowing how to write the letters of the alphabet and spell correctly does not in itself enable you to write 'high quality' stories. This is the very point that Margaret Meek made when she wrote:

> Our failure to expect that children can acquire power in written language derives, in part, from too great a preoccupation with their spelling and punctuation — the power we exert over them — rather than a sufficient concern for their productions — their skill in using language and in making plain what they are reading and writing *about*. [original emphasis]
> (Meek, 1991, p. 185)

There are very few reported instances of television and video supporting very young children's development of spelling or punctuation or understanding of layout etc. despite explicit 'lessons' being included in some programmes such as *Sesame Street*. To begin to understand why television does not appear to help children with these aspects of writing it is necessary to reflect briefly on the logic of different scripts. When a *Sesame Street* programme included a scene of a young child being taught to write in Chinese, Rehana was able to recall how to write 'rain' and 'stream' and yet, despite the fact that the same programme provided numerous opportunities to see words written in English, often supported by emphasis on the onset and rime (e.g. 'W-alk, w-alk, walk, walk! T-all, t-all, tall, tall! Walk tall! Walk Tall!'), she did not remember how to write these words. Gunther Kress has persuasively argued that children beginning to represent their ideas start off as 'pictographers', and has provided examples of how children express their ideas in a physical form (Kress, 1997). Pat Gura has also recorded numerous examples of how children have used blocks to represent their ideas (Gura, 1992). Children move on to drawing their ideas and, Gunther Kress argues, the step from drawing ideas to drawing the characters in pictographic scripts is a much easier one than the move that children writing in alphabetic scripts must make. Children writing in alphabetic scripts have to learn to draw pictures of sounds, not pictures of ideas which, according to Kress opens up a 'vast conceptual-cognitive gap which is difficult to bridge' (Kress, 1997, p. 84). The fact that the Chinese characters shown on *Sesame Street* represented ideas, albeit in a highly stylized form, meant it was possible for a 3 or 4 year-old to see how the character for rain, for example, included dots that looked like rain drops. The written word 'walk', however, does not given any clues as to what it might refer.

I would argue that television and videos can provide significant support to young writers' development, not through providing lessons, explicit or implicit, in the physical aspects of writing but rather through providing children with a rich experience of stories told in different ways to different audiences and also an experience of different genres. This experience of stories helps develop children's understanding of the structure of narrative. Fox made the point that the young children in her study were using knowledge of how narratives are told, knowledge that they did not know they possessed. This knowledge:

> . . . of how to tell a story is not only grounded in all the other stories that they have ever heard, but also in their everyday social experiences, the conversations they have listened to and participated in, the games they have played, everything they have observed and heard.
> (Fox, 1993, p. 25)

Rowe Wells highlights how Goodman's research (1990) showed how children used familiar stories as the basis for playscripts and Goodman concluded, following her analysis of these playscripts, that dramatic play provides opportunities to develop and practise narrative skills. Gordon Wells has also argued that children's 'inner storying is sustained and enriched' thorough dramatic play and makes the point that stories seen on television have a powerful influence on the content of children's dramatic play (Wells, 1987, p. 200). Hall and Robinson (1995) have also argued that role play is about authorship and the mutual composition of narrative texts.

On the basis of my observations of young children between the ages of 2 and 7 and conversations with children involved in the study, I would argue that it is necessary to acknowledge that what children watch on videos and television offers potential dramatic playscripts, and that videos and television should be included in the 'everyday social experiences' and 'everything they have observed and heard'.

Videos as the catalyst for dramatic play and storytelling

My contention is that videos, television and books each provide children with examples of ways in which narratives can be told. Research by Wells Rowe (1998) has identified ways in which books can be the starting point for dramatic play through which children can explore the '*content*' of books (Wells Rowe, p. 31). My research would suggest that televisual texts also stimulate children's imaginations and may provide the spark for dramatic play and storytelling. Through observing young children, playing and talking to them about what or who they pretended to be, it was very apparent that for children of the late 1990s, videos and television are the catalyst for a great deal of their dramatic play:

Hannah:	Well, me and my brother [aged 2] pretend to be fairies and butterflies because he has got fairy wings and I've got some coloured butterfly wings.
Lauren:	I sometimes pretend to be Noddy and Tinkerbell . . .
NB:	What from *Peter Pan*?
Lauren:	Yes, and Peter Pan and sometimes I pretend to be Pocahontas and sometimes I pretend to be Barbie.
NB:	You pretend to be a lot don't you? This is at home, yeah? Have you got any clothes or costumes?
Lauren:	I have Pocahontas, Barbie and Tinkerbell.
Hannah:	I've got a Barbie dress.
NB:	Right, all of those are videos and books, have you got the books and the videos?
Hannah:	I got the video of *Peter Pan*.
Lauren:	I've got the video of *Peter Pan* and I don't know about *Pocahontas*.
NB:	So do you pretend to be whatever you've seen on the video or do you make it up as well?
Lauren:	Or, whatever I've seen on a video or a film or a book that somebody's read to me. And if I have the costume I pretend to be it in that and if I don't I just pretend to be it normal.
Hannah:	I've got, my mum, she made me, we got this brown felt and she made me a Pocahontas dress. I've got the video of *Peter Pan*, *Pocahontas* and I've got the book of, I haven't started reading it, but I've got the book of *Peter Pan*.

[Girls aged 6, TSE, pp. 10–11]

Two younger boys made it clear that their ideas came from both books and television:

NB:	Do you ever pretend to be somebody?
Gary and John:	Yeah.
Gary:	I pretend to be a pirate with a shotgun.
NB:	Where did you get that idea from?
Gary:	Mmm, my mummy. I saw a picture of a big, big pirate and a big bit of snow dropping in their face.
John:	I pretend to be all of the characters.
NB:	What do you mean 'all of the characters'?
John:	I pretend to be all the characters on films.
Gary:	I pretend to be Batman.
John:	I pretend to be Batman as well.

[Boys aged 5, TSJ, p. 2]

A number of children took on roles from both television *and* books but many children I spoke to only mentioned television or video-related roles. These children told me that they pretended to be Belle, Sleeping Beauty, Woody, presenters of children's programmes, Thomas (the Tank Engine), Teletubbies, one of the Power Rangers, Wallace, Gromit, Feather McGraw, Winnie the Pooh, Sera from *Land Before Time*, characters from *The Worst Witch*, *The Last Unicorn*, Robin (from *Batman and Robin*), Spiderman, Barbie and Ariel. The range of characters children pretend to be seems to be heavily weighted towards those seen on the television screen. Instead of worrying about the fact that children are not exploring characters from books and therefore possibly not deepening their understanding of the written texts they encounter, perhaps we ought to consider what children are gaining from dramatic play centred around their experiences of videos.

Videos and dramatic play

Observing a number of young children between the ages of 2 and 6 it is clear that watching a particular video can help to initially structure a child's imaginative play and the child may mirror what is happening on screen. A colleague related how her young grandson would watch *Thomas the Tank Engine* videos whilst simultaneously replicating the screen text with his own train track and engines. Helen Bromley has told of how she too observed a small boy making direct connections between what he was watching on video with his own play with his train set and, furthermore, making links between Thomas the Tank Engine's experiences and his own real-life experiences with his mother (Bromley, 1996, p. 72). After having watched *The Wind in the Willows* on television, another mother described how her 2-year-old son asked her to make him some mole-shaped paws from cardboard and how, equipped with these and a long scarf, he played for the whole afternoon at being Mole.

From the time Rehana first began to watch television and videos it was clear that videos provided added stimuli for her imaginative play and she adopted a range of roles when watching various videos. At the age of 3 she watched the video of *Mary Poppins* repeatedly until, on adopting the role of Mary Poppins, she was not only word-perfect, but she could also duplicate what was happening on screen. Before she settled down to watch the video she collected all the necessary props: hat, coat (to be taken off and hung up at the correct moment), measuring tape, medicine spoons etc. She enlisted my help in ensuring that her costume was as accurate as possible. On one level she was gaining a thorough knowledge of the sequence of events in the story and opportunities to repeatedly hear language outside her every-day experience. On a deeper level, through dramatic reconstruction of what she saw being depicted on the screen, she was attempting to gain a better understanding of the deeper meanings of the story itself and to explore emotions and motives such as those of loss and rejection precipitated by Mary Poppins's departure at the end of the film. Teachers and parents will be familiar with young children's insistence that a particular book is read and reread. One explanation for this is that the book is satisfying at a deep emotional level because it enables the child to confront, explore and acknowledge uncomfortable emotions at a safe distance. Sendak's book *Where the Wild Things Are* would appear to be one such book (Meek, 1991, p. 98). Access to videos means that young children are able to revisit a story as they would a book, as many are very adept at fast forwarding or rewinding the video tape to enable them to focus on key points of the story. This re-viewing of specific parts of a video is comparable to the way in which children may return to specific pictures in picture books or reread certain passages. Freud (1920) and Bruno Bettelheim (1978) discussed the importance of stories and dramatic role play in enabling children to reflect on fundamental, universal themes such as separation, loss, greed and envy. It is not appropriate at this point to digress into the realms of psychoanalytic theories, but it is important bear in mind that opportunities for reflections of this sort are not only important for children's emotional well-being and development but will also influence their response to and understanding of what they read, what they write and what they watch on video. It is clear that the stories the children find emotionally satisfying are not confined to oral stories or written stories in books.

Developing a deeper understanding of plot and characterization

Adopting a role and playing it out enables the child to take control of it and, in so doing, work towards a resolution in terms of the fear or anxiety induced by the character or the situation or the video or television programme. As the story and characters become more familiar the children's play may gradually diversify in order to explore further possibilities. Playing out a story or assuming a role in order to explore a character has an important part to play helping a child develop a deeper understanding of the plot or motivations of the characters.

At the age of 3 Rehana as Mary Poppins explored the notions of 'leaving':

[Rehana, aged 3.6, dressed as Mary Poppins playing with her mother in the garden]
Father: Who are you?
Rehana: I'm Mary Poppins and I gotta go now but I won't leave you for such a
            long time. [Walked down garden path and then returned singing 'Just a
            spoonful of sugar'. Opened door to a little house in garden. Mother was
            already inside house]
Mother: It looks like Mary Poppins has arrived!
Rehana: You don't know it's Mary Poppins.
Mother: Oh.
Rehana: You don't recognize me.
Mother: Oh, sorry.
[Mary Poppins sat down as if for an interview, as seen on the video of *Mary
Poppins*]
Mother: What is your name?
Rehana: Mary Poppins and, er, I'm practically perfect in every way.
Mother: Oh, would you look after my children?
Rehana: Yes, that's quite satisfactory.
[She clearly responds as if her terms of employment had just been outlined, as on
the video, but since her main focus in this instance was not accuracy, she allowed
the error to pass without comment]

Rehana:	You go to work now.
Mother:	Bye! I'm off to work now.
Rehana:	Don't be quick.
Mother:	Well, I'll be as long as my work takes me. Be good for Mary Poppins.
Rehana:	[Left house too] I'm going.
Mother:	You've left the children!
Rehana:	I know.
Mother:	Why?
Rehana:	This is the other room.
Mother:	Oh I see, why are you looking so fed up?
Rehana:	They're being naughty for me — NO! You mustn't hear me!
Mother:	I was just asking, I was just being curious.
Rehana:	I didn't want you to be curious.
Mother:	All right, I won't be like the oysters – we know what happened to the oysters, don't we? [Reference to the oysters in recently-seen Disney video of *Alice in Wonderland*]
Rehana:	Yes!
[Mary Poppins returns to house and then leaves again]	
Rehana:	I'm going to go into the other room, you mustn't see.
Mother:	I'm at work, I'm not here.
Rehana:	Oh.

Those familiar with the video will recognize certain phrases such as 'practically perfect' and 'quite satisfactory'. The video stimulated her role play and, in so doing, provided the arena for her to experiment with words and use language she would not normally use herself. In addition, this extract from a much longer session of role play demonstrates very clearly how she was moving away from the supportive framework of the video and beginning to explore the character and the underlying themes more on her own terms and in ways that made sense to her.

From the age of 3, Rehana took on a wide range of roles in her dramatic play, many of which were related to videos (e.g. Belle, Snow White, Minnie Mouse, Cinderella, Wizard of Oz) and some of which were book-related (e.g. characters from Jill Murphy's *The Worst Witch* series). At the age of 5 Rehana was still heavily involved in dramatic play and a particularly memorable role she explored a this stage was that of the White Witch in *The Lion, the Witch and the Wardrobe*. This was a character to whom she had an ambivalent response, on the one hand fascinated by her whilst, on the other, frightened by her. Rehana played out the role of the White Witch again and again both at home and in school until she had 'neutralized' the character. As Rehana began to feel more at ease with the character of the White Witch she extended her dialogue and actions until she was exploring how the White Witch would respond to new and imagined situations. As she took more control over the character her fear was diminished and she relished exploring being wicked, telling me 'It's good fun pretending to be bad'. Her last instance of playing the Witch coincided with a fancy dress party to which she went dressed as the White Witch. Before leaving she said, 'I'd better not pretend to be her because the other children may be frightened'. She never again took on this role for a sustained period of time and it was as if she felt she had exhausted all the possibilities and was no longer emotionally engaged by the character. At the age of 7 whilst watching the video of the *The Lion, the Witch and the Wardrobe* she could still remember the dialogue sufficiently well to be able to join in, and when the White Witch was at her most unpleasant she recalled how she used to be 'really scared by this bit'.

When Rehana was 6 a frequently present character in our home was the teenager, Melody. Rehana first encountered this particular fictional character whilst watching a TV adaptation of Dick King-Smith's book *The Queen's Nose*. Melody is aptly likened to Barbie by another character in the series and I suspect that herein lay her attraction. Through identifying with this particular character, imitating her mannerisms, body language and verbal language, Rehana was able to explore what it means to be 'nearly grown up'. The video provided the initial stimulus for dramatic play but this was then followed up with numerous questions: 'How old is Melody supposed to be?', 'Do you think she looks nice in that?', 'Why is she making that sort of face?', 'I think Gregory's nice, Melody's being mean isn't she?' and so on. Her dramatic play could be viewed in Vygotskian terms as providing her with the opportunity to rehearse a version of a role she may play for real in the years to come, but her identification with Melody also enabled her to reflect on the narrative from a different standpoint. Rehana's interest in Melody was important in terms of her literacy development as it motivated her to attempt to interpret the narrative from Melody's perspective rather than from her own position or even that of Harmony, the main protagonist.

When we read *The Queen's Nose*, after having watched the television adaptation, Rehana expressed disappointment with the characters, mainly because the two sisters were much younger than those portrayed on television. Reading only the book would not have sparked Rehana's imagination and provided her with the opportunity to rehearse future roles and possibly develop her ability to explore how the events and relationships within a narrative may have a different impact on the characters involved. This ability to decentre and be able to consider alternative viewpoints is important for storytelling and writing. I would argue that creators of powerful stories, be these oral or written, need to have developed an ability to consider the viewpoints of the various characters in their narratives. Without this ability the dialogue and characterization is likely to result in 'cardboard cut-outs' rather than convincing personalities. This ability to consider and take account of different viewpoints is also necessary for writing non-narrative texts as these may require a well-reasoned argument that acknowledges the possibility of alternative views.

Visual cues provided by videos

When reading about the beavers in *The Lion, the Witch and the Wardrobe*, Rehana was struck by their kindness and helpfulness but it was only after close observation of the beavers on the video that she began to mimic their expressions and explore moving like a beaver. The video opened up this possibility in a way that the book did not. Whilst she could draw on her experience of the written text to confidently and accurately reproduce the beavers' dialogue she needed the visual support provided by the video in order to know how to move, she needed to see what the words meant in the same way as she did when asking about facial expressions (see p. 89).

Similarly, when watching the video of *Prince Caspian* she stated 'I'm going to pretend to be King Miraz in this next bit 'cos I want to see what it feel likes to die'. Seeing King Miraz 'die' led to a range of questions about the physical aspects of death (e.g. 'why do people close their eyes when they die?' 'Do people always stick their tongues out when they die?') Reading the same section in the book had prompted questions about the motivations of the two Lords who betray the king, but watching the video made it possible to consider another aspect of the same event.

The majority of children involved in my study not only talked about the roles they adopted from television and video but also made very positive comments about the role of videos in terms of providing ideas for dramatic play:

NB: Do you get more ideas from books or from videos?
Rehana: Normally from videos because I know what their costumes look like and what they act like but once, once I dressed up, but you were in bed, I got up early and I read the Ms Wiz story and dressed up as Ms Wiz.
NB: Mmm.
Rehana: But usually I get ideas from videos . . . like Belle.
[Rehana, aged 7.2]

However, one child I spoke to felt that videos did not help her to 'act things out':

Charlotte: Books are, um more easy to act out if you really want to act them out when someone's reading the book and videos aren't because they go a bit too fast because you'll have to press um, stop, um, and do the parts you have to do to say the parts you have to.
[Girl aged 6, TSA, p. 3]

Some of the children, especially the girls, talked about how videos helped them engage in a more organized form of dramatic play:

Isobel: Videos are good because say you wanted to do a play, you could see what they were doing, you could see how they move, but in books you can't and, and, and in books, books gets, in videos it, it say you want to to . . . er . . . to . . . er do a play you can see how they move and all that and what they're wearing . . .
Davinder: Yeah, but if you want to do the play, if it's early tomorrow in the morning how will you remember these things?
Isobel: In the morning? You *can* remember the movements, *easy*.
[Girl and boy aged 7, TSK, p. 1]

A younger child also talked about the potential of videos for stimulating plays:

NB: Do television programmes or videos ever give you ideas about games to play?
Sasha: Well videos are quite good because you can do plays from them.

NB: Have you ever done a play?
Sasha: Yes, at school we did *Cinderella*.
[Girl aged 5, TSF, p. 5]

Children are also stimulated to work out playscripts based on books but the visual nature of videos and the high levels of dialogue probably makes it easier to base a play on a video than on a book. This could have implications for classroom practice as Year 4 children may be expected to write playscripts (see National Literacy Strategy Framework for Teaching, DfEE, p. 38). I would argue that children who are experienced in interpreting televisual texts are likely to be better placed to understand what a playscript may involve than children whose reading experiences have been limited to narratives written in continuous prose in the form of short stories or novels.

When she was 5, Rehana performed a show which was based on books she had read about *The Twitches*. This show or performance involved a step away from the dramatic role play she had hitherto been engaged in, as it was clear that she had an awareness of the audience and consciously structured the narrative to take account of the audience. Her main aim was to tell a good story rather than explore an emotion or character in more depth. The performance was similar to dramatic role play in that she was still able to physically experience movements through space and changes in body language. Through the performance she was exploring how to carry a narrative through dialogue, action and visual cues, which is a feature of both televisual texts and stage plays and it is precisely because of this that it is difficult to read the partial transcript of the drama (see below) and also to follow the story from the transcript. The visual cues played an important part in supporting the audience's understanding. The performance was interesting in terms of her literacy development because of the strategies she employed to sustain the story and the ways in which she overcame a number of difficult problems.

Two witches were involved in the story and Rehana took on both roles, switching effortlessly from one character to the other. She overcame the absence of an ever-present narrator in a variety of ways. One strategy she used was to physically reposition herself as appropriate (e.g. if acting out the role of Lil talking to Gert she stood to the left of a footstool and when Gert responded she moved to the right hand side of the stool). She appeared to be very conscious of the need to retain the integrity of the spatial relationship between the two characters and it would appear that reference to a mental map she had created of the various scenes helped her to maintain this integrity. An additional signal to the audience about who was speaking was provided by her use of different 'voices' and her characterizations which were heavily dependent upon her body language and tone of speech. It was only with the entry of a third character, that of the narrator's voice, that she found it difficult to indicate who was speaking without providing verbal cues for the audience. Watching the video of her drama it was interesting to note how, although conscious of the video camera, she talked to the 'other' (invisible) characters rather than her audience or the camera. When watching video narratives on television, the characters also talk to each other and the audience assumes the role of onlooker and eavesdropper. Similarly, when reading a book the reader can only look on, they can not alter the course of events or interrupt the characters' conversations. This notion of a 'distant' but engaged audience is an important one for writers of both televisual and written texts as it requires the writer to consider what needs to be made explicit in order to facilitate the readers' or viewers' understanding. As this was a performance rather than a written text, she did not explain what each of her limited props symbolized as the drama unfolded, but ensured that this was apparent from the way in which she used them. The footstool, for example, began as a bed in which she lay and then climbed out of; it changed into an aeroplane which she 'boarded' by pretending to climb some steps, sat down in and pretended to buckle up her seat belt. She indicated that the 'plane' had taken off by the way in which she peered down on the ground and pointed out things through a 'window'.

[To facilitate the reading of the transcript I have only noted her actions in the initial exchanges. Rehana as Gert is denoted by standard font, Rehana as Lil is denoted by italics]

[Rehana began in narrator role and directly addressed the audience]

The show of *The Twitches*! There are two twitches in this, one called Gert and one called Lil. There's only one actor and that is — Miss Rehana Browne! [bows and smiles] You will meet the Twitches when they are in bed. The Twitches' Horrorween. Instead of the Twitches' Halloween it's Horrorween because it's a horror day, because it's a horror for the witches.

[Lies on footstool covered with tablecloth] This, yuk! Lil get up! [sits up] I believe we are going on holiday today. Get your suitcase, Lil. Ugh! [Stands up and 'makes' bed] For the first time in my life I've made the bed. [Picks up small suitcase] Get your suitcase, Lil!

[Lies down and then stretches and yawns] Okay

[Walks around room] Now, we'd better get the aeroplane, bettern't we! It's quicker than going on the bus. Last time we scared the people out of their wits when we did that. [Sits down on footstool and buckles imaginary seat belt. Turns to her left] Put your seat belt on because we're going to launch. [Looks ahead and then turns to her right, cranes her neck and and peers down at floor] I think there's the castle tower where we go [Points]

[Moves onto left side of footstool] Mmm [stands up]

[Moves to right side of footstool and turns to left to talk] Sit down! Here we are and off we go. [Stands up. Puts tape of children's songs on] What is that pretty music I can hear? [Mimics singing] Everybody in the ring, la,la, la,la,la, la, Ugh! What's that revolting smell? I think that revolting smell, Lil, is . . . soap! Yuk, Ugh, the cover's got flowers on it.

So has the duvet

So have the sheets. That was the most uncomfortablist night I have ever spent. These sheets have been washed you know, Lil. Horrible isn't it? What are *you* doing in here?

[Unnamed third character speaks in high-pitched voice] I've come in here to clean the hotel.

Oh really? said Gert, Well, we don't normally have a cleaner at our hotel so this is going to be the smelliest holiday in the world.

[. . .]

Well, we can't expect it can we? As it's Horrorween

Oh really? We'll see about that. The absolute scenery of it all. Last year we had a party.

Did we?

Yes, of course we did. You know we did.

Mmm, did we?

Yes!

Shall we go and have a swim?

No way. Last time they all wanted to give us a bath.

[Aged 5.10, partial transcript of performance, 7 December 1997]

Six months later Rehana became particularly interested in writing plays. In the example (Figure 6.1) it is clear that she understands how it is possible to carry the narrative through dialogue and action and she appears to have begun to explore the use of stage directions. I would suggest that Rehana's experience of watching televisual narrative was reflected in her shows, as televisual narratives are heavily dependent upon dialogue and action and there is generally no narrator, which contrasts with the way in which narratives are usually carried in written texts in books. Is it possible that children learn incidental lessons from televisual narratives that they may not learn from books? Rehana appeared to have been developing an understanding of screen plays and playscripts. If this is the case teachers may need to reflect on what sorts of texts provide the most appropriate medium for developing children's understanding of different written forms.

Figure 6.1   Example of writing playscripts

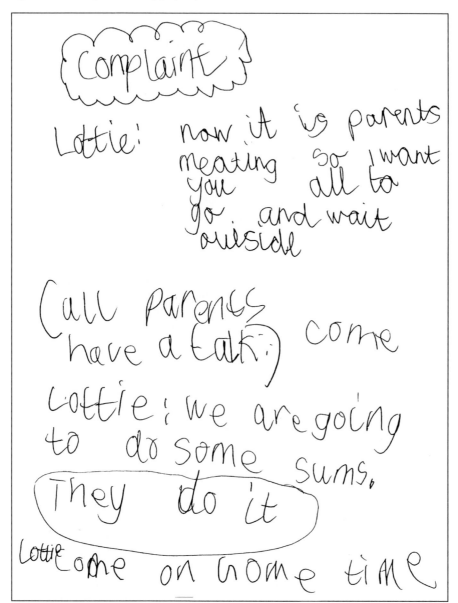

Intertextual nature of dramatic play

Carol Fox has demonstrated clearly how young children's narratives may draw on a range of experiences, some real and some experienced through the medium of books. It has been argued that this 'borrowing' (Meek, 1991), or 'transformation' (Fox, 1993), is a valuable part of a child's literacy development. Observations of young children's dramatic play has yielded evidence of intertextuality. Children engaged in dramatic play make connections between videos as they do between books. An illustration of this is derived from an observation of a Rehana's re-enactment of *The Little Princess* after having seen the film. It was interesting to note how she integrated elements of Disney's *Cinderella* with *The Little Princess* through her commentary and dialogue whilst pretending to be Sarah in her attic room:

> The bell's ringing to tell me to get up. All right, I hear you, killjoy. Time to start another day. [Moves around 'tidying up'].
> Pretend I'm a servant already . . .

Rehana also drew on books in attempting to make sense of Sarah's experiences. As the dramatic play continued to unfold I found some of the connections she made were unexpected. She commented on how Miss Minchin, Sarah's hard-hearted school principal, was similar to the strict form teacher, Miss Hardbroom in the *Worst Witch* stories. She also recognized the experience of evacuation in three separate books and videos (*The Little Princess*, a BBC *Look and Read* series *Spy Watch* and *The Lion, the Witch and the Wardrobe*). This ability to analyse stories, books and videos; identify salient features; utilize 'book' language and be sensitive to commonalities between texts videos and real life and then to manipulate what they have read, heard and seen to create something new is an essential aspect of literacy. It would appear that dramatic play may provide an ideal forum for this valuable process.

Questions of reality, genre and response to texts

As with books, children can explore and ultimately decide to opt in or out of the fantasy presented on screen. A vivid example of this was provided by two 5-year-olds who, on watching the appearance of a werewolf in *Prince Caspian*, either demonstrated or sought confirmation of, their understanding that the characters were in reality actors dressed up. The two children made matter of fact remarks to the adult such as 'It's like Maugrim [a wolf in *The Lion, the Witch and the Wardrobe*] . . . I think it must be the same costume'. This comment suggested that they were aware of the weak modality of the scene. This comment was instantly followed by both girls clutching each other and saying, 'I'm scared!' in suitably dramatic voices. This second comment could indicate that the children's judgments about the modality of what they were watching were unstable and very easily altered, or, possibly, that they were fully aware that what they were watching was not 'real' but were willing to 'play the game' in order to sustain their enjoyment of the scene. To continue watching, the children needed to opt back into the fantasy, to *choose* to judge the modality as strong in order to be able to respond emotionally and enjoy being scared. At the age of 7 Rehana appeared to have remained drawn to the character of Aslan. Interestingly, when watching *The Lion, the Witch and the Wardrobe* at the age of 7, she recalled her visit to the Theatre Museum in London and talked about how she had seen and stroked 'the actual head of Aslan at the museum' but was still sufficiently engaged with the story to choose to fast forward the scene when Aslan dies saying 'it's too sad'.

The concept of modality is important as it is related to children's development of a more refined understanding of genre. Barrie Gunter and Jill McAleer (1997) provide an overview of the research into children's growing ability to make distinctions between real-life or true television programmes, and fantasy or fictional programmes, and also children's awareness of the different genres of television programming. Some research indicates that children may be able to distinguish between fiction and non-fiction in written texts at an early age and adapt their language accordingly, although there is a degree of disparity in the research findings focusing on young children's understanding of genres (e.g. Pappas, 1991, Fisher, 1997). At the age of 3, when Rehana read a known non-fictional text, she did not open with any of the traditional story openings that she was familiar with at the time and the language she used was close to that of non-fictional texts for small children:

> Long, long ago dinosaurs was living and people was digging up their bones. People found them in rocks. That's true you know. This is called a Tegosaurus, it ate other dinosaurs and plants and this only ate plants but it does look a bit fierce. This is a mummy one. Baby ones, baby dinosaurs hatch-ed from eggs. And this only ate plants, it had a long neck for it to — you know Mummy? Sometimes its neck was so long it could eat right on top of this house and for breakfast 'em would eat all of them plants. And this one only ate other dinosaurs and insects. And this one ate only plants and this one only ate plants.
> [Rehana reading *Dinosaurs*, aged 3.7]

She only stepped 'outside' the genre on two occasions. The first was when she commented 'That's true you know' and the second when she introduced a piece of information with the words 'you know Mummy?' The assertion about the truthfulness of the text may have been because she was not sufficiently confident in her ability to signal the veracity of the statements or possibly because she thought it was a feature of this particular genre. Alternatively, both comments may have been prompted by her experiences of having this genre read to her by adults who tended to attempt to alleviate the vapidness of the non-fictional text by drawing the child in and relating difficult concepts to the child's own experiences.

In the case of television, recent research findings are not consistent, although a number of researchers have suggested that Key Stage 2 children had some understanding of genre (Buckingham, 1993; Dorr, 1983; Robinson 1997). Whilst children may be able to make some distinctions between different types of programmes, such as the news and a drama programme, it is more difficult to make the finer distinctions between different types of narratives. How, for example, is a mystery different from a horror story, how are these different from adventure stories or from historical accounts based on rigorous research? By exploring and playing with the modality of both screen texts and written texts, children may begin to form and refine their ideas about the features of different genres and develop a realization of how screenwriters and directors and also, I would argue, authors, manipulate the watchers' or readers' modality judgments, (e.g. leading them on only to confound their expectations). This relatively sophisticated level of understanding is necessary for developing a refined understanding of the more subtle characteristics of different genres and I would argue that children's engagement with televisual texts may provide some with an incipient understanding of the concepts of modality and genre. I would also suggest then, that children's developing knowledge about modality and genres, gained from both written and televisual texts, is explored and utilized in their oral storytelling and their written stories (see Rehana's Disneyland story on p. 132).

Gunther Kress has argued that learning about genres and learning to write in particular genres is a means of socializing children into organizing knowledge in acceptable ways (Kress, 1994). Knowledge about genres is a double-edged sword, in that the knowledge facilitates communication with others with similar concerns and interests, but it can serve to impede the development of new and different ways of thinking and responding.

I would suggest that exploring writing for different purposes during dramatic role play may lay the foundations for writing in a range of different genres. Between the ages of 5 and 7 Rehana's self-initiated writing at home encompassed a wide range of genres including stories, poems, jokes, playscripts, diary entries, instructions about how to make a model and information labels for a toy museum. Some of this writing was prompted by books but there were instances when it was a screen-based text that acted as a catalyst for the writing. One very clear instance of a film generating an interest in a particular genre occurred after having watched the film of *Harriet the Spy*. Immediately after seeing this film Rehana collected the requisite equipment (binoculars, note book and coat etc.) to enable her to engage in dramatic play in which she was a spy. Part of the play involved keeping a diary of her observations. I was fascinated to see how her diary entries were so dissimilar to her usual form of writing (Figure 6.2). She seems to have been exploring how to write in note form without an emotional element (see Figure 6.3). She also read the book and it is clear that the experience of both the film and the book helped her to get to grips with this unfamiliar form of writing. Approximately 15 months after having seen the film at the cinema the video was released and she watched it, to the exclusion of all else, for almost three weeks. Her involvement in dramatic play, which had somewhat diminished during the previous year, resurfaced as she was prompted to adopt the role of a spy. Her new entries in her spy notebook show how she had developed her understanding of the genre (Figure 6.4). A few weeks prior to watching the video of *Harriet the Spy* she had been reading *Skinny Melon and Me* (Ure, 1996) and was puzzled by a specific aspect of the book and asked, 'If the book is supposed to be like her diary, why are her mummy's letters in it, because she's not supposed to know what her mummy has written, is she?' The author had attempted to overcome the problems of a book written in diary form and the consequent absence of the voice

Figure 6.2   *Example of a usual form of writing*

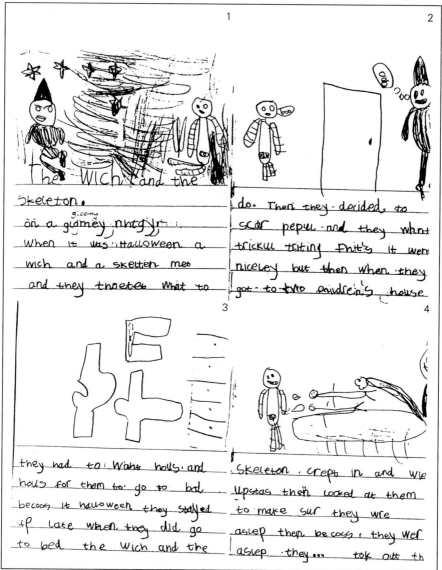

Age 5.7

of an omniscient narrator, by including the mother's letters, which provided the reader with cues about future events and dramas. Rehana's growing familiarity with the form of diaries which had begun at the age of 6 with her experience of the televisual text of *Harriet the Spy* and the resulting role play, was explored in more depth through written texts such as Anne Fine's *The Diary of a Killer Cat* and *Jennifer's Diary*, Clive Dickinson's *The Lost Diary of Tutankhamun's Mummy*, all of which

Figure 6.3   Example of writing in note form

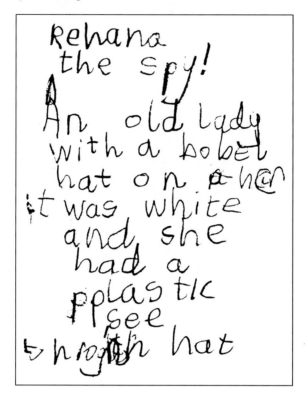

had made it possible for her to identify the reason she was finding it difficult to locate *Skinny Melon* within a genre. At the age of 7- and-a-half, watching the video of *Harriet the Spy*; her previous experiences of a range of written texts within the genre and her role play, had clearly contributed to her development as a writer.

Knowledge of genre is an important element of literacy development as it influences the reader's expectations of a given text, which, in turn, influences the reader's approach and response to the text. Authors, even inexperienced authors, need to have an awareness of the influence of genre on reader response.

The final example of her exploring genres involves a brief discussion and an instance of dramatic play with dolls at the age of 7. As with other children, (Robinson, 1997) Rehana is in the process of developing and refining her understanding of genres and, furthermore, is exploring who are the main audiences for different types of television programme. After watching and episode of *The Demon Headmaster*, the following interchange occurred:

Rehana: Is *The Demon Headmaster* a soap?
NB: Um, what do you think?
Rehana: No . . . I'm not sure.

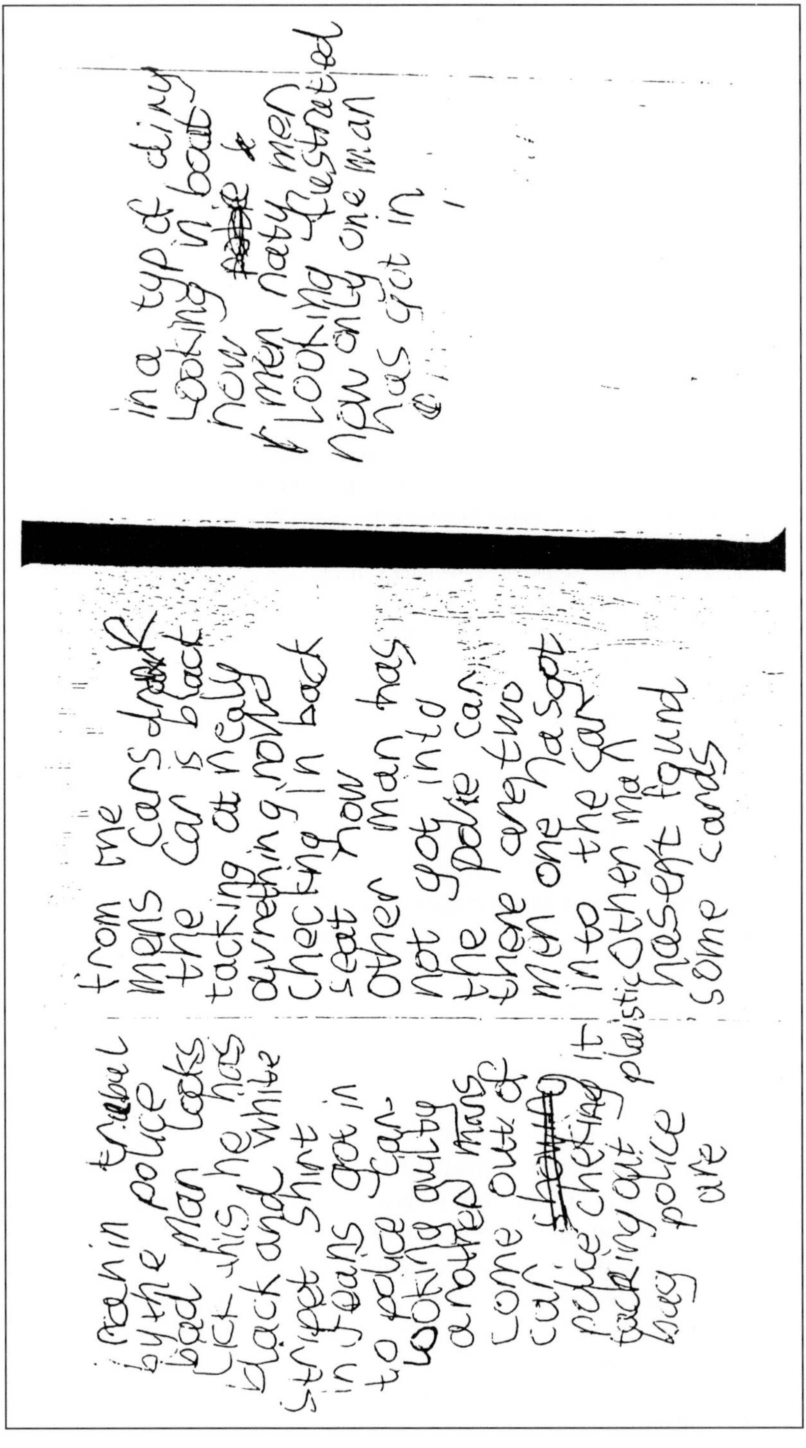

Figure 6.4   Example of writing showing understanding of the genre

man in travel
by the police
bad man looks
Let this he has
black and white
striped shirt
in jeans got in
to police car
looking quite
another mans
come out of
car
police checking it
taking out plaistic
bag police
are

from the
mans cars drunk
the car is black
tacking at really
everything now
checking in back
seat now
other man has
not got in to
the police car
there are two
mun one has got
into the car
other man
hasent found
some cards

in a typ of ding
Looking in bout
how r men
r men hav men
looking frustrated
now only one man
has got in

NB: What is a soap?

Rehana: When it's about everyday life, so no, *The Demon Headmaster* isn't . . . And they're not kissing and stuff in *the Demon Headmaster*, so no.

The following exchanges were part of an imaginative game that took place a few days later. Two dolls, Barbie and Steve were involved and initially Rehana provided the 'voice' for Barbie and I was Steve, but she soon took on both roles:

[Rehana had established that Steve was watching football]

Steve: (sitting watching TV): GOAL!

Barbie: That's enough, you'll get square eyes.

Steve: But grown ups can't get square eyes.

Barbie: I know, but I think you've watched enough football.

Steve: But the match hasn't finished yet!

Barbie: I don't care, now hurry along, hurry along!

[Rehana now moves both dolls and takes on both roles]

Barbie: I'm going to watch *Neighbours*.

[Rehana steps out of role to ask: 'Mummy, she's about twenty, nearly grown up, but she'd still like *Neighbours*, wouldn't she?']

NB: Yes, plenty of grown ups enjoy it.

Steve: Nei . . . ei . . . ei . . . bours [sings theme tune in mocking tone]

Barbie: Be quiet!

Steve: It's a load of rubbish, they all live on the same street and all they do is kiss and stuff.

Barbie: No.

Steve: Well, what's happening now? [Pause] You can't tell me because nothing is.

Barbie: Be quiet!

Rehana's interest in notions of audience has important implications for her writing development since authors always need to have an audience in mind.

Oral storytelling and the moves into writing

In order to write imaginatively and with enthusiasm, children need to feel motivated and confident. Experienced storytellers are likely to be confident about their ability to 'tell a good story' which is likely to be well received by the audience. I am not suggesting that writing is merely a case of assigning written symbols to spoken language. It goes without saying that children have to learn how writing and speech are different and also the various conventions regarding spelling, punctuation, layout etc. However, the fact remains that in order to unlock a child's potential with regard to writing she must feel that she is writing for a genuine purpose and that she has something to communicate. Children with a story to tell are more likely to write than children with no story in their heads. Carol Fox has this to say about developing children's imaginative writing:

... it should be possible to make some of the techniques employed by good story-tellers more explicit as children grow older. This does not mean giving lessons on analysing literary texts. On the contrary, we can accomplish it both pleasurably and rigorously through *role play, story-telling, retelling and changing stories.* [My emphasis]
(Fox, 1993, p. 197)

Important research by Gordon Wells in the 1980s, highlighted how experience of story is a key factor in young children's literacy development (Wells, 1981, 1985, 1987). Gordon Wells has argued that children's ability to make meaning using words alone is developed through their growing understanding of stories. An understanding of, and facility with, narrative forms enables young children's literacy to develop apace. In order to write stories they need to know how stories 'work' and Margaret Meek has argued that television helps beginner readers and writers, not least because of what children can learn about narratives through watching television and videos:

TV programmes are episodic; they are rounded off in organized time slots, so that watching becomes a complete act with its own conventions, the very thing we say children have to discover about reading and writing. In addition, TV teaches children to keep the story going, just as readers learn to do.
(Meek, 1991, p. 218)

The writers of the National Literacy Strategy have acknowledged the importance of oral work in relation to the composition of texts:

Good oral work enhances pupils' understanding of language in both oral and written forms and of the way language can be used to communicate. It is also an important part of the process through which pupils read and compose texts.
(DfEE, 1998, p. 3)

The following sections look at how Rehana's development as a storyteller was supported by the dual experience of books and videos.

Storytelling with puppets

In order to move into writing stories, I would suggest that a child needs to be able to make the transition from dramatic play, in which she takes an active part in the narrative, to more abstract thinking in which the various possibilities and dramatic 'moves' are imagined and played out in her head. Performing short plays to an audience may be one stepping stone to this more abstract storying (pp. 115–16) but in reviewing Rehana's development as a storyteller, reader and writer, I was struck by the role that puppets also played in helping her move into the realms of the more abstract thinking required for oral storytelling and writing stories. At this point it is important to note that Rehana watched *Sesame Street* every weekday and therefore she was familiar with the way in which 'real' people can interact with puppets and how puppets themselves can have distinct personalities, tell stories and ask questions.

[Context: Rehana (aged 3.4) performing a puppet show for a small audience.]

Story One:

> [Opens curtains of puppet theatre to reveal empty stage]
> Once upon a time, in the land of wood. . . . there was a donkey [shows donkey puppet]. Eeeaw, ee-aw he said. Singing to himself he went on his way. There was a cat [show cat puppet] Miaow, miaow she said and she went on her way. And a fox [waves fox's tail]. And a hedgehog and . . . [no clear end]

Story Two:

> [Opens curtains to reveal cat puppet]
> *Rehana*:   Once upon a time there was a very sad pussy cat. He was sad because he had no friends. Soon along came Goofy.
> [Goofy puppet appears] 'Why are you sad?' asked Goofy.
> *Cat*:   Because I've got no friends
> *Goofy*:   'That's OK I'll be your friend.
> *Rehana*:   And that's the end of the story

Immediately after performing this playlet she searched through the collection of puppets and props and started a new story.

Story Three:

> Once upon a time [introduces mouse puppet carrying small pink plastic chest] there was a mouse carrying a treasure box and it had in it some very dear little friends. I'm come around to show you all [does so and then retreats behind screen once more]
> [Introduces fox puppet] 'Stop your mumbling'. Said the fox in a silky voice.
> [Introduces a little teddy] A little teddy was walking down the road minding his own business and he saw a treasure box and do you know what? He kept it for himself for ever and ever [teddy and treasure box disappear from view].
> [Reintroduces mouse] Mouse was very sad.
> [Introduces small Father Christmas toy] Father Christmas came along and said, 'Don't be sad, I'll give you another treasure box.'
> And that's the end of the story.

These three stories with puppets were told within the space of approximately half an hour. It is worth considering how each time Rehana told a story using the puppets the story became longer and more complex. In each of the three 'episodes' Rehana seems to have been exploring different elements of narrative acts through the medium of puppets. In the first example she appears to be experimenting with ways in which she could use the puppets to make contact with and communicate with the audience, but she makes no attempt to establish and maintain a discernible story line. In the second puppet show her focus appears to have shifted as she moved on to exploring the dramatic potential of the medium. In this second story the curtains are pulled back to reveal, not an empty stage, but a character. Employing this visually dramatic strategy serves to instantly draw the audience into the story as they ask themselves 'Why is the cat sitting there?' Most *Sesame Street* episodes and many of her videos at the time (e.g. Noddy) opened with a character already in place as the narrator orientated the audience. It would seem that this was a technique that Rehana may have been exploring. Through her opening statement she orientates the audience temporally and introduces the main character. A story is told, albeit a very brief one, and she signals the end with the words 'and that's the end of my story'. In the third episode she seems to have been exploring a number of narrative conventions, including the use of storybook language (e.g. the use of 'silky' to describe the voice, and inversions such as 'and it had in it some very dear little friends'). In the third puppet show she tells a story with at least two events linked in terms of time and there is a clear beginning which introduces the main character and establishes the theme.

What is also very apparent in the third story is that she was experimenting with her role as narrator and what this meant in terms of the control that she had in relation to the direction of the story, the pace of the story and the audience's response. Very early on she established her role as narrator and that of her audience as listeners and watchers (i.e. 'receivers' of her narrative). At the start the narrator was high profile, in that Rehana decided that it was herself as the narrator who would allow the audience to share the secret of the contents of the mouse's treasure box but later, in asking 'and do you know what?' she simultaneously explicitly acknowledged her role as narrator and also experimented with ways in which the narrator can communicate with the audience in a less direct manner, more reminiscent of the narrator on videos of *Noddy* and *Old Bear*. Although her mother was watching her puppet show, it was clear that Rehana had invented an audience of young children for her narrative. This was clear from the somewhat condescending tone in which she spoke when directly addressing the audience and also when she promised to 'come around to show you *all*'. In creating an imagined audience for her story, Rehana had, unknowingly, done what writers need to do. When writing a story the author needs to imagine who the audience might be and what their responses might be and also what they might like to know. Bereiter and Scardamalia (1982 and 1983) identified this challenging feat as one of a series that inexperienced writers have to accomplish in order to become fluent, proficient writers. In imagining a child audience for her story Rehana adapted her telling to accommodate the audience by, for example, altering her tone of voice and predicted that children would be very interested in the contents of the treasure box.

In the third story there is also the mystery of the fox. It is not possible to state with any certainty whether she introduced the fox to add an element of suspense or whether she simply did not develop his role because she forgot about him, or because the fox had no place in the narrative as it developed. It is interesting to note how she introduced the suggestion of danger through the mismatch between the unpleasantness of what the fox said and how he said it, 'in a silky voice'. Is this an example of her experimenting with what Barthes identified as the hermeneutic code which, in very simplistic terms, is a structuring technique aimed at keeping the reader guessing and involved and wanting to know more (Barthes, 1970)? This short story also shows evidence of intertexuality in that she is probably drawing on her knowledge of the conniving fox from her video of *Jemima Puddle-Duck* and the fox in the storybook *Dinner with Fox* (Paul and Wyllie, 1990).

Two months later her puppet show was considerably longer than on previous occasions and demonstrates that she has made the transition from being the ever-present narrator to being able to adopt the roles of the various characters in the story.

[R at the start of the utterance indicates that Rehana was speaking as herself. When Rehana was speaking 'in character', I have named the character concerned].

R:	One, two, three four.
Goofy:	Hallo.
R:	This is a different story.
G:	Hallo, I'm Goofy. Bow! I'm very good. I can eat really fine. You haven't got any meat ready have you?
R:	There's some under here.
Goofy:	[Eats pretend food] Bye! I gotta go now.
[Long pause]	
NB:	Is that the end of the show?
R:	No, I'm just fitting things in.
[Another long pause and then three finger puppets and a troll appear]	
R:	Hallo everybody!
NB:	Hallo!
R:	You know us don't you?
NB:	I'm not sure.
R:	[Waggling the appropriate puppet] I'm the strong Billy Goat, I'm the troll, I'm the baby and the mother. I'm the Three Billy Goats. I'm not going to read the story today, I'm going to start off with the troll.
R:	[as troll]: Hallo everybody, you haven't saw Billy Goats out here have you?
NB:	No!
Troll:	Well, watch out 'cos I'm come to eat them up.
R:	Trip-trap, trip-trap
Troll:	Who's that walking on MY bridge?

Little Billy Goat:	It's only me the little Billy Goat
Troll:	Okay. I'm going to eat you up.
Little Billy Goat:	No! No! I'm, you will find me very bony. Wait 'til the other one comes along, he, she much stronger than me.
R:	[singing off stage] Gruff Billy Goat Gruff where are you? Here you are!
R:	Trip trap, trip, trap.
Troll:	Who's that walking on MY bridge?
Middle Billy Goat:	It's only me the middle-sized . . .
Troll:	And I'm come to eat you up!
Middle Billy Goat:	No, No! You won't see me, very bony. Wait until the bigger one comes he's much more stronger than me.
[Big Billy Goat makes an appearance]	
Troll:	Now I'm come to eat you up.
Big Billy Goat:	No!
Troll:	I'm stuck near the hill. Help! Help!
[The troll disappears and all three Billy Goats are on stage]	
All three:	[singing and dancing] Hallo everybody, we'll stay here, we're never going to walk on that bridge just in case the tro-o-o-o-o-ll did come back.
[Curtains are closed]	

This last story is interesting as it not only drew on her knowledge of the story of *The Three Billy Goats Gruff* which she had been read, but also drew on her growing knowledge of televisual narratives. The language of stories is very evident throughout this puppet show, but the manner in which the story was told was very reminiscent of the retellings of fairytales that she has watched on *Sesame Street*. Instead of ending the story with her usual 'and that's the end of the story', her ending involves singing and dancing as the curtain falls. On television, stories rarely end with the words 'and that's the end of the story' or even 'they lived happily ever after', other signals are used such as ensemble singing, coupled with fade out. This was the sort of ending Rehana appears to have been playing with.

During the next three years, some of her stories with puppets consisted of stories with good characterization and clear story structures, but many were exploratory in nature. Although she enjoyed having an audience, her intentions were not always to amuse the audience. Sometimes she focused on the relationships between puppets to the detriment of a story. On other occasions she continued what she began with her Billy Goats Gruff story and worked on alternative versions. At other times she was concerned with exploring themes which she was unable to explore through dramatic play. One such theme was that of friendship. Attempting to work out the complexities of what constitutes friendship is difficult when you cast yourself in the role of one of the 'friends' and then do not have another person to play the other 'friend'. If she had explored such an idea with another child the 'rules' of the dramatic play would have to have been very clearly understood by both parties: it was only 'pretend'. Furthermore, I would suggest that young children need a safe setting within which to explore the more negative aspects of relationships. Playing with puppets and weaving stories incorporating the theme of friendship provided the opportunity to explore these ideas safely but in so doing deepened her under-standing of relationships and motivations that govern people's actions, both in real life and in stories as presented in books and on screen. As adults we are able to play a scene through in our heads, we can mentally run through the 'what ifs' and the consequences. Young children need to experience it or see it happening.

Having some idea about how Rehana used puppets to tell stories when she was 3 it is interesting to reflect on what stories she was telling with puppets at the age of 7 years. The following extracts are taken from a story that is quoted in full in Appendix D. The story gives a sense of not only how far children move on in terms of length of story but also in terms of their confidence in handling the narrative form. This story also provides an interesting example of Rehana pulling together a range of her literary experiences: oral stories, stories in books, narratives on videos, puppet shows, pantomime and plays at the theatre.

Rehana was very clear that the audience needed to be put in the picture and was conscious of the limitations presented by small wine-cork sized puppets on a theatre stage made of a shoebox. She was presented with some of the challenges that face an oral storyteller, not least how she was going to breathe life and character into the puppets and sustain her narrative. Analysis of the puppet show (*The Wolfie Story*) reveals that Rehana used a range of 'narrator functions' (Fox, 1993, p. 18) to deal with some of the problems and, in so doing, was developing her ability to use the language of stories. In narrator mode she told the story, directed the narrative, evaluated the narrative and occasionally directed the dialogue through reported speech. Whilst, for example, she could manoeuvre the puppets around the stage, she found it difficult to show other types of movements but, by adopting the role of narrator as storyteller, she was able to provide this type of information and retain the tension of the story:

> *Rehana*:   Polly couldn't resist. Anyway the wolf had grabbed her again — he had a great thing with grabbing — and he pulled and tugged her into the next room. This was lightly lit by two candles . . . had a wooden floor and an arrow slit and another arrow slit.

She did not always use the narrator mode to overcome difficulties. To overcome the problem that the puppets could not signal changes in their emotional state through, for example, facial expressions or other forms of body language, Rehana opted to use a wide range of voices and intonations in order to communicate the characters' emotions and moods. On first meeting Polly the wolf talks in a friendly, even wheedling tone which becomes increasingly more insistent, unfriendly, threatening and soon we were told he is 'cackling evilly'. In contrast, on meeting the Queen the wolf's tone is more subservient:

Rehana:	*(as narrator)* Her voice drained away as Polly walked further and further out. First she had to go . . . through a wood then she went up a big path. Suddenly, she came to a wolf and the wolf said 'Hello little girl, would you like to come with me and I'll give you some sweeties?'
[. . .]	
Wolf:	Oh come on. Come on! Come on!
Rehana:	Finally the wolf dragged her away until she couldn't put up any more. Suddenly she found herself outside a great big castle. 'Heh, heh, heh' said the wolf, cackling evilly. She went inside. Well she couldn't help it, the wolf was dragging her!
Queen:	Oh you've done a good job, Wolfie.
Wolf:	Thank you, Oh Mighty One.

That Rehana has drawn ideas from both written and televisual texts is clear. On a very superficial level her choice of name for the protagonist is drawn from the *Clever Polly* stories, as are some of the more comic aspects of the wolf's behaviour (e.g. burning his paw on the candles). At the outset there are clear connections between Rehana's story and the traditional tale of Red Riding Hood (e.g. the mother warning her daughter to be careful, the path or magic road through the forest and the wolf tempting the little girl). In the two stories she is also exploring the idea that the wolf can be 'good' or 'bad' and again, here she is doubtless drawing on her numerous readings of *Clever Polly and the Stupid Wolf, Red Riding Hood, The Three Little Pigs* etc. and possibly also *The Narnia Chronicles* in which the wicked queen's chief helper is Maugrim, a wolf. Ranged against these wicked or naughty wolves she has read books such as *The Little Wolf* and *The Three Little Wolves* and *The Big Bad Wolf*. The idea of 'catchers', people who catch others to make them into slaves is derived from the video of *The Legend of the Lost Keys*. Children's unwillingness to reveal to their parents what they have been doing was an idea that intrigued her when watching *The Sound of Music*. The language that she uses is reminiscent of storybooks (e.g. the use of the word 'mother' rather than mum and phrases such as '. . . they walked through the deep forest . . .' and '. . . the wolf cackled evilly . . .'). There is also evidence of her experience of pantomime and live theatre. The 'Yes you are, No I'm not' interchange, so common in children's pantomimes, is utilized by Rehana as is the communicative narrative function she uses at the end of the story to suggest that the audience and the protagonist share a secret which is not known to other characters in the play (e.g. 'Shall I tell her?').

The story moves through a range of settings, Polly's home, the forest, the queen's castle, inside the castle, and the inner 'thinking' room. Rehana used eight backdrops during the course of the story and each was slipped into place at appropriate points in the story with minimal disruption to the flow of the narrative. This awareness of the importance of scene could be traced to her familiarity with videos or live theatre, but the way in which she chose to change the scene suggests that she employed a screen device to show characters' movement through place and time. In a theatrical performance scene changes are frequently accompanied by a break in the narrative (e.g. either a new act or there is clear recognition of a new scene within an act) but on television, videos and films there is frequently no such break, especially when the movement of a character is traced continuously and it is this option that Rehana had chosen.

Telling stories

The move into a sustained period of telling oral stories happened to coincide with Rehana noticing that I was writing down her puppet stories. She asked me to write a story as she told it to me and was totally fascinated with the process and wanted me to read her story back to her. So began a period of her telling stories to herself, her toys, to me and on to tape.

> *Rehana*:   Tell me story.
>
> *NB*:   Why don't you tell us a story?
>
> *Rehana*:   OK. . . . um. . . . I was just thinking 'bout what story to tell you [long pause]. Um . . . Once upon a time there was Mary Poppins, Donald, Donald Duck and a parade. Mummy and Daddy and Rehana were at Disneyland and having a fine day then they came home, they got on an aeroplane, met Granny and Papa came home and that's it. But *Goofy* didn't come home did he?
>
> [Rehana aged 3.5]

The first point that is interesting is that she articulated the fact that she was 'thinking' about what story to tell. This implies that she is either making up a story in her head or sorting through her 'store' of stories and deciding which one to tell. Either way it would seem that she had formulated a plan in her head. This supposition was borne out by the fact that from the moment she began to tell the story she appeared to have a clear idea about the characters involved and what was going to happen as there were virtually no pauses, stumbles or false starts. A cursory reading of this story could lead one to conclude that it was a very brief, autobiographical narrative and, apart from the fact that it is told by a third -person narrator, it is reminiscent of Monday morning news offerings of many Key Stage 1 children. The short story certainly demonstrated that Rehana was able to use story conventions in terms of some of the language, in that she established it is a story with her opening phrase, she utilized the slightly formal, 'bookish' phrase 'and having a fine day', which does not map onto the everyday speech patterns of a 3-year-old, and she appeared to have understood the need to introduce the characters and establish a setting while her sequencing of the events is both accurate and logical. However, what drew me back to the story and what I found intriguing is the question at the end, 'But *Goofy* didn't come home did he?' The addition of this last sentence may be a simple statement of fact, a rhetorical question or it may be an example of Rehana experimenting with different ways of closing a story. The fact that she emphasized Goofy and the tone in which the question was asked does raise other possibilities. Rehana could have been exploring techniques for introducing and creating suspense or, bearing in mind her age at the time, it could have been a relatively sophisticated and, I might add, successful attempt at employing what Barthes has defined as the hermeneutic code.

The question may lead the listener to ask '*Why* didn't Goofy come home' or 'Why should *Goofy* have come home — how is he different to all the other Disneyland characters?' or 'Where *is* Goofy's home?' She did not embed the mystery within the story and it may be that she added the question spontaneously, as an afterthought as she had already signalled the end of the story with the words 'and that's it'. She may, therefore, have been experimenting with the techniques to see what the listeners' responses were going to be — would they ask her to continue? It is not clear why she decided to introduce the mystery at the end rather than in the middle. She may have been exploring a technique she had seen on numerous occasions on *Sesame Street* in which a problem or dilemma introduced at the start of each episode and sorted out in the Fix-It Shop is put 'on hold' and interspersed with cartoons, films and songs and language and a number of film clips. She may also have been experimenting with ways of moving a story from the realms of real-life experiences into the realms of fantasy. Interestingly, when Rehana read this story at the age of 7, she was struck by the apparent incongruity of the final sentence as she said, 'But I never mentioned Goofy so why did I say that?'

Other stories she told clearly showed the influence of videos in her choice of characters:

> Princess Jasmine. Once upon a time there was a little princess and she lived in a castle. She was going to marry a prince but not today. She went to the prince's castle and lifted the knocker and let it fall back silently. She went upstairs and. . . . the prince was in BED! And it was the middle of the afternoon! She said, 'Will you marry me?' The prince said 'Yes'. They went to the genie's garden and found a lamp. A lamp is something you shine. They lit the lamp and they got married and lived happily ever after.
> [Rehana aged 3.8]

She had not seen the video of *Aladdin* but had watched a *Sing-Along* video of songs from *Aladdin* and had, therefore, seen excerpts which included Jasmine and the genie emerging from the lamp. She had not been read the story of *Aladdin* and to my knowledge had not come across genies or magic lamps in any of her books up until this time and so it would appear that the inclusion of these elements is attributable to her experience of videos rather than books. In this story she adopts the narrative function as the narrator and as the one who knows what is to come and as 'explainer' or, what Genette defined as narrator in the directing function, in that she shows metalinguistic awareness (e.g. 'A lamp is something you shine'). She also makes use of the communicative function of the narrator's voice in that she draws the listener into the story not, in this instance, through the use of phrases such as 'Do you know what?' but instead through her use of pauses for dramatic effect (e.g. She went upstairs and . . . the prince was in BED!). This ability to adopt different functions as a narrator has important implications for children's writing development.

Some of her stories show that she was exploring alternative endings. It is not possible to state with any certainty whether she was influenced by the, so called, *Sesame Street News*, which involved Kermit the Frog reporting on a fairy story or interviewing a nursery rhyme character. During these mini-versions of a news report, alternative versions of the story or rhyme were presented. These were very much enjoyed by Rehana and she would rewind the tape to enable her to rewatch this part of the programme. The following two stories are examples of her early attempts at alternative versions:

The Three Little Pigs

Once upon a time there was a very sad mother . . . and the mother said to her children, 'You must go and build your own houses now' and they said, 'Do we?' and they, and they jumped, two jumped to their mummy and the little one, the little clever one didn't jump, she went hugging and the other two little piggies were quite careless and they were with their mummy, I'm making this story up, so the other little, so a wolf climbed down the chimney and the piggy had a hot cup of water and they, so 'em, and the wolf was died and they lived happily ever after, the end. [Rehana, aged 3.6]

The Three Billy Goats Gruff

It's called the Three Billy Goats Gruff. The Three Billy Goats Gruff was lived quite happily so the Three Little Billy Goats *didn't* get eaten up, the troll *wasn't* under there it was *already* died. And they trotted along and that's the end of the story. [Rehana, aged 3.6]

At the age of three she was not reading chapter books and had not had any read to her. She had, however, had experience of *watching* a story in small episodes or chunks and the following story is perhaps an exploration of this form of story:

Rehana: Once upon a time in a faraway land lived a family of pigs. A mummy one, a daddy one and a baby and Rehana and Mummy and daddy went to the a piggy farm. And the mummy piggy was lying there in a little hutch and the babies were lying in the little hutch too. And Rehana throw some carrots and, did I throw some lettuce?
NB: Some lettuce, some cabbage or . . . ?
Rehana: And then Rehana throwed some cabbage and Daddy said 'Here we go!' and then the piggy don't come out and so they went to see the goats. But one of the grown up goats was being a billy — a bully and when and when it saw the little one got some bread it pushed it out of the way and Rehana run after it and Mummy said, 'Shall we tell Daddy to keep the big goats busy?' And when, when, and when they went home Rehana had their tea and got into bed and then the next morning she run into Daddy and Mummy's bedroom and gave them a big hug and that's the end of the story. Snip, snap snout, my story's out.

[Listened to story on tape and then started on next one]

One upon a time in a faraway land there was a piggy farm. When Mummy and Daddy woke up again and Rehana woke up again Rehana said to Mummy, 'I could go to the exhibition again. But I wanting you to pick me up till we're going home,' she said. And Mummy said, 'But you won't be scared of them this time?' And Rehana said, 'I will!' Do we have to go to school tomorrow?

There is a clear sense of Rehana exploring ways in which it is possible to create and sustain longer narratives by using chapters or episodes. The first story and second story both start with the form of words she used at the time to signify a story opening but, whereas the first story could stand alone, the second story follows on from the first with connections in terms of the characters involved and the temporal relationship of the first story with the second. The first story or episode draws to a close not at the end of the day, which is a more usual ending, but in the morning of the following day. The second story then starts with the family waking up in the morning following the visit to the farm. As the parent I know that this story is based on her own experiences, the exhibition being referred to was a half-term visit to a museum-based exhibition and, furthermore, Rehana alludes to the fact that she herself found the exhibition very frightening (hence the mother's comments in the story and the child's response). The story does not have a neat ending as she was distracted by something she saw which prompted the question about school.

Four years later she was a confident oral storyteller. The story of *The Faraway Tree* (see Appendix E) is an example of one of her long oral stories which clearly illustrates her understanding of narrative structures and devices. She orientates the listener at the start of the story, uses story conventions such as the tripling device (e.g. 'down, down, down,' 'tumble, tumble, tumble' and the inclusion of three witches). She uses suspense to sustain the narrative but is careful to ensure that all of the problems are neatly resolved before the end of the story. For example she introduces the idea of a potential calamity:

> And the witches were talking. Next to them was another, no, a little wooden box . . . On top of it was a tablecloth with frogs on it and on top of that was a big, black cauldron. Inside these was some whitey, greeny, turquoisy, reddy, bluey liquid bubbling away. They ran back and thought we'll go back there later to sort out what they're planning to do.

The witches' evil plans are outlined later and the problem is also resolved:

> They went along the corridor. Then they saw the witches again. The cauldron had got filled up even more. They managed to catch a snip of what the witches were saying. They said, 'If we can, if we turn the whole kingdom into frogs, heh, heh, heh, heh, we will be able to take it over.' 'Oh no,' thought Charlotte and then she said that to William. Luckily the mixture had now turned to white. 'Now,' said the witches, 'We'd better just go away while these bubbles set. We'll go somewhere else, we'll go on a trip.' 'Okay' said the other witches, 'But remember we must do it when they are asleep.' 'Of course I will, Dummy,' said one of the other witches and off they went. The colour of the cauldron was a milky kind of colour. Charlotte went over to the sink and there were two taps, one of them says 'milk' and the other says 'water'. She turned on the water tap but only water came out.

> She turned it off. She turned on the milk tap and the *exact* colour of milk and *exact* colour that the cauldron was came falling out. She tipped all of the contents of the cauldron down the sink as the cats had gone as well and she put the cauldron under the tap and so it filled up with milk. Then she put it down, she put it down on the table and went back to the door to see what would happen. 'Now they will only feed them milk in the night and they're sure to wake up,' she said.

There is no doubt that her experiences of written texts had supported her understanding of narrative and also provided some ideas for the story. The picture of the cat doing the washing up in Janet and Allan Ahlberg's *The Jolly Christmas Postman* had always been a favourite and she introduces such a cat into her story:

> On the table were little cups of green liquidy stuff, it was yuk. In the right hand corner there was a sink and cat was doing the washing up with an apron on.

Her title was possibly influenced by the Enid Blyton books about *The Faraway Tree*, with which she was familiar, although she had never read any of them. There is similarly little doubt that her experience of televisual texts influenced her story (e.g. the idea of falling down a hole into another world may well have been derived from the video of *Alice in Wonderland*). I was interested to establish whether Rehana was able to reflect on her own stories and asked her whether she could identify where and how video, television and books had influenced her. She listened to the story on tape and as she did so she told me that she had been going to say a yellow brick road, 'like in *The Wizard of Oz*' but had changed it to a stone road. The idea about time in the land of *The Faraway Tree* as being different to real time she told me came from the *Narnia Chronicles*, which she had read but had also watched avidly on video. She was very quick to tell me that the ideas of trapdoors 'were from *The Queen's Nose*, when Harmony falls down that hole in that scary house', which is a clear reference to one of her favourite videos (*Harmony's Return*). Rehana was equally clear about when ideas came from books: 'And I got the idea for all the different doors from that book we're reading [*The Phantom Tollbooth*]'.

I would also suggest that her story is influenced by her experiences of televisual texts in that there is a great deal of movement through space which is described in detail and suggests that she not only had a clear picture of the physical layout of the setting, but also felt that the characters' movements were an important feature of this particular narrative. She describes the characters' movements in detail and, in view of the fact that this is an oral story, with a high degree of consistency. The route to the witches den for example was described thus:

> There were spider webs everywhere and when they went in the door creaked open, the steps were steep. They went along a long, narrow corridor . . . soon they came along to a lit — a big wooden door. She opened it, there was another passageway but this time it was sloping. She went up, down the steps, along the straight and then there was a stone door. When she opened it it clanked back because it banged against the stone wall.

And the route away from the witches was described in the following way:

> They went through another path, up a slope, down the steps, through the corridor out of the stone door, which didn't clang because they were careful, along the corridor, up the stairs, down the slope through the wooden door.

I would suggest that in many books the return journey would simply have been summarized with a phrase such as 'And they retraced their steps'. Rehana's decision to reiterate the details of the route would seem to be an example of her exploring the dramatic devices used in televisual texts in which movement is generally communicated through the device of 'cutting' to a different scene unless, as in this case, the characters' movements form part of the drama, in which case continuity demands that both the outward and the return journey are shown. Reviewing the *Twitches* story, the *Wolfie Story* (Appendix D) and the story of *The Faraway Tree* it is possible to detect a line of development regarding her ability to visualize and articulate characters' movements through space. As discussed earlier (pp. 115–16) Rehana's awareness of spatial relationships, which television and video texts may have developed, was evident in her body positioning. In the Wolfie stories she had refined this aspect of her storytelling and used the puppets' movements and scene changes to indicate changes in location or spatial relationships. Ways of communicating this predominantly visual element of a story through language is then explored in *The Faraway Tree*. Rehana's ability to visualize the characters' movements is akin to rerunning a film in one's head and it is interesting to consider whether she would have explored this potentially useful dramatic device had she only had experience of written texts.

Young children's experience of telling their own made-up stories is very important in terms of developing literacy as is it through these stories that children are able to deal with issues of importance to them and also to experiment with ways of telling, to learn to use words, explore how language works, be creative with language, take risks and develop their ability to communicate a range of meanings. I would suggest that the examples provide evidence of how experience of watching television and videos contributes to children's storytelling.

Retelling stories from videos and books

Retelling stories from books and videos is a valuable experience for children as it is through retelling that meanings may become clearer and they also have the opportunity to tell it in the way they want to. Wolfgang Iser has argued that with narrative 'the reader receives it by composing it'. Iser describes fictional texts as 'indeterminate' and it is this indeterminancy of a narrative text 'that evokes the text to "communicate" with the reader, in the sense that they induce her to participate both in the production and the comprehension of this work's intention' (Iser cited in Bruner, 1986). Jerome Bruner also argues that readers construct 'virtual texts' of their own. Bruner has likened the construction of these virtual texts or retellings to a journey:

As our readers read, as they begin to construct a virtual text of their own, it is as if they were embarking on a journey without maps — and yet possess a stock of maps that *might* give hints . . . first impressions of the new terrain are, of course, based on older journeys already taken. In time the new journey becomes the thing in itself, however much its initial shape was borrowed from the past. The virtual text becomes the story of its own, its very strangeness only a contrast with the reader's sense of the ordinary. The fictional landscape, finally, must be given a 'reality' of its own — the ontological step. It is then that the reader asks 'what's it all about?' But what 'it' is, of course, is not the actual text, however great its literary power — but the text that the reader has constructed under its sway.
(Bruner, 1986, pp. 36–7)

Bruner goes on to argue that narratives lead to conclusions 'not about certainties in an aboriginal sense but about *the varying perspectives that can be constructed to make experience comprehensible . . .*' [my emphasis]. (Bruner, 1986, p. 37) Such a view accords with my view of reading and although I make some comments on what the child has remembered in retelling a story the main focus of the following section is to illustrate how *videos* can be a text that encourages the creation of virtual texts which, according to both Barthes and Bruner, helps make writers. The book or video may help the development of storytelling because the child has had experience of a story that they have already gone some way to 'recreating' whilst listening to the story or watching it unfold on the television screen. There is a supportive framework in that the story is not completely new to the child and the book or video may also have provided some of the words with which to retell the story, an important factor to consider when thinking about young children's ability to tell or retell a story.

The first example we will consider is of Rehana retelling a story that occurred when she was 3 years and eight months old, when she told me the story of Jeremy Fisher without the book to provide prompts or cues.

Jeremy Fisher. Once upon a time there was a little frog called Jeremy Fisher. He was very good until Mrs. Tiggy-Winkle came along and she said, 'Oh, Jeremy Fisher, have you been bitten by a swordfish?' So he said, 'Well, I've been bitten by a swordfish in the sea.' So, Mrs. Tiggy-Winkle ran off so Jeremy Fisher got ready to go for fishing. So then he digged some worms and then he put one on his fishing rod and then he floated to look for a convenient place to do some fishing. And then he pulled out a big shark. And then he didn't see a big fish and then he ate him up and then he ran away. And then he got out of the water and then Mrs. Tiggy-Winkle came back. And then, right at the very end he met his friends and they said, 'Oh! How did you do that? How did you do that? How did you hurt your fingers?' That's all I'm going to say.

This retelling represents a synthesis of the two slightly different versions of the same story (i.e. the original book and the video) with the addition of some original ideas (e.g. Mrs. Tiggy-Winkle's involvement reflects the video). The increasing amount of detail in the middle section is probably due to her growing familiarity with both the book and the video, as are the instances of 'book' language such as

'. . . to look for a convenient place'. The retelling also illustrates how she was able to sequence a story and how she was able to incorporate details gleaned from reading two texts, the book and the video. The high levels of conversation are a feature she has possibly picked up from the video as in the book there is no direct speech. Meek has argued that videos enable children to follow a story through dialogue and in the story above there is an example of dialogue being used to 'tell the story' (Meek, 1991).

Within a few days of her retelling *Jeremy Fisher* she was given some stickers showing characters from the story of Jemima Puddle Duck and these motivated her to retell the story. I scribed her story as she told it but for reasons of clarity for the reader I have not included hesitations or stumbles and have inserted punctuation in order to maintain what I perceived to be her intended sense.

> Jemima Puddle Duck was very sad because they didn't let her bring her eggs. First she flied and flied and flied and then she came to a big part of the woods. And then she met a fox reading a newspaper. He picked his head up to look at her and she said, 'I'm looking for a place to lay my eggs.' 'Certainly my madam' so he led [her] to the woodshed and said 'You can go anywhere you like.' And then she laid her eggs. And then she comed out and the foxy gentleman was reading the newspaper again. And she said, 'I'll be back in the morning' and he said 'OK the madam'. And he turned the eggs over and counted them one by one. And he said to her 'Go shopping' and so she said 'Go away and fancy you my dog'. And then she flied back and then he got very cross with her. Then the big dog who met her went to find the bulldogs. They were all chatting to the octopus. Jemima said 'What am I going to do? What am I going to do?' Then some dogs came in and ate all her eggs and she was very sad. But she had some chickens and they lived happily ever after.
> [Rehana aged 3.8]

By the time she retold the story I had read the book to her frequently and watched the video with her on numerous occasions. A study of the language she uses, the relationships between the characters and the emotional highs and lows in her retelling suggests that, as with readings of Mrs Tiggy-Winkle and her earlier reading of Jemima Puddle Duck, this retelling of the story consists of a synthesis of elements from both the book and the video. In the book, but even more visibly on the video, Jemima is shown carrying what Rehana interprets to be a shopping bag. The fox's instruction to 'Go shopping' which is not a feature of either the book or the video is possibly a result of Rehana attempting to make sense of a fairly difficult part of the story. There were sufficient clues on the video that the fox was planning to eat Jemima but she did not understand the significance of Jemima being sent to collect the herbs and vegetables necessary for stuffing roast duck and probably recalled an image which she found particularly humorous: the sight of a duck with a shopping bag.

Rehana's retelling of The Tale of Jemima Puddle Duck differs from her retelling of The Tale of Jeremy Fisher in that there is very clear evidence of intertextuality. Earlier in the day Rehana had seen the Disney video of *The Little Mermaid* for the first time at a friend's house. She and her friend had then spent most of the afternoon engaged in imaginative role play, wearing mermaid costumes. For many months afterwards Rehana was very frightened by Ursula the Sea Queen, a wicked octopus, and it is interesting to note that not only does she include an octopus in her retelling of Jemima but also that the point at which the octopus is mentioned coincides with the point of high danger for Jemima. Thus, not only did Rehana include an element of another narrative text, in this case a televisual text, but by introducing an octopus when she did, she also appears to have recognized that the foxy gentleman and the octopus were similar in that they were both sly, villains of the piece, intent on harming the gentle, harmless protagonist. It is not possible to state with any degree of certainty whether Rehana had an explicit understanding of the links between the roles and characters of the fox and the octopus but this is certainly an example of the two-way traffic between stories that Carol Fox has noted in relation to young children's' storytelling (Fox, 1993, p. 12) What is of particular interest here is that the texts drawn on for this version include a book and two videos.

Almost two years later Rehana's storying skills had developed sufficiently for her to make an attempt at retelling the story of *Pollyanna* (Appendix F). She had seen the video a number of times and I had just started to read her the book. Rehana's version of *Pollyanna* reveals how she was able to include precise visual details about the characters (e.g. 'the checked skirt') and also how she was able to interpret expressions she saw on the video and draw on her experience of the language of books and stories to provide an exact description of the expression (e.g. '. . . mouth shut and pursed lips . . .'). What is not evident from the transcript, but is a strong feature of the taped story, is that Rehana also used a range of entirely appropriate vocal expressions and intonations when different characters were speaking. It is also apparent that she has remembered chunks of the screenplay and attempts to include sections of it in her telling (e.g. Nancy's comments about the doll and crutches). Videos such as *Pollyanna* are rich in language and new words are introduced within a meaningful context. The advantage of this is that children are introduced to new words which they may decide to experiment with in their dramatic play and story-telling. In Rehana's version of *Pollyanna* she tried out unfamiliar words and some-times coupled them with familiar words to ensure that the meaning was clear and that the momentum of the story was not lost. An example of this is when she states that Aunt Polly says to Pollyanna, 'I annore you . . .' On the video, the aunt says 'I implore you . . .' Rehana grasped the sense of what the aunt says, tries out the new phrase, and then uses a phrase she feels comfortable with. Carol Fox has pro-vided examples of how children play with words and phrases they meet in books (Fox, 1993, p. 49) and what I am suggesting is that it is important not to overlook the role of videos in stimulating this valuable word play.

Describing emotions is difficult, even for experienced storytellers or writers. Rehana did not find it easy to express how Pollyanna betrayed the depth of emotion she felt about her father. On the video, Pollyanna's voice breaks, she stops mid sentence and she is clearly seen to be struggling to control her emotions and pre-vent herself from crying. Rehana attempted to convey this by stating that 'Suddenly Pollyanna turned off very quickly and thought' and followed this sentence with a deliberate pause to provide dramatic emphasis. In the book the author wrote:

'Pollyanna laughed again, but sighed too; and in the gathering twilight her face looked thin and wistful'. (*Pollyanna*, p. 40). It appears that Rehana's description is closer to the author's despite not yet being familiar with the book. Rehana had not focused on the surface features of the video text (e.g. Pollyanna trying to be brave) but had instead focused on how mention of her father served to heighten Pollyanna's sense of loneliness and isolation. It is important to note at this point that, when watching this particular scene on video, Rehana had asked numerous questions about Pollyanna's response and the subsequent discussions, coupled with her growing familiarity with the video text, had enabled her to interpret and understand scenes within the context of her knowledge of some of the important themes running throughout both video and book. She did not explicitly articulate her awareness of these themes and it was therefore enlightening to listen to and then read the transcript of her retelling of the story as it revealed the complexity of her ideas about the story. She had clearly not been watching 'mindlessly' but had been actively attempting to read the video text and create a meaningful narrative.

It is also very clear that Rehana is aware of the need to orientate the listener. At the beginning she signals the start of the story by stating the title and following this with what can only be described as theme music. Throughout the telling of the story she works hard to create visual images for the listener. These careful descriptions have a variety of purposes. In some instances they serve to evoke an emotional response (e.g. the description of the aunt's demeanour when Pollyanna first meets her). At other times she uses careful description to ensure that points she considered essential were unequivocally stated. By contrasting Pollyanna's family home, which is never described in the book or seen on the video but merely alluded to, with her aunt's home, Rehana was possibly attempting to symbolize the difference between Pollyanna's past life and her new life: '. . . her aunt's home just like her own little cottage but much fancier. And she walked down the garden path which was curved like in the swimming pool when you go round and you see a big crowd in the swimming pool but it was like the path in the swimming pool and it could be curved, it was all curved'. Without the words in her personal repertoire to describe the carriage drive she has seen on the video she draws on her own life experiences, and those of her audience, in order to arrive at a shared understanding of the appearance of the 'path'. Her third use of visual imagery reveals a sophisticated understanding of imagery and symbolism which, in a young child, would have been difficult to develop through books alone. Her description of the little girl, journeying to meet her aunt:

> . . . and then she went out walking and walking with her bruised, scratched legs and with her beautiful straw hat on, her beautiful checked skirt on and her beautiful checked blouse . . .

was perhaps an attempt to capture Pollyanna's optimism, vulnerability and personal hurt. Whilst remaining fairly true to the concept of the original story Rehana has made this story her own through the addition of meaningful details and her own explorations with symbols and metaphors.

For obvious reasons to do with length, as Rehana became a more fluent reader and watched lengthier videos it was not so easy for her to retell me stories. Her retellings consisted of very brief outlines of the key points. It is clear, however, that watching videos is as likely to provide the stimulus for retelling as is a book. In fact, when talking to the children in my study, the most animated conversations occurred when the children discussed shared experiences of watching a particular video. This often led to collaborative retellings of the story with a sharing of the 'best moments':

John: I've got a favourite video which is called *Hercules*.
NB: Right . . .
John: And in *Hercules* I like the bit when [indistinct] says [mimics tone of voice of character] 'Ello, ello, am I talking to an outta space.
Gary: [laughs]
John: And I like the bit where, um, Pegasus the horse, which is 'Ercules's horse he goes and and says to [indistinct] and he says 'What with my 'air cut? And I like the bit where 'Ercules punches 'im like that! [Mimes a fight]
NB: Have *you* seen Hercules?
Gary: I like the bit were, yeah, where the horse goes, he goes [makes face] and when Hercules's hair right, when the wind blows his hair and it goes [makes his hair stand on end]
[Both boys giggle]
John: What, you mean, you mean the bit where 'e goes in that green water?
Gary: Yeah.
John: He gets old in that green water and when he gets mend he picks himself up and that's the bit when he says 'Hercules, Hercules stop, you can't do this to me, BANG!'And he goes [mimes falling down]
NB: Is that your favourite bit?
John: Yeah.
[2 boys aged 5, TSJ p. 2]

And two slightly older girls discussing what sort of video they liked:

Elizabeth: I like story ones. My favourite story one is *Bedknobs and Broomsticks*.
Natasha: Yeah, I *love* that one, *Bedknobs and Broomsticks*.
NB: Can you tell me the story of *Bedknobs and Broomsticks*?
Elizabeth: No, it's long!
Natasha: Well, there's this lady and . . .
Elizabeth: And she . . .
Natasha: And she comes to collect her present and um, there's this other lady and she's looking after some children and they don't have a mum and dad and . . .
Elizabeth: And so they go home with her.
Natasha: And they go like 'I ain't silly', it seems like a funny language. And her present is a broomstick and then when she gets home she tries it but she takes one hand off and then she takes both and then she just crashes down and the broomstick breaks and the boy, he says, 'Nice flying last night' because he's came out and looked at her fly.

NB:	Mmm.
Natasha:	And um, when they're on the magic bed 'cos the boy's got the knob, the lady gave him the knob, so they put it on the bed and they want to go somewhere, I can't remember where it is ...
Elizabeth:	To the, to the book store.
Natasha:	And they get the other half of this magic book and ...
Elizabeth:	And then there's this man and it's really the lady's friend and he says, 'Let's see,' and he puts a paper bag and he has some glass, a glass, and he pokes it and they can hear that the glass smashes and he tries to break in so that it doesn't smash and then they go on the magic bed again and they land in this place, they land in the deep sea and they win it and then they go back up 'cos this fish, this man pulls them up by the hook, the bed ...
Natasha:	It's not a man it's a little dinosaur, a bear ...
Elizabeth:	A bear, yeah, and the, he hooks onto the bed and the children are in the bed are they're dancing so they have to run off and catch the bed and go up. Then he brings them to the king and they play ... baseball ... with the king.
NB:	Mmmm. And then what happens at the end?
Elizabeth:	They go back.
Natasha:	Yeah, they go back to their own land
Elizabeth:	And then, and then um, and they have supper and man cooks who was with them and he tries to juggle and he has this soup underneath him which he juggles three apples and one splats there and all the soup comes on his face.

[Both children laugh]

[Girl aged 6, girl aged 5, TSE, pp. 2–3]

Both Muriel Robinson (1997) and Gordon Wells (1987) have discussed the purpose of mutual retellings. In collaborative retellings children may affirm or challenge the interpretations of others, may have the opportunity to draw on and utilize the outside-text experiences others bring to the interpretation of the text in order to shape their understanding of it. Children's different responses to characters in a televisual text are underpinned by the complex web of influences, expectations and experiences that each child brings to the viewing of programme or video. After watching the film adaptation of Roald Dahl's *Matilda*, a friend of Rehana stated that her favourite character was the kind and gentle Miss Honey, but Rehana was unimpresssed by this character who she dismissed as a 'goody-goody', instead, to the surprise of her friend, Rehana was fascinated by the less central character of Zinnia Wormwood, Matilda's somewhat unmaternal and narcissistic mother. Rehana's interest in Zinnia makes more sense when one considers that seeing the film coincided with her interest in Melody, from the BBC series *The Queen's Nose* (see p. 112). The question in Rehana's mind may have been, was Zinnia a grown-up version of Melody? (see also Chapter 7) A key point, however, is that the different responses of the two children influenced how they interpreted the story. Some critics of the value of television argue that:

> Reading a book allows one to create one's own unique picture of events and people, at one's own pace, and encourages a more profound understanding. Television imposes the same standard interpretation of a novel, such as *The Secret Garden* for millions of viewers. The same people reading the book would have created millions of different versions . . .
>
> (Large, 1990, p. 75)

Such arguments are based on the premise that watching television is an intellectually passive process and the 'message' on the screen, unlike in books, is simply transmitted and absorbed intact and unchanged by viewer. Observations of children watching and talking about televisual texts would suggest that this is not the case and, as discussed in the Introduction (Chapter 1), Fiske has argued that television texts are both polysemic and fluid. In working with others, children are involved in developing an understanding of how texts may be interpreted differently by others coming with a different set of experiences and expectations and also how it is possible to arrive at a negotiated meaning of the text. Shared retellings do not serve to fossilize the meanings of televisual texts but instead can open up new possibilities and new vantage points for children

Influence of videos and TV on children's story writing

Brian Cambourne has put forward the notion of an individual's 'linguistic data pool', which includes knowledge about words, syntactic knowledge, and features of narratives, and from which the child draws when writing (Cambourne, Cited in Smith and Elley (1997)). In view of what has been written in the earlier part of this book it is not difficult to envisage how children's experiences of screen texts will supplement the knowledge they gain from oral stories and books. By the time Rehana was writing independently she had had a great deal of experience of both written texts and televisual texts of a specific nature, namely fictional narratives.

   This fund of knowledge about fictional narratives was utilized when writing her own stories. When writing The flower fairies book, for example, Rehana was clearly influenced by televisual texts not only in terms of ideas but also language structures. For example the idea of matching the patterns on the box and the key was drawn from *The Legend of the Lost Keys* (a current favourite BBC look and read programme). An instance of a phrase prompting a connection between text and video occurred when she was planning her ending to the story and said, before typing the words, 'when they got back the sun was setting and flower fairies say goodbye'. She then laughed and said, 'No, not really the sun was setting and the flower fairies went to bed after a busy day, that's what I'll write'. When I asked her why she had changed her mind about what to write she simply replied, 'No I can't'. She had obviously borrowed a key phrase from *Teletubbies* (a BBC programme for very young children) in that the phrase 'The sun is setting in the sky, Teletubbies say goodbye' is the signal that the *Teletubbies* programme is drawing to a close. I wondered whether she was conscious of where the phrase originated and why she

So they flew down the path . Suddenly they saw a treasure chest. "The only way to open this chest is to get a key" said Zinnia. "But how do we that?" said Bluebell."I know" said sunflower. They fluttered to an old sea cabin. They pushed the rusty door open. It creaked open. It took three of them to open it.

There in front of them was a wooden box they lifted up the top. There was the key. They knew it was the key because there was a key because there was a pattern on the chest and the key was shaped in that Pattern. They took the key and glided back to the chest. They unlocked the chest . There were some jewls worth lots of money. And also if you rubbed

them and told them where you wanted to go they took you there. "Come on " said Sunflower "Lets go to giantworld". "Ok" said the others. So they agreed. Sunflower rubbed a purple jewl and said "We wish for you take us to giantworld ." They went wizzing across the sky. Millions of differant colours rushed

Figure 6.5   Example of writing demonstrating breadth of knowledge about fictional narratives

had chosen not to use the phrase. Four months later she was reading The Flower Fairies book and the following conversation took place during which it was clear that she *was* aware of the origin of the phrase and also remembered why she had opted not to use it:

Rehana: [reading] The sun was setting in the west . . . [starts to laugh]
NB: Can you remember what you were going to write?
Rehana: The sun was setting in the sky, Teletubbies say good . . . flower fairies say goodbye! [laughs]
NB: So why didn't you write flower fairies say goodbye?
Rehana: I don't know. I thought people would laugh because it was for school.

I asked her to read the book and see whether she could tell me where some of the ideas had come from and it became apparent that not only was she conscious of where ideas or phrases were derived from but also that she adopts an eclectic approach to her writing in that it is influenced by written text, televisual texts and her own original ideas:

Rehana: Ah ha! One of the names of the flowers I chose was Zinnia and Matilda's mummy in Matilda is called Zinnia. And, in . . . Matilda's mummy was quite lazy and Zinnia's quite lazy as well.
NB: What in your book?
Rehana: Yeah.
Me: Mmmmm.
Rehana: Oh, the treasure chest! The pattern on it I got from, the chest from, what's it called? The Legend of the Lost Keys.
NB: What about things like this 'They pushed the rusty door open. It *creaked* open'? Where did that come from?
Rehana: From my head
[Continues reading]
Rehana: 'She rubbed the jewels' It was from Aladdin like rubbing the lamp.
NB: You've not read the Aladdin story have you? You've just seen the video.
Rehana: Mmmm.
[Continues reading]
Rehana: And with the purple fruit 'pluckers' I thought of snozzcumbers from the BFG and I thought pluckers would be good.
NB: Is that from the BFG video or the book?
R: Well really the book because I didn't really like the video.

By the age of seven her lack of experience of certain televisual texts was also apparent in that, unlike Josh in Carol Fox's book (1993), she would not have been able to approximate, let alone parody, certain forms of televisual texts such as the weather forecast or the news as she seldom watched either of these. From the age of 6, however, despite her relatively limited experience of watching live television, she was able to able to make up advertisements for different products around the home and would not only cue the advert in terms of her body language and possibly some music, but she was able to use appropriate linguistic forms:

This is the most soft, silky shampoo . . . Mmm, smell the bubbles. It will be kind on your skin. Mmm, Feel it. It will make your hair look wonderful.
(Aged 6.4)

Summary

The preceding sections highlight how watching videos, talking about what she saw, engaging in dramatic role play and storytelling in various ways, supported Rehana's development as a writer, not only of stories but of other genres too (e.g. dairies, playscripts). Since she was involved in reading written texts and watching televisual narratives on a daily basis it is not possible to state whether she would have developed her current range of understandings had her experience been limited to either written texts or televisual texts. In the late 1990s and early in the twenty-first century such a question may be redundant, given that written texts, television, and other screen texts are woven into the fabric of the vast majority of children's everyday lives, albeit in different proportions. This chapter however, would suggest that young children's literacy development may owe much to their experience of televisual texts.

Chapter 7

Gender Issues

This chapter discusses the clear gender-based patterns that emerged from the research, but it does so with an awareness that what is written does not have universal applicability to every child in all contexts. It is important to read this chapter with the consciousness that each child's developmental path is unique and dependent upon the interplay of a wide range of factors (e.g. social class, culture, gender, ethnicity, physical factors, environment and life experiences). Society may constrain an individual's actions and choices, not least through a highly gender-polarized social structure, but rather than viewing girls and boys as polar opposites, one needs to recognize that individuals experience 'multiple, diverse and contradictory ways of being' (Davies, 1989, p. 140). In terms of viewing and reading preferences and responses to various texts the multiplicity of 'ways of being' results in an overlap in terms of the interests, concerns and capabilities of girls and boys. Although some writers such as Bronwyn Davies (1989) have argued that this bi-modal model of gender does not go far enough, I would suggest that it is the furthest point that this society has currently reached in terms of constructing and understanding gender and, as such, the young children involved in the study will be attempting to understand and conform with this conception of what counts as 'gender appropriate'. The children's expressed preferences and responses are probably indicative of their struggle to position themselves 'correctly' in gender terms within a society where such positioning is seen to be important.

Research has highlighted some of the differences that exist between girls and boys in terms of their reading and writing. Myra Barrs (1993) outlined three main differences which research has confirmed exist between girls and boys. Differences in achievement have long been recognized, with girls outperforming boys in reading and writing at all ages, and the other two major differences highlighted by Myra Barrs are that girls and boys tend to choose to read different sorts of books and other reading material, and that girls read more than boys. This chapter examines how, and to what extent, girls' and boys' reading and writing development may be influenced by their experiences of watching television and videos. An analysis of viewing preferences is a necessary first step to developing our understanding of what girls and boys watch and particularly enjoy. The possible consequences of children's viewing preferences are explored, as is the way in which children's role play may be influenced by the television programmes and videos they watch. The appeal of the superhero figure and genre is examined and the chapter closes with some thoughts about ways in which teachers can develop children's literacy whilst recognizing the influences and powerful attractions of aspects of popular culture.

Viewing preferences

As discussed in Chapters 5 and 6, televisual texts may provide the impetus for socio-dramatic role play, storytelling, reading written versions of the screen texts and writing, all of which are rich experiences in terms of literacy development. This section explores how and to what extent girls' and boys' viewing preferences differ, as this could be a crucial factor in terms of the range of literacy activities they may engage in as a result of watching the small screen. Moreover, an awareness of what types of narratives or other texts children find particularly appealing, may provide ideas about the role of popular culture in developing children's literacy.

It soon became very apparent in my conversations with children that girls and boys had different viewing preferences. In total the girls identified a far greater number of different videos and TV programmes as favourites than did boys. The girls' list of favourite videos totalled 53, whilst that of the boys was just over half as long, at 28 (Figure 7.1). The situation regarding television programmes was similar, with the girls mentioning 37 different programmes as 'favourites' and the boys listing only 22 (Figure 7.2).

In Figures 7.1 and 7.2 the programmes written in ordinary font were mentioned by girls, those in italics mentioned by boys and those in italics and underlined mentioned by girls and boys.

It was also evident that girls appeared to watch a wider *range* of videos and television programmes than did the boys. Both girls and boys mentioned Disney

Figure 7.1   List of favourite videos

Videos mentioned as favourites by children	Videos parents identified as children's favourites
Drama (long):	**Drama:**
Babe, BFG, *E.T.*	The Amazing Mr. Blunden
Enchanted Lands, Fern Gully, Flight of the Navigator	Black Beauty
	Dumb and Dumber
Free Willy, Home Alone	Enchanted Lands
<u>*Jurassic Park*</u> James and the Giant Peach	Free Willy
Jason and the Argonauts, Matilda	Fly Away Home
Pippi Longstocking, *Police Academy*	Herbie
The Lion, the Witch and the Wardrobe.	*Home Alone*
The Secret Garden, *Twister* [16]	Hook
	Matilda
Disney videos	Pippi Longstocking
	Spy Hard
101 Dalmations	The BFG
American Tale, The Aristocats	The Famous Five
<u>*Aladdin*</u>	*The Last Unicorn*
Bedknobs and Broomsticks	The Lion, the Witch and the Wardrobe.
Chitty Chitty Bang Bang, *Goofy Movie*	The Never Ending Story
Hercules, Hocus Pocus	The Phoenix and the Carpet
The Jungle Book, Lady and the Tramp	The Railway Children
Land Before Time, Land Before Time III	The Return of the Psammead
Mary Poppins, <u>*Peter Pan*</u>	The Secret Garden [16]
<u>*Space Jam*</u>, Pocahontas	

Sleeping Beauty, *The Lion King*
The Little Mermaid The Sword in the Stone
Toy Story, Winnie the Pooh [22]

Musicals

Wizard of Oz*, Sound of Music, Grease
Lord of the Dance, Riverdance [5]

Comedy

Mr. Bean, Andre [2]

Toons

Tom and Jerry, Pink Panther,
Scooby Doo [3]

Action cartoons/Superhero programmes:

Power Rangers, Power Rangers: the Movie
Batman, Superman, Turtles, Spiderman [6]

Other

Animal Hospital, 'A French video'
'One about an Otter', Care Bears, Noddy
The Black Sheep, The Tailor of Gloucester
'Dorling Kindersly set' (Cooking, Science and Nature)
Thomas the Tank Engine, Old Bear, Tots TV
The Flintstones, *The Last Unicorn*,
Pet Rescue
Simpsons, Wallace and Gromit,
Fireman Sam
Rosie and Jim, *Black Sheep, Sonic, Sinbad and the Musketeers*
Sesame Street [21]

Disney videos

101 Dalmatians
Aladdin
Alice in Wonderland
An American Tale
Aristocats
Bambi
Beauty and the Beast
Bedknobs and Broomsticks
Cinderella
Gladiators
Hocus Pocus
Jungle Book
Mary Poppins
Mickey's Christmas Carol
Peter Pan
Pluto's Tales
Pocahontas
Sleeping Beauty
Snow White
The Hunch Back of Notre Dame
The Lion King
The Little Mermaid
The Sword in the Stone
Winnie the Pooh [22]

Comedy

Mr. Bean [1]

Toons

'Loony Toons', Beano
Pink Panther Scooby Doo

Action cartoons/Superhero programmes

Action Man
Spiderman

Other

Art Attack, Little Bear, Noddy, Sooty, Spot
Nellie the Elephant, Paddington Bear, Rainbow
Riverdance Rosie and Jim, Ruff, The Little Toaster
Sesame Street, Sinbad and the Musketeers, Singing Kettle
The Nutcracker,Thomas the Tank Engine,
Wallace and Gromit, William's Wish Wellingtons

videos and those mentioned most often by the children in the study were *Toy Story*, *Aladdin*, *Space Jam*, *101 Dalmatians* and *Bedknobs and Broomsticks*. Whilst girls aged from 4 to 7-years-old included Disney videos such as *The Little Mermaid*, *Sleeping Beauty*, *Winnie the Pooh*, *Bedknobs and Broomsticks*, *101 Dalmatians* and *Aladdin* amongst their favourites, no boy did so beyond the age of 5. However, in conversation, many of the 5 to 7-year-old boys in the study acknowledged that they had enjoyed *Toy Story* or *Space Jam*:

Penny: I've got another favourite video it's called *Space Jam*.
Luke: Oh yeah, I seen that at my auntie's. That's really cool.
[Girl and boy aged 5, TSI, p. 1]

Figure 7.2   List of favourite TV programmes

TV programmes mentioned as favourites by children	TV programmes parents identified as children's favourites
Animal Shelf, Art Attack	*Animal Shelf*
Beetleborgs Metallix,	Art Attack
The Bill, Bewitched	Bewitched
Black Beauty, Blue Peter,	Blue Peter
Bodger and Badger	Bodger and Badger
Captain Caveman, *Cartoons*, CBBC Caspar	*Cartoon Network*
Coronation Street,	CBBC
East Enders, Enchanted Lands	Come Outside
Farthing Wood Flintstones, *Football*	Coronation Street
Gladiators, *Ghostbusters*	Enchanted Lands
Havakazoo, *Hero Turtles*	Havakazoo
Hey Arnold!, How Goes 2	Juliet Jekyll and Harriet Hyde
Juliet Jekyll and Harriet Hyde	Little Bear
Knight Rider	The Little Vampire
Light Lunch, Local Hero	Local Hero
Neighbours, Newsround Nickelodeon	Neighbours
cartoons	Newsround
Night Fever, *Ninja Turtles,* No Sweat Noddy	*Nickelodeon cartoons*
Playdays Power Rangers *Rugrats*	Playdays
Sabrina the Teenage Witch, *Sam and Max*	Potomas Park
Scooby Doo, *Sesame Street*	*Power Rangers*
Simpsons, Sister, Sister,	*Rugrats*
Skippy Smart Guy Star Trek	Scratchy and Co.
Stars in Their Eyes *Superman: the movie*	*Sabrina the Teenage Witch*
Teen Angel *Teletubbies*	Sesame Street
The Really Wild House *Tom and Jerry*	Skippy
Tots TV	Stars in their eyes
Wizadora Wombles	Sooty
	Teletubbies
	The Bill
	The Really Wild House
	Tom and Jerry
	Woof

Conversely, some of the videos that were particularly popular with the boys (e.g. *Fireman Sam, Thomas the Tank Engine* or Disney's *Hercules*) were not included by any girl in her list of favourites. The most clearly apparent gender division occurred in relation to action cartoons and superhero films. No girl named an action cartoon or superhero video as a favourite but the majority of boys aged between 5 and 7-years-old named at least one action cartoon video or superhero film and many boys' lists of favourites was composed solely of these, with the most popular being *Batman, Power Rangers* and *Superman*. In one particular school, where the majority of the children were bilingual, many of the children reported that they watched films in Hindi at home. When, with the help of the bilingual classroom assistant,

I asked the children in the reception class what their favourite Hindi film was, most could not name a film, or simply told me about the most recent film they had watched. A number of the 5-year-old boys talked excitedly about 'Sharu Khan films', the classroom assistant explained that this was the name of an actor who 'does all action films. An Action Man!' The boys confirmed that this was how they viewed him, too, telling me that 'He fight every day. And they fight all night.' (TSQ, p. 13). Interestingly, none of the girls in class had mentioned this actor or his films.

Apart from the Disney videos already mentioned, there were five further videos enjoyed by both girls and boys. Three of these videos were based on television programmes that both girls and boys stated they enjoyed (*Tots TV*, *Sesame Street* and *The Simpsons*) and the remaining two were *The Last Unicorn* (an animated story) and *Jurassic Park*. It is important to bear in mind that the gender of the interviewer may have influenced the children's responses. It would be interesting to explore how boys' responses may differ when interviewed by men.

There was also a noticeable gender division in terms of the favourite television programmes. Only a limited number of programmes were mentioned by both girls and boys as favourites. Girls and boys aged 5 and under appeared to particularly enjoy *Sesame Street*, *Playdays* and *Teletubbies*. In the case of the slightly older children, between the ages of 5 and 7, only four programmes were mentioned as favourites by both girls and boys and these were all cartoons: *Tom and Jerry*, *Rugrats*, *Scooby Doo* and *Caspar*. Most boys over the age of 5 talked about watching various action cartoons but very few girls did so and those that did so only mentioned watching *Power Rangers*. The findings of this study are in line with those of recent research by the Independent Television Commission (ITC). The ITC report *Cartoon Crazy?* noted that the 'core viewers' of action cartoons are boys aged from 5 to 7-years-old and that 'girls in general' do not like action cartoons for a range of reasons (Chambers et al., 1998, p. 40).

Factual or 'how to make or do' television programmes were not frequently mentioned by either girls or boys. A small number of both girls and boys included *Art Attack* amongst their favourite television programmes and a few girls aged 6 and over identified *Blue Peter* and *Newsround* as one of their favourite television programmes. Only girls mentioned factual animal programmes such as *Pet Rescue* and *Animal Hospital*. On one level it was encouraging to find that some girls claimed to enjoy watching factual programmes, as research has shown that when it comes to reading girls tend not to choose to read non-fiction (e.g. APU, 1984; Osmont and Davis, 1987). Conversations with the girls, however, revealed that the girls focused on the 'caring' aspect of these programmes rather than the factual side and the television programmes did not seem to be kindling an interest in reading non-fiction texts about animals:

Elizabeth: I like *Animal Hospital* because it's got, it's about animals and it's got lots of animals and they do operations to help them . . .
Natasha: I like that one too.
Elizabeth: And I like it . . .
Natasha: And there's this dog and he had all his skin come off because it was infected so it was all pink and all his fur came off and now he's all fluffy.

NB:	Do you ever read any books about animals?
Elizabeth:	Sometimes.
NB:	What books have you read? I think you can get some books about *Animal Hospital*.
Elizabeth:	No, you can get magazines but I don't. . . .
Natasha:	I like the magazines about *Tom and Jerry*. I like *the Pink Panther* too.

[Girls aged 6 and 5, TSE, p. 1]

This brief interchange highlighted how children may read texts, both visual and written, in a variety of different ways. One cannot assume that two children watching the same programme are constructing the same message or perceiving the programme in similar ways. The two girls quoted in the extract above appear to have been drawn to the programmes because of the caring element and Natasha's obvious delight in the fact that the dog was 'all fluffy' once more led me to wonder whether boys would have focused on the same elements of the programme. Hilary Minns (1993) has provided a wonderful account of how a 10-year-old boy chose to distance himself emotionally when discussing the moving story of *Charlotte's Web* by moving into the realms of facts about spiders. Sue Adler, in her analysis of 'feminine' and 'masculine' experiences of reading felt that this 'outward-looking' or 'efferent' (Rosenblatt, 1979) experience of reading was how boys and men tend to approach and respond to texts (Adler, 1993). Bronwyn Davies has also provided a vivid account of how girls and boys may understand the same written text in different ways, which are mediated by their gender and their understanding of gender positionings and relations within society (Davies, 1989). Although Sue Adler and Bronwyn Davies were discussing written texts, children's comments to me would suggest that this difference in approach is not confined to written texts as children appeared to construct very different meanings from the same televisual text. Comparing what two 5-year-olds had to say about *Sesame Street* illustrates the point:

NB:	Have you got a favourite character in *Sesame Street*?
Luke:	Um, yeah.
NB:	Who's your favourite?
Luke:	Errr.......
Penny:	I watch *Sesame Street*.
NB:	Do you? Have you got a favourite bit of *Sesame Street*? What bits do you like best?
Luke:	Er well, my favourite bit is when [indistinct] and he runs away and he knocks over all the things that man has got.
NB:	So that you like that bit? Have you got a favourite bit?
Penny:	Yeah. When we watched *Sesame Street* there's, um, this monster and these two men and one of them was writing a letter and then he got tired of writing 'cos his hand was tied up and then other one [who] was writing and then we saw another bit and then we came back to the bit we were watching and then the man who was writing he write about that much letters [uses hands to indicate how high the pile of letters was].

[Girl and boy aged 5, TSI, p. 3]

What I found intriguing was the way the girl described the factual and number and language sections as 'another bit' and talked about returning 'to the bit we were watching' rather as one might talk about the commercial breaks in a film or TV drama. Penny seems to be focusing on the relationships and problems explored in the Fix It Shop on *Sesame Street*, and earlier in the conversation, had been able to name many of the characters. In contrast Luke appeared unable to name even his favourite character, did not talk about the sections which were of such concern to Penny and instead focused on one of the 'educational' sections.

As discussed in Chapter 3, young children's television and video viewing may be fairly tightly controlled by parents and this may account for some of the children's stated preferences. It is interesting to note that the children and parents identified very few 'general interest' or 'family entertainment' programmes or videos as favourites, although the children talked about watching a range of such programmes (e.g. *Top of the Pops* and *You've Been Framed.*). There could be a number of explanations for this, including the young age of the children concerned and parents' possible unwillingness to reveal that their young children regularly watched programmes and videos not specifically produced for their age group. Despite the relatively small numbers of children naming family entertainment programmes, it was possible to detect a noticeable gender-based division in terms of such programmes children reported enjoying. British and Australian 'soaps' were only mentioned by girls, whilst it was only boys who said they enjoyed sport programmes, particularly football and rugby.

Most of the children were very conscious about how viewing preferences may be related to gender:

NB: Do you think you have a lot of videos?
India: Yes, but most of the videos are stupid football.
NB: Why do you say they're stupid football?
India: Because it's really boring and, but that's what my brother watches and goes 'Hurray!' and things like that.
[Girl aged 5, TSF, p. 2]

Another girl talking about her own preferences and those of her 7-year-old brother:

Catherine: My favourite video is *Grease*.
NB: Why do you like it?
Catherine: Because they sing lovely songs and at the end, she is small before but at the end she is tall with curly blond hair.
NB: Does your brother like it?
Catherine: No. He likes *Batman* and *Action Man* and that's it.
NB: Do you like those as well?
Catherine: No.
NB: So do you watch different things?
Catherine: Yes
[Girl aged 5, TSB, p. 1]

When two 5-year-old boys in a reception class were asked whether there were any programmes they would not watch it was interesting that Gary immediately chose to focus on the issue of gender rather than talk about programmes that he felt were 'babyish' or frightening or boring:

NB: Is there anything you wouldn't watch?
Gary: Yeah! *Barbie Girl*, um, *Magical Princess* . . .
NB: Why wouldn't you watch those programmes?
Gary: 'Cause they're for girls. Because they're . . . because *The Care Bears* and all them other ones are for the girls to watch so they'll be very, very loving.
[Boys aged 5, TSJ, pp. 3–4]

Gary's comments were interesting as they suggest that not only was he developing a good understanding of what sort of programme would be defined as being 'for girls', but also was able to express his ideas with astonishing clarity. A number of other children spontaneously raised gender issues which would imply that gender was an important issue for the 4 to 7-year-olds in this study. Sue Pidgeon (1993) found a similar concern amongst young children when she listened to their ideas about the links between gender and reading but, as she pointed out, this perhaps ought not to be surprising in view of the fact that the various psychological theories which seek to explain the development of gender identity tend to highlight the age of 5 or thereabouts as being of considerable importance in terms of children's learning about gender. This is an issue that older children continue to find intriguing (Robinson, 1997), possibly because having established a secure gender identity they are then able to consider the contradictions in their own and other's positioning.

Some factors influencing viewing preferences

Children's ideas about what girls and boys and women and men tend to enjoy watching develop for a range of reasons and through a range of processes. Fiske has argued that there are 'gender-specific' forms of television which have been developed by the medium itself (Fiske, 1987, p. 179). The children's comments in conjunction with the children's stated preferences would tend to suggest that very young children were aware that certain programmes tend to appeal to either a female or male audience. Furthemore, the young children's opinions seemed to accord closely with those of Fiske in that they related soap operas and narratives about relationships and caring with girls and action and adventure narratives with boys. Fiske has argued that 'feeling-centred' narratives are feminine, whereas 'action-centred' narratives are masculine (Fiske, p. 215). Muriel Robinson's research highlighted how some of the children she spoke to were conscious of the stereotypical views of their peers, but were also convinced that some television programmes were specifically designed for females or males yet, as group, were not able to name any of these programmes (Robinson, p. 75). Recent research has highlighted how children also categorize written texts as 'for girls' and 'for boys' (Pidgeon, 1993; Urquhart, 1996).

There was evidence that the children in this study were learning about what counts as 'gender-appropriate' viewing from their peers and parents. When interviewing in same-sex pairings, both girls and boys would receive confirmation of the 'appropriateness' of their choice through the positive response of their interview partner:

> *John*: And I like the bit where 'e, um, Pegasus the horse, which is 'Ercules horse he goes and and says to [indistinct] and he says 'What with my 'air cut? And I like the bit where 'Ercules punches 'im like that! [Mimes a fight]
> *Gary*: I like the bit where, yeah, where the horse goes, he goes [makes face] and when Hercules hair right, when the wind blows his hair and it goes [makes his hair stand on end]
> [Both boys giggle]
> [Boys aged 5, TSJ, p. 1]

Girls also responded enthusiastically to each other's choices:

> *Elizabeth*: I like story ones. My favourite story one is *Bedknobs and Broomsticks*.
> *Natasha*: Yeah, I *love* that one, *Bedknobs and Broomsticks*.
> [Girls aged 6 and 5, TSE, p. 1]

Girls in same-sex interview situations were not overtly judgmental about their partner's choices and did not challenge them on the grounds of gender or age inappropriateness. The boys however, were less tolerant of other boys' individual preferences and would challenge their interview partner. Some of the younger boys appeared either less willing to conform or had not yet learnt all the 'rules' of being a boy. When 5-year-old Gary commented that *Care Bears* was a 'girls' programme John drew on his personal experiences and countered with:

> *John*: No! I got *Care Bears*. *Care Bears* are for boys and girls, *Care Bears* are.
> *NB*: You think *Care Bears* are for boys and girls?
> *John*: Yeah, they are, 'cause I got it.
> [Boy aged 5, TSJ, p. 4]

When interviewing the children in girl–boy pairs a different set of dynamics seemed to operate within some pairings as several children, particularly girls, appeared to be somewhat tentative about revealing what their favourite video or television programme was, possibly because they were unsure of the other child's response. In the girl–boy pairings I found that the girls made no comment about the boys' viewing preferences, whereas the boys frequently laughed about the girls' choices and suggested that the girls' favourite videos or television programmes were 'for babies':

> *NB*: What's your favourite television programme?
> *Meena*: *Rugrats*.

Anthony:	*Superman: The movie.*
NB:	What did you say? *Rugrats?*
Meena:	Mmm.
Anthony:	That's only for babies!

[Girl and boy aged 7, TSL, p. 2]

A younger boy was equally dismissive of Teletubbies but was unable to explain his reasoning:

Shafiq:	I don't like *Teletubbies.*
NB:	Why?
Shafiq:	It's babies. . . . and girls!
NB:	Why is it for babies and girls?
Shafiq:	Because they like the *Teletubbies.*

[Boy aged 4, TSQ, p. 6]

Boys made no negative comment if a girl stated that she liked programmes also enjoyed by boys (e.g. *Power Rangers*) and in these instances the boy occasionally started to discuss the programme with the girl or helped out with the explanation:

NB:	Have you got a favourite programme on Nickelodeon?
Alicia:	Um, *Beetlebugs.*
NB:	*Beetlebugs?*
William:	*Beetleborgs*, you know, like the *Power Rangers*. I like *Beetleborgs* as well.
NB:	And these are like *Power Rangers* are they?
Alicia:	Yes.
NB:	Do they turn into something?
William:	They changing into bugs.
NB:	They're people who change into bugs are they?
Alicia:	They've got . . . um, one is silver, one is gold, one is purple.

[Girl and boy aged 4, TSO, p. 3]

What was taking place during these interviews can be partially explained through recourse to cognitive-developmental theory. At around the age of 3 children are able to identify themselves as a girl or boy. At around the age of 5 or 6 the concept of gender constancy is established and for the next few years children maintain a stable gender identity by adhering to what they perceive as 'gender-appropriate' behaviour and censuring 'inappropriate' behaviour in others (Marcus and Overton, 1978; Meyer, 1980). It is not until around the age of 10 that children are able to view gender roles as social rather than biological constructs. Thus, according to cognitive-developmental theories, most nursery and Key Stage 1 children may appear to hold extremely sexist views in their attempt to conserve a stable gender identity and knowledge of what is gender-appropriate is gleaned from interactions with, and observation of, peers and adults. Without knowing where the children were in terms of their development of gender identity, it is still possible to speculate on the possible consequences of the children's different responses. The lack of feed-back to the boys, for example, may simply act to confirm the 'appropriateness' of their choice whereas the boys' somewhat negative feedback to the girls may prompt the girls to reflect further on the reasons for their choice or, alternatively, may suggest that the girls are immature or that their choices are poor. Peer pressure on girls to watch 'girls' programmes was less than that experienced by boys to watch 'boys' programmes. One consequence of this is that from a young age girls seem to be provided with a 'licence' by other children to watch a wide range of pro-grammes whereas boys exert pressure on each other to conform to a more narrow definition of what is gender-appropriate. The implications of this are explored later in the chapter.

Children occasionally mentioned parents when justifying their views about specific television programmes. Hilary Minns conducted research with 10-year-old boys in the field of reading and concluded that '. . . what underpins the focus of the boys' reading choices . . . is the influence of their fathers. The boys, consciously or otherwise, model some of their own reading behaviour on their father's particular reading styles and preferences' (Minns, 1993, p. 70). This pattern appeared to be mirrored in younger boys' viewing preferences. A number of boys emphasized that they particularly enjoyed football and there were a few instances of children explicitly stating that they did not like a video or television programme because their same-sex parent did not either:

NB:	Why don't you like *Teletubbies*?
David:	Just . . . don't. Same as my Dad.
NB:	Same as your dad?
David:	I just don't grow up, didn't grow up liking the *Teletubbies*.
NB:	So your dad doesn't like it . . .
David:	And my great, great grandfather.
NB:	And you don't like it either? What don't you like about it? . . . Have you ever watched it?
D:	Yeah, I watched it a couple of times but I just don't like it.

[Boy aged 4, TSP, p. 3]

In order to develop our understanding of why many young girls and boys respond to, and appear to be drawn to, different types of stories it is necessary to consider how pyschoanalytic theories, originated by Freud and refined and rewritten since then, provide a model of how the *unconscious* mind plays a role in the development of gender identity and sexuality. The pyschoanalytic theory developed through Nancy Chodorow's transmutation of Freudian theory provides a persuasive model of the process of gender identification and is useful in understanding why and how gender and genre may be linked and also why, despite the most earnest efforts by parents and teachers, young children's activities, including those related to literacy, can continue to be so gender-specific. Why, for example do boys want to watch so many action cartoons and why are they so drawn to superheroes? Why are girls happy to watch and read narratives about emotions, caring and relationships and why do so many young girls play with Barbie?

Although there is not space here to discuss the theories in detail, suffice it to say that it is possible that children's gender-based toy, role play, reading and viewing preferences may be attributable to the process children go through in developing their sense of individuality from their mother, their identity and sexuality. In very simple terms, in the case of girls this process results in a close identification with the mother and mothers 'fusing' with their daughters, which results in girls developing a sense of empathy, a concern with and interest in relationships and an unconscious desire to identify with their mothers in terms of their role in attracting the father. In the case of boys the development of individual identity is accompanied by a curtailment of the close relationship with the mother who relates to her sons as different and separate. For boys, this process results in unconscious violent fantasies against their mother. Both girls and boys experience anxiety about the world represented by the father, but this anxiety is managed in different ways. In the case of boys this anxiety may be dealt with through aggression. These desires and fantasies, which are constructs of the *unconscious* mind, may be played out in dramatic role play or narrative play involving toys. Books, videos and films also provide an arena for exploring fantasies; the notion of the different desires and fantasies of girls and boys may be used to explain why girls and boys and women and men are drawn to different screen and written texts. Girls and women are more drawn to texts which provide opportunities to dwell on relationships, feelings and fantasies of family life, while boys and men are more likely to read texts with high levels of action and possibly destruction and violence. The links between gender and genre are clearly demonstrated by the girls' and boys' very different viewing preferences discussed earlier in the chapter.

Possible consequences of children's preferences

In view of how the opportunity to read different texts, both screen and written, may enhance children's understanding of a specific narrative and support their literacy development in more general terms, (see Chapters 5 and 6) it is interesting to note that the girls' list is more wide-ranging than the boys' list in terms of genre and types of narratives. In addition, many of the videos mentioned by the girls are based on children's books (Figure 7.1), and familiarity with the televisual versions of texts may mean that girls are more likely to contemplate reading a wide range of stimulating, challenging and well-written texts and in the process uncover, or arrive at, new and possibly more refined understandings of both the televisual and written texts. In contrast, relatively few of the videos favoured by the boys are tied to books in the same way, although boys do read books based on the films (see Chapter 4).

The relatively narrow *range* of videos and television programmes particularly favoured by boys would suggest that television and videos will play a very limited role in acquainting boys with a wide range of authors. If girls were to read the various books that were tied in with their favourite videos they would be introduced to writers such as Dick-King Smith, Roald Dahl, C.S. Lewis, Frances Hodgson

Burnett, E. Nesbit, P.L. Travers, J.M. Barrie, Enid Blyton, T.H. White, L. Frank Baum, Jane Hissey and A.A. Milne. In contrast, boys would be introduced to a much more limited range of authors (e.g. Roald Dahl, Rudyard Kipling, A.A. Milne, Beatrix Potter, Rev. Awdry).

Experience of a wide range of *types*, or forms of narratives, is more likely to accrue from reading a wide range of authors. Girls therefore, may be advantaged by their viewing experiences, whilst boys' reluctance to engage with what they classify as 'girls' television programmes, videos and books is likely to result in experience of a relatively narrow range of televisual and written texts and types of narratives. It has been argued in earlier chapters that children may be stimulated to read specific books on the basis of having watched and enjoyed a video or television version of a story or book and, if this is true, then the range of types of narratives boys are likely to read may be narrow in comparison with girls.

Margaret Clark (1976), in her study of young fluent readers, found that boys tended to learn to read using environmental print and informational texts, whereas girls were drawn more to fiction, especially that dealing with relationships and feelings. A similar pattern with regard to video and television preference was evident in the study, as only a limited number of boys' choices and many of the girls' choices were fictional narratives focusing on issues such as friendship, loss and family relationships.

Girls may be further advantaged by the fact that the primary school curriculum and the responses of primary teachers to girls' reading and viewing preferences may serve to confirm that what girls want to read is valid, interesting and worthwhile. Furthemore, many of the books that tie in with the girls' favourite videos are likely to be easily accessible in school and children will be encouraged to read them. In contrast, the types of narratives that capture the boys' imaginations may not have such a high profile in school. The superficial explanation for this difference is that in primary schools teachers, predominantly female, have always placed a high value on narrative, and on particular types of fictional narratives. Children are alive to the messages conveyed by the contents of the book corner or school library. In addition, storytime in school tends to be exactly that, with the teacher, usually female, reading fictional stories to the class. Although there has been a growing awareness of the importance of introducing children to a wide range of genres and this is recognized in the National Curriculum for English, it is rare to find teachers reading non-fictional texts or non-narrative texts to their class. This may be due in part to the fact that publishers have only recently begun to produce informational texts and other non-narrative texts which bear being read aloud, but I would suggest it is also due to teachers' own preferences and what they themselves find appealing and enjoyable. Many primary teachers will also be familiar with the views of influential thinkers in the field such as Margaret Meek (1988), Henrietta Dombey (1983) and Carol Fox (1993). Henrietta Dombey and Margaret Meek have both argued strongly that reading stories results in 'skilful, powerful readers' (Meek, p. 40) and Carol Fox's study of children's stories led her to conclude that 'stories ought to be regarded as a central resource' (Fox, 1993, p. 194). Whilst not taking issue with these views, if we are concerned with ensuring that both girls and boys become powerful readers I think it is important to consider the types of stories that are made available to children in school, bearing in mind the different sorts of stories girls and boys appear to connect with.

As was demonstrated in the previous chapter, dramatic role play is a powerful way in which children can explore stories and is:

> . . . a process of discovery, which allows children to linger within the tale, to examine its issues and dig beneath the surface of the words in order to create new meanings, [and] new understandings . . .
> [Grainger, 1997, p. 98]

The following section examines the links between gender and children's role play and the implications of this for literacy development.

Dramatic role play, gender and literacy

The ways in which televisual texts may provide the stimulus for imaginative, dramatic role play and the positive consequences such play has for the development of literacy has been explored in the previous chapter. When I asked children and their parents what roles their children had adopted, it was apparent that both books, television and video provided potential ideas for roles. Some children claimed that they never pretended to be someone from a book or a television programme/video. Whilst some parents stated that their child had never pretended to be someone from a book or television, others claimed that their children derived most of their ideas from books. The majority of the responses, however, made it clear that children adopted roles they had seen on television and videos rather than of characters they had read about in books (see Figures 7.3 and 7.4). There are a number of possible explanations for this pattern of role play. It could be that the visual nature of television and videos provide children with easily accessible cues regarding behaviour, appearance and context. In the case of heavily gender-specific roles, it is possible that children come across these on the small screen more often than in books. Glen Cupit (1996, p. 22) has argued that superhero narratives provide very detailed play scripts which are reinforced regularly, due to the fact that children may watch superhero narratives every day on television. This supposition was borne out in the interviews:

William: Can I tell you a secret?
NB: Mmm.
William: I watch *Power Rangers*.
NB: Why is that a secret?
William: 'Cause I watch it every day and it's real good and they have to fight the monsters who get to fight the Power Rangers.
NB: Mmm
William: And they use their secret weapons to destroy that, the monster.
[Boy aged 4, TSO, p. 3]

Figure 7.3   Characters on video or television that children pretend to be

Girls	Boys
The Last Unicorn	Action Man
Nola (*The Lion King*)	Robin (from Batman and Robin)
Lala (*Teletubbies*)	Spiderman
Po (*Teletubbies*)	Superman
Esmerelda (*Hunchback of Notre Dame*)	Power Rangers
Ariel (*The Little Mermaid*)	Ghostbusters
Belle (*Beauty and the Beast*)	Batman
Snow White	Hercules
Cinderella	The Lion King
Sera (from *Land before Time*)	Julian
Silky (*Magic Faraway Tree*)	Little Bear
Tinkerbell	Noddy
Pocahontas	Gromit
Barbie	Postman Pat [14]
Mr. Bean	
Minnie Mouse	
Pippi Longstocking	
Teletubbies	
Sleeping Beauty	
'far too many' [6-year-old girl's comment]	
Rabbits	
Power Rangers [22]	

Figure 7.4   Characters from books that children pretend to be

Girls	Boys
Alice in Wonderland	Reepicheep (from *Narnia* Chronicles)
Lucy (from Narnia Chronicles)	Edmund (from Narnia Chronicles)
Cinderella	Julian (Famous Five)
Little Mermaid	Winnie the Pooh
Sky Dancers	Christopher Robin
'All sorts, some combinations,	Piglet
some not' [parent's comment]	Pirates [7]
a bird	
Silky (Magic Faraway Tree)	
Goldilocks	
Butterfly Children from *Summer Sleep*	
Tinkerbell	
'most fairy tale princesses' [parent's comment]	
Dog in *Cinderella*	
Alice in Wonderland's cat	
Sleeping Beauty [15]	

It is also possible that, for young children today, television is part of a shared culture and the likelihood that their friend will have seen the same television programme the night before is higher than that they would have read the same book. Such shared experiences can then be explored jointly in school without the need for too many explanations and making of rules.

Figures 7.3 and 7.4 highlight the different roles that girls and boys explore. Not only did the girls and their parents list more characters in total, but also the girls mentioned more characters from books than did the boys. It is important to note that all of the characters from books were listed by four boys all aged 4. No boy over the age of 4 mentioned characters from books. Only one of the 4-year-old boys mentioned pretending to be a pirate he had seen in a book, and all the Winnie the Pooh characters' roles were taken on by one boy, who would involve his mother in his socio-dramatic play. The remaining two boys both had sisters aged 7 and no brothers and it was these two boys who mentioned the characters from the Narnia Chronicles and Julian (of Famous Five fame). One of the boys' sisters mentioned that she took on the role of Lucy from the Narnia Chronicles and this would suggest that some of the socio-dramatic play these very young boys engaged in was led by their older sisters rather than self-initiated.

A closer examination of the lists for the girls and boys makes it clear what type of role the girls and boys were, in general, exploring. In the case of the girls highly feminized characters such as Minnie Mouse, princesses, potential princesses (Cinderella, Ariel, Belle) feature strongly in the list but there are also a few female characters who fall outside these categories (e.g. Pippi Longstocking) and some animals. There is less variation in the boys' list in which superheroes predominate. Vivian Gussin Paley (1984) also found that, with the 5-year-olds she taught, it was television that provided boys with the ingredients for their role play in terms of actions and characters. For girls these ingredients were drawn from everyday domestic life and fairy tales.

Most of the examples in the previous chapter were of girls' dramatic play and it was very apparent how such dramatic play can play a valuable part in children's literacy development but this may have been due in part to the fact that the child concerned explored a wide range of roles. An interesting question to reflect on is whether boys' superhero dramatic play, stimulated by television and videos, can play a valuable role in boys' literacy development.

Glen Cupit (1996, p. 22) has argued that superhero scripts for television are very limited in terms of variety of plot, situations and dialogue which results in rigid playscripts or narrative structures. Vivian Gussin Paley noted this when observing 5-year-olds:

> Superhero drama is dynamic and satisfying but . . . the only change came about through bringing in a new superhero or killing more bad guys. The stories [of the boys] . . . are used to mask, not reveal individuality'.
> (Paley, 1981, p. 129)

Glen Cupit asserts that peer pressure enforces the rigidity and children very soon learn that there is a 'right' way to play specific superhero games (Cupit, p. 22). If children are not exploring the various possibilities of the superhero's character and experimenting with different ways of responding to situations in superhero role it could be argued that such play is of only limited value. On one hand the children are certainly involved in symbolic representation which is crucially important for literacy development (see Chapter 5). On the other hand, if the superhero play scripts are rigid and non-negotiable then there are only limited opportunities to make changes and adapt the story, to explore a range of alternative scenarios and responses and to develop a range of narrative competences.

In documenting her grandson's imaginative play, Sue Pidgeon has argued that he developed an understanding of plot and story-line and the roles of good and evil characters within stories through superhero play. What it did not do was 'develop the affective side of his understanding' (Pidgeon, 1998). Similarly, Vivian Gussin Paley's observations of 5-year-old girls and boys led her to conclude that for girls 'taboos in play are few' but much of what girls experience at an intense level through role play is not explicitly included in the stories that they tell (Paley, 1984, p. 110). Instead in girls' stories intense experiences are hidden but the metaphors of fairy tales may be used. In contrast, boys' superhero play cloaks sensitive issues and superhero themes provide the basis for boys' stories. Vivain Gussin Paley goes on to describe how boys deal with emotional issues:

> When something makes a boy sad, he simply becomes a more powerful superhero.
> He is not compelled to act out confusing events face to face, as are the girls.
> (Paley, 1984, p. 111)

It is possible that boys seek to overcome their feelings of anxiety and vulnerability through identification with superheroes and this identification is a necessary part of a boy's emotional development.

Another important issue that Sue Pidgeon raises is that, as a result of seeing other videos such as *Peter Pan* and *Sleeping Beauty*, her grandson moved on to exploring other roles which were not so rigidly defined and which offered the opportunity to explore more complex themes such as jealousy and kindness.

Batman in the book corner?

If superhero narratives and the role play that it sparks off can be shown to have some value in terms of children's literacy development, should teachers incorporate the genre in the school-based body of literature children are encouraged to read or should they eject superheroes from the school? In attempting to answer this question it is possible that some insights will be gained into how teachers' response to aspects of popular culture and, in particular, certain types of televisual narratives, may have an impact on children's literacy development, especially that of boys.

Whilst teachers and parents are not disturbed to observe small girls adopting highly-feminized roles or developing playscripts which facilitate the exploration of emotions and relationships, the sight of small boys adopting superhero roles tends to arouse concern amongst many adults (Cupit, 1996). Why is it that teachers react so strongly to boys' superhero play and yet tolerate girls' heavily sex stereotyped role play? I do not think there is a neat answer to this question, as the explanation will be different for individual teachers, and is likely to consist of permutations or versions of some of the factors listed below, mediated by context and their own professional and personal experiences.

Drawing on the psychoanalytical theories outlined earlier, it is possible that nursery and primary teachers, most of whom are women, feel uncomfortable with superhero type games simply because they do not understand the children's unconscious need to adopt such roles and the satisfaction and enjoyment children, particularly boys, derive from it — whereas these same teachers do have some understanding of girls' need to play out highly feminized fantasies. It is also conceivable that teachers' antipathy to superhero play is based upon the view that superhero fantasies celebrate a hegemonic masculinity. This concept of masculinity defines masculinity in terms of dominance, strength and power and perceives men and women as 'opposites' and for many teachers this is unacceptably sexist. Perhaps teachers do not wish to endorse the exploitation of young children by the entertainment industry, a view that is based on the premise that young children are passive, powerless consumers of what is offered on television. It could also be that teachers make negative assumptions about the superhero narratives children find so appealing because they, as adults, have never watched them on television or read the related comics and books. This is an indicative rather than an exhaustive list of the possible reasons for many teachers' aversion to superhero role play and the televisual and written texts which provide the playscripts.

Not all adults and teachers hold uncompromisingly negative views about the value of the superhero narrative genre. Cathy Pompe has argued that children are not powerless consumers but rather the entertainment industry has the economic resources to 'find what touches us' and then creates and markets products to fulfil our desires and fantasies (Pompe, 1996, p. 98). Furthemore, Cathy Pompe believes that children will move on from 'low-nutrient' cultural products (e.g. a specific superhero or even the genre of superheroes) when they have had enough. The key issue is that of 'what touches us'. Children who find that written texts in school resonate with their own concerns, interests or current obsession will be more drawn to read than those who find little common ground between themselves and the teacher-chosen written texts they encounter in school. It should now be clear that girls are more likely than boys to find that their reading and viewing preferences are approved of and understood by their teachers. Furthermore, since the staff in primary and nursery schools are predominantly female it is likely that it is women who make the decisions about what texts should feature in library and classroom book areas. Research by Osmont and Davis (1987) found that in Key Stage 2, girls were generally happy with the range of books available in school but boys were less happy and commented on the absence of media-related fictions and comics. When teachers have clarified in their own minds the basis for their views on heavily gendered texts drawn from popular culture they will be better placed to decide on the stance to adopt with respect to these texts.

Should such texts be used in school? Possibly. Recognizing boys' and girls' different desires and fantasies ought to result in provision of reading material that satisfies children's differing needs. Vivian Gussin Paley's perception that girls are 'compelled' to explore emotions and relationships, coupled with her assertion that whilst television has an observable impact on boys' play it 'does not invent the way boys play, but fits the mode comfortably' (Paley, 1984, p. 106) could be important ideas to reflect on, as they resonate with the psychoanalytical theory outlined earlier. Girls, unlike boys, may have an internal drive to explore emotional issues and relationships and boys, even without the influence of television and videos, may need to play in a certain way. If this is the case, can we and indeed, ought we, as teachers, prevent children from engaging in forms of role play and reading texts that they find deeply satisfying? This is not to suggest that all boys will want to read Batman books or Superman comics or that all girls will be interested to read about My Little Pony, but it may be that sharing a text which has a particular potency for a particular child may provide the route into reading for that child. The provision of such material in school may provide a stepping-stone for some reluctant readers, who may begin to see that reading can be enjoyable, satisfying and possibly linked to pleasurable out-of-school experiences, such as watching television or videos.

Alternatively, drawing certain aspects of popular culture into the school curriculum may simply ruin their 'deliciously school-free connotations' (Pompe, p. 102). It may be that instead of introducing Power Ranger and My Little Pony comics into the book corner, teachers need to be sensitive to the underlying themes of children's current interests evidenced by their role play, imaginative play and book and viewing preferences, and to utilize this knowledge to provide written texts that work to complement and extend the child's televisual experiences. A boy particularly keen on Superman could be introduced to child-friendly versions of Greek myths complete with monsters, flying horses and adventure. Margaret Meek has stated that, for her, the move from 'more of the same, to something different'; is a sign of reading development (Meek, 1988, p. 30). By simply providing in school what children experience at home when watching television and videos may not facilitate this move to 'something different'.

Cathy Pompe has highlighted how the introduction of Annabelle Dixon's idea of story boxes have been successful in inspiring a range of narratives which draw on the totality of the children's experiences of narratives, at home and school, written and televisual (Pompe, p. 120). Talking with the children about their favourite television programmes, videos and books and their reasons for their preferences may play an important part in ensuring that children develop an understanding of different narrative genres. A discussion with two 4-year-old boys, part of which is quoted here, demonstrated to me that even very young children are actively attempting to understand concepts related to genres. The two boys discussed how one could recognize a superhero:

Paul: Hercules is a superhero.
David: He can't fly can 'e?
Paul: No, but he's a superhero who can walk with a flying horse, right?
David: No.
Paul: Yes, he can.

Later in the conversation the boys explored some of the inherent contradictions in the superhero genre, not least the notion that superheros are supposed to be 'good' and yet are violent and aggressive:

NB: Are superheroes always good or are they sometimes bad?
David: Good always.
NB: Do *you* think superheroes are always good?
Paul: Well I think sometimes they're good and sometimes they're not horrible but they, sometimes they save dinosaurs from, um . . .
David: Bad things.
Paul: Yeah, bad things. And once something . . .
David: I suppose the other thing, he's mean sometimes . . .

Where do superheros reside? In the world of every day life or equally important realms of fantasy?

Paul: I pretend to be . . . oh yes, policeman.
David: Oh, but they is a superhero.
Paul: No. You know . . .
NB: Do you think a policeman is a superhero?
Paul: Yeah, but, no, no . . .
David: Yes, course they are!
Paul: No, no, no, police . . .
David: Yes they are!
Paul: No police, police, no. Police are *not* superheroes. Police arrest people.
David: No, pleeease Paul! That's why they're superheroes.

It is interesting to note how David is adamant that superheroes can exist in everyday life (e.g. as police officers or fire fighters) and yet later in the same conversation his comments suggest that his concept of superheroes is somewhat fluid in that he states that superheroes' brains are plastic:

David: How can you see superheroes' brains.?
Paul: I seen, you might see in . . .
David: No, let me say what I have to say. You might see 'em in a museum . . .
Paul: Yeah, that's what, that's what!
David: But they're not, Paul, they are *plastic*!
[Boys aged 4 years]

Where to from here?

Vivian Gussin Paley's opinions may match some readers' stance:

Let the boys be robbers, then, or tough guys in space. It is the natural, universal, and essential play of little boys. Everything is make-believe except the obvious feelings of well-being that emerge from fantasy play.
 Can the superhero controversy yield to so simple a solution? Have I come to like the characters and the plot more than I admire a quiet room?
(Paley, 1984, p. 116)

Teachers adopting such an approach may ensure that the literacy experiences of the children affirms the children's sense of self being defined in gender terms, which accords with the current view of the female–male dualism and also recognizes children's need to 'work through' their anxieties arising from the realization that they are individuals.

Having met children's needs it is possible that teachers could begin to adopt an alternative approach implied in Bronwyn Davies' argument that:

> Children need to be given access to a discourse which frees them from the burden of the liberalist humanist obligations of coming to know a fixed reality in which they have a unified and rationally coherent identity separate and distinct from the social world . . . They need to have access to imaginary worlds in which new metaphors, new forms of social relations and new patterns of power and desire are explored . . . They need the freedom to position themselves in multiple ways . . . (Davies, 1989, p. 141)

Teachers and parents may ask themselves how realistic this is in the current context and Bronwyn Davies herself recognizes she is describing a Utopia.

I would suggest that it is possible to acknowledge the strengths of both these polarized viewpoints without compromising teachers' own views and values or ignoring children's needs and interests. Accepting that children position themselves in different contexts in diverse and multiple ways (e.g. sometimes caring, sometimes aggressive, sometimes 'little', sometimes 'nearly grown-up' etc.), aiming to be informed about the children's concerns, building on what the children bring to school in terms of their experience and understanding of different narrative forms and other literary experiences, is one aspect of this 'middle road' approach. The second, which is equally important, is to offer children alternatives. This second element involves introducing children to a wide range of texts, both televisual and written, interesting and inspiring children to try writing in different ways, encouraging children to explore other roles and explore the range of meanings that readers of a text may create and to develop both their critical abilities and their emotional responsiveness. We need to provide children with the opportunity to make a range of choices and in so doing they may come to realize that, although they may have a favourite form of narrative or even a favourite story or book, there are a range of possible fantasies, narrative genres and texts which are satisfying in different ways and which can be turned to and enjoyed when they find that a different side of themselves is looking for fulfilment.

Afterword

In writing this book I have sought to explore the ways in which televisual texts may support children's literacy development and in so doing have questioned the validity of some of the 'common sense' arguments about the detrimental effects of television.

The book raises many questions, some of which are answered with reference to specific children within particular contexts, but these 'answers' may not be universally valid. Looking in depth at one child's literacy development in relation to her experience of televisual texts has yielded a wealth of detail which is lacking from more quantitative studies but there is clearly a need to look in more depth at how televisual texts impact on the literacy development of a wider range of children in diverse contexts.

The study has thrown certain issues into sharp relief. Firstly, it is clear that children's 'literacy lessons' are not confined to school. Children's literacy development is influenced by their interaction with different forms of texts (written and televisual) in a variety of contexts. Meek (1988) has cogently argued that readers learn to read because they become involved in what they read and share what they read with others (Meek, p. 7). Meek focused on written texts and their role in encouraging the emergence of 'literary competences'. In the light of the findings from this study, which provide numerous examples of televisual texts developing important elements of children's literacy (e.g. oral storytelling, understanding of genre, narrative structures, dramatic devices, characterization, modality, metalinguistic awareness), it would appear that both written and televisual texts play a crucial role in developing children's 'literary competences'.

Secondly, there is a paucity of convincing research findings to support the contention that regular television viewing reduces the likelihood of children reading for pleasure and, furthermore, there is no clear causal relationship between children's viewing patterns and their reading patterns. This is an important issue, because television plays an important part in the lives of many children and adults and acknowledgment of this does not devalue the reading of written texts.

There was evidence that children in the study watched television and videos in ways characterized by high levels of intellectual, emotional and sometimes physical engagement: the children were discerning viewers and, with the increasing availability of video recorders, children were also selective viewers both in terms of what they watched and also how often a favourite video was watched. Furthermore, it was evident from talking to and observing the children involved in this study that gender influenced children's responses to texts (especially between the ages of 3 and 7).

The findings of this study would lend support to the notion that books and television may be mutually supportive, in that each form of text may support children's literacy development in different ways and with this in mind the need to adopt extreme positions (i.e. anti-television or anti-books) becomes unnecessary. Experience of a televisual text can serve to enhance children's enjoyment and understanding of linked written texts and vice versa. Experience of the 'same' narrative in different textual forms is also a powerful means by which children's critical analysis, reflection and conscious awareness of response may be developed.

In the same way that adults or more experienced readers mediate written texts for young children or inexperienced readers, it would seem that children's viewing experiences also need to be mediated in order to realize the full educational potential of the televisual texts. I would suggest that, rather than reject a powerful medium, we need to look at ways in which we can use it differently in order to maximize the learning and entertainment potential. Adult involvement is important since it is through watching television with children, talking about what is seen, helping children to make sense of what they see by encouraging them to draw on previous life experiences and experiences of texts (both written and televisual) that children are enabled to engage at a deep level with the mutually constructed meanings of televisual texts. A key point is that televisual texts, like books, are open to a range of interpretations and the meanings we create are personal and unique. Recognizing the polysemic nature of televisual texts and helping children make connections between written and televisual texts is an important aspect of their literacy development.

It is also possible that we need to reflect on how current educational practices are taking account of the need to develop children's ability to become adaptable and creative thinkers, which are necessary attributes during periods of rapid change. The technological changes alluded to in the introduction include the more widespread use of computers and developments such as access to the internet, which have resulted in readers and writers needing to deal with texts which are less linear and more visual. A continuing emphasis on the development of print literacy (i.e. the reading of books) ignores the range of ways in which meanings are carried and encoded.

This book may be viewed as providing a preliminary map of the terrain. As a result of future research or technological developments, some features on this 'map' may prove to be out of scale (i.e. the relative importance of the issues discussed may shift) and some 'landmarks' may have to be added. The book does not provide ready-made answers to the questions besetting those concerned with early literacy development (e.g. how to overcome boys' underachievement in reading, how to encourage all children to read for enjoyment, how to make constructive use of the out-of-school experiences, skills and knowledge and understandings young children bring to school every day) but, it is hoped, the book clarifies some of the pertinent issues whilst simultaneously provoking discussion amongst those concerned with the literacy development of young children.

References

ADAM, N. and WILD, M. (1997) 'Applying CD-ROM interactive storybooks to learning to read', *Journal of Computer Assisted Learning*, **13**, 2, June, pp. 119–32.

ADLER, S. (1993) 'Great adventures and everyday events', in BARRS, M. and PIDGEON, S. (eds) *Reading the Difference: Gender and Reading in Primary School*, London: Centre for Language in Primary Education.

ARIES, P. (1962) *Centuries of Childhood, London*, London: Jonathan Cape.

ASSESSMENT OF PERFORMANCE UNIT (1984) *Language Performance in Schools, 1982 Primary Survey Report*, London: HMSO.

BANDURA, A., ROSS, D. and ROSS, S.A. (1963) 'Imitation of film-mediated aggressive models', *Journal of Abnormal and Social Pyschology*, **65**, pp. 575–82.

BARRS, M. (1993) 'Introduction: Reading the difference', in BARRS, M. and PIDGEON, S. *Reading the Difference: Gender and Reading in the Primary School*, London: Centre for Language in Primary Education.

BARRS, M. and PIDGEON, S. (eds) (1993) *Reading the Difference: Gender and Reading in the Primary School*, London: Centre for Language in Primary Education.

BARRS, M. and THOMAS, A. (eds) (1991) *The Reading Book*, London: Centre for Language in Primary Education.

BARTHES, R. (1970) *S/Z: An Essay*, New York: Hill and Wang.

BAZALGETTE, C. and BUCKINGHAM, D. (eds) (1995) *In Front of the Children: Screen Entertainment and Young Audiences*, London: British Film Institute.

BEREITER, C. and SCARDAMALIA, M. (1982) 'From conversation to composition: the role of instruction in a developmental process' in GLASER, R. (ed.) *Advances in Instructional Pyschology*, Hillsdale, NJ: Lawrence Erlbaum.

BEREITER, C. and SCARDAMALIA, M. (1983) 'Does learning to write have to be so difficult?' in FREEDMAN, A., PRINGLE, I. and YALDEN, J. (eds) *Learning to Write: First Language/ Second Language*, London: Longman,

BERKOWITZ, L. (1965) 'Some aspects of observed aggression', *Journal of Personality and Social Psychology*, **2**, pp. 359–69.

BETTELHEIM, B. (1978) *The Uses of Enchantment: The Meaning and Importance of Fairy Tales*, London: Penguin.

BOYATZIS, C.J., MATILLO, G.M. and NESBITT, K.M. (1995) 'Effects of the "Mighty Morphin Power Rangers" on children's aggression with peers', *Child Study Journal*, **25**, 1, pp. 45–55.

BRITTON, J. (1970) *Language and Learning*, London: Allen Lane.

BROMLEY, H. (1996) 'Video narratives in the early years' in HILTON, M. (ed.) *Potent Fictions: Children's Literacy and the Challenge of Popular Culture*, London: Routledge.

BROOKS, G., SCHAGEN, I. and NASTAT, P. (1997) *Trends in Reading at Eight*, Slough: N.F.E.R.

References

BRUNER, J. (1986) *Actual Minds, Possible Worlds*, London: Harvard University Press.

BRYANT, J. and ANDERSON, D.R. (eds) (1983) *Children's Understanding of Television: Research on Attention and Comprehension*, New York: Harcourt Brace and Jovanovich.

BUCKINGHAM, D. (1993) *Children Talking Television: The Making of Television Literacy*, London: Falmer Press.

CHAMBERS, S., KARET, N., SAMSON, N. and SANCHO-ALDRIDGE, J. (1998) *Cartoon Crazy?: Children's Perceptions of Action Cartoons*, London: Independent Television Commission.

CHODOROW, N. (1978) *The Reproduction of Mothering*, Berkeley, CA: University of California Press.

CLARK, M. (1976) *Young Fluent Readers*, London: Heinemann.

COVENEY, P. (1957) *Poor Monkey*, London: Rockcliff.

COWARD, R. (1998) 'Everybody say "Uh-oh"', *The Guardian*, 4 March.

CUPIT, C.G. (1996) 'Superhero play and very human children', *Early Years*, **16**, 2, Spring pp. 22–5.

DAVIES, B. (1989) *Frogs and Snails and Feminist Tales: Pre-school Children and Gender*, Sydney, NSW: Allen and Unwin.

DAVIES, M.M. (1989) *Television is Good for Your Kids*, London: Hilary Shipman.

DEPARTMENT FOR EDUCATION and EMPLOYMENT (1997) *Excellence in Schools, (White Paper:)*, London: HMSO.

DEPARTMENT OF EDUCATION and SCIENCE (1991) *Testing 7 year olds in 1991: Results of the National Curriculum Assessments in England*, London: DES.

DEPARTMENT FOR EDUCATION and EMPLOYMENT (1998) *The National Literacy Strategy: Framework for Teaching*, London: HMSO.

DOMBEY, H. (1983) 'Learning the language of books', in MEEK, M. (ed.) *Opening Moves*, Bedford way Papers, 17, London: Institute of Education, University of London.

DOMBEY, H. (1998) 'A totalitarian approach to literacy education?' in *Forum*, **40**, 2, Summer, pp. 36–41.

DORR, A. (1983) 'No shortcuts to judging reality', in BRYANT, J. and ANDERSON, D.R. (eds) *Children's Understanding of Television: Research on Attention and Comprehension*, New York: Harcourt Brace and Jovanovich.

DORR, A., KOVARIC, P. and DOUBLEDAY, C. (1989) 'Parent–child co-viewing of television', *Journal of Broadcasting and Electronic Media*, **33**, pp. 35–51.

DRABMAN, R.S. and THOMAS, M.H. (1975) 'Does TV violence breed indifference?', *Journal of Communication*, **25**, 4, pp. 86–9.

EGAN, K. (1988) *Teaching as Storytelling*, London: Routledge.

EISNER, E.W. (1996) *Cognition and Curriculum Reconsidered*, London: Paul Chapman.

FILM EDUCATION, *Mulan: Filming Folktales*, 2 October 1998, Film Education for BBC Learning Zone.

FISHER, R. (1997) 'Children's understanding of narrative and information genres on starting school', *Early Years*, **18**, 1, Autumn, pp. 15–19.

FISKE, J. (1987) *Television Culture*, London: Methuen.

FISKE, J. and HARTLEY, J. (1978) *Reading Television*, London: Methuen.

FOX, C. (1993) *At the Very Edge of the Forest: The Influence of Literature on Storytelling by Children*, London: Cassell.

FREEDMAN, A., PRINGLE, I. and YALDEN, J. (eds) *Learning to Write: First Language/Second Language*, London: Longman.

FREEMANTLE, S. (1993) 'The power of the picture book', in PINSET, P. (ed.) *The Power of the Page, Children's Books and Their Readers*, London: David Fulton.

FREIRE, P. (1972) *Pedagogy of the Oppressed*, Harmondsworth: Penguin.

FREUD, S. (1920) *Beyond the Pleasure Principle*, London: Hogarth.

FRY, A. (1998) 'Not in front of the children', *Television Europe*, **4**, March, pp. xi–xiii.

FURU, T. (1962) *Television and Children's Life: A Before–After Study*, Tokyo: Japan Broadcasting Corporation.

FURU, T. (1977) *The Function of Television for Children and Adolescents*, Tokyo: Sophia University Press.

GALDA, L. et al. (1989) 'Preschoolers, emergent literacy: A short term longitudinal study', *Research in the Teaching of English*, **23**, pp. 292–310.

GANTZ, W. and MASLAND, J. (1986) 'Television as babysitter', *Journalism Quarterly*, **63**, 3, pp. 530–6.

GENETTE, G. (1980) *Narrative Discourse*, Oxford: Basil Blackwell.

GOLDSMITH, E. (1987) 'Differences in reciprocal peer relations among children who view low, moderate and high amounts of television', *Home Economics Research Journal*, **15**, pp. 207–14.

GRAINGER, T. (1997) *Traditional Storytelling in the Primary Classroom*, Warwickshire: Scholastic.

GREGORY, E. (1996) *Making Sense of a New World: Learning to Read in a Second Language*, London: Paul Chapman.

GUNTER, B. and MCALEER, J. (1997) *Children and Television*, Second Edition, London: Routledge.

GURA, P. (ed.) (1992) *Exploring Learning: Young Children and Block Play*, London: Paul Chapman.

HALL, N. and ROBINSON, A. (1995) *Exploring Writing and Play in the Early Years*, London: David Fulton.

HARDING, D.W. (1977) 'What happens when we read?', in MEEK, M., WARLOW, A. and BARTON, G. (eds) *The Cool Web. The Pattern of Children's Reading*, London: The Bodley Head.

HEATH, S.B. (1982) 'What no bedtime story means: narrative skills at home and school', *Language in Society*, **11**, pp. 49–76.

HEATH, S.B. (1983) *Ways with Words: Language, Life and Work in Communities and Classrooms*, Cambridge: Cambridge University Press.

HILTON, M. (1996) 'Manufacturing make-believe. Notes on the toy and media industry for children', in HILTON, M. (ed.) *Potent Fictions: Children's Literacy and the Challenge of Popular Culture*, London: Routledge.

HILTON, M. (ed.) (1996) *Potent Fictions: Children's Literacy and the Challenge of Popular Culture*, London: Routledge.

HIMMELWEIT, H.T., OPPENHEIM, A.N. and VINCE, A.N. (1958) *Television and the Child: An Empirical Study of the Effects of Television on the Young*, London: Oxford University Press.

HINCKS, T. and BALDWIN, J.W. (1988) 'On the relationship between television viewing time and book reading for pleasure: the self reported behaviour of 11 to 16-year-olds', *Reading*, **22**, 1, pp. 40–50.

HOLDAWAY, D. (1979) *The Foundations of Literacy*, Gosford, NSW: Ashton Scholastic.

ISER, W. (1974) The Implied Reader: Patterns of Communication in Prose Fiction from Bunyan to Beckett, Baltimore, MD: Johns Hopkins University Press.

JAMES, A., JENKS, C. and PROUT, A. (1998) *Theorizing Childhood*, Cambridge: Polity Press.

KELLEY, P. (1998) *The Future of Schools' Television*, London: Independent Television Commission.

KIRK, L. and PEARSON, H. (1996) 'Genres and Learning to Read', *Reading*, April, pp. 37–40.

KITSON, N. (1997) 'Adult intervention in children's socio-dramatic fantasy play', *Education 3–13*, **25**, 1, March, pp. 32–6.

KLINE, S.C. (1995) 'The empire of play' in BAZALGETTE, C. and BUCKINGHAM, D. (eds) *In Front of the Children, Screen Entertainment and Young Audiences,* London: British Film Institute.

KLUGMAN, E. and SMILANSKY, S. (1990) *Children's Play and Learning Perspectives and Policy Implications*, New York: Teachers' College Press.

KRESS, G. (1994) *Learning to Write*, London: Routledge.

KRESS, G. (1997) *Before Writing: Rethinking the Paths to Literacy*, London: Routledge.

LARGE, M. (1990) *Who's Bringing Them Up? Television and Child Development: How to Break the TV Habit*, Stroud, Gloucs: Hawthorn Press.

LIFE, R. (1998) 'Facing the heavens', *Television Europe*, **4**, March, pp. iv–vi.

LULL, J. (1990) *Inside Family Viewing: Ethnographic Research on Television's Audiences*, London: Routledge.

MACOBY, E. (1951) 'Television: Its impact on school children', *Public Opinion Quarterly*, **32**, pp. 102–12.

MARCUS, D.E. and OVERTON, W.F. (1978) 'The development of cognitive gender constancy and sex role preferences', *Child Development*, **49**, pp. 434–44.

MARKS GREENFIELD, P. (1984) *Mind and Media: The Effects of Television, Videos and Computer Games*, Bucks: Fontana.

MEEK, M., WARLOW, A. and BARTON, G. (eds) (1977) *The Cool Web. The Pattern of Children's Reading*, London: The Bodley Head.

MEEK, M. (1988) *How Texts Teach What Readers Learn*, Stroud, Gloucs: Thimble Press.

MEEK, M. (1991) *On Being Literate*, London: Bodley Head.

MEYER, B. (1980) 'The development of girls' sex-role attitudes', *Child Development*, **51**, pp. 508–14.

MILLARD, E. (1997) 'Differently literate: Gender identity and the construction of the developing reader', *Gender in Education*, **9**, 1, pp. 31–49.

MILLER, L. (1996) *Towards Reading*, Buckingham: Open University Press.

MINNS, H. (1993) 'Three ten year old boys and their reading', in BARRS, M. and PIDGEON, S. (eds) *Reading the Difference: Gender and Reading in the Primary School*, London: Centre for Language in Primary Education.

MURPHY, C. (1983) *Talking About Television: Opportunities for Language Development in Young Children*, London: IBA.

MURRAY, J.P. and KIPPAX, S. (1978) 'Children's social behaviour in three towns with different television experience', *Journal of Communication*, **28**, pp. 18–29.

NEELands, J. (1984) *Making Sense of Drama*, Oxford: Heinemann Educational Books.

NEELands, J. (1992) *Learning Through Imagined Experience*, London: Hodder and Stoughton.

NEUMAN, S.B. (1986) 'Television and reading: a research synthesis'. Paper given to International Television Studies Conference, London, 1986.

OFSTED (1993) *The Use of Educational Broadcasts in Primary Schools*, HMSO.

OFSTED (1996) *The Teaching of Reading in 45 Inner London Primary Schools*, London: HMSO.

OSMONT, P. and DAVIS, J. (1987) *Stop, Look and Listen: An Account of Girls' and Boys' Achievements in Reading and Mathematics in the Primary School*, London: Inner London Education Authority.

PALEY, V.G. (1981) *Walley's Stories: Conversations in the Kindergarten*, Cambridge, MA: Harvard University Press.

PALEY, V.G. (1984) *Boys and Girls: Superheroes in the Doll Corner*, Chicago: University of Chicago Press.

PALMER, S. (1997) 'Turned on and switched off', *Times Educational Supplement*, 18 April.

PAPPAS, C. (1991) 'Fostering full access to literacy by including information books', *Language Arts*, **68**, October.

PELLEGRINI, A.D. et al. (1991) 'A longitudinal study of the predictive relations among symbolic play, linguistic verbs, and early literacy', *Research in the Teaching of English*, **25**, pp. 215–35.

PELLEGRINI, A.D. and GALDA, L. (1993) 'Ten years after: A re-examination of symbolic play and literacy research', *Reading Research*, April–June, pp. 163–75.

PIDGEON, S. (1993) 'Learning reading and learning gender' in BARRS, M. and PIDGEON, S. (eds) *Reading the Difference: Gender and Reading in the Primary School*, London: Centre for Language in Primary Education.

PIDGEON, S. (1998) 'Super hero or prince', in BARRS, M. and PIDGEON, S. (ed.) *Boys and Reading*, London: CLPE.

PINSET, P. (ed.) (1993) *The Power of the Page: Children's Books and Their Readers*, London: David Fulton Publishers.

POLLOCK, L. (1983) *Forgotten Children: Parent–Child Relations 1500–1900*, Cambridge: Cambridge University Press.

POMPE, C. (1996) '"But they're pink!" — "Who cares!": Popular culture in the primary years', in HILTON, M. (ed.) *Potent Fictions: Children's Literacy and the Challenge of Popular Culture*, London: Routledge.

POSTMAN, H. (1984) *The Disappearance of Childhood*, London: W.H. Allen.

POTTER, G. (1996) 'From symbolic play to symbolic representation in early literacy: Clarifying the links', *Early Years*, **16**, 2, Spring, pp. 13–16.

POTTER, R.L. (1979) 'Television and teaching: the emerging partnership', *Television and Children*, **5**, pp. 24–5.

QUALIFICATIONS AND CURRICULUM AUTHORITY (QCA) (1998) *The Baseline Assessment Information Pack*, Part 3, London: QCA.

RICHARDS, C. (1995) 'Room to dance: Girls' play and *The Little Mermaid*', in BAZALGETTE, C. and BUCKINGHAM, D. (eds) *In Front of the Children, Screen Entertainment and Young Audiences*, London: British Film Institute.

ROBINSON, M. (1997) *Children Reading Print and Television*, London: Falmer Press.

ROSENBLATT, L.M. (1979) *The Reader, the Text, the Poem: The Transactional Theory of the Literary Work*, Carbondale, IL: Southern Illinois University Press.

SANGER, J. with WILSON, J., DAVIES, B. and WHITTAKER, R. (1997) *Young Children, Videos and Computer Games: Issues for Teachers and Parents*, London: Falmer Press.

SCHRAMM, W., LYLE, J. and PARKER, E.B. (1961) *Television in the Lives of Our Children*, Stanford, CA: Stanford University Press.

SHASTRI, J. and MOHITE, P. (1997) 'Television viewing pattern of primary school children and its relationship to academic performance and cognitive skills', *International Journal of Early Years Education*, **5**, 2, pp. 153–60.

SINGER, J.L. (1980) 'The power and limitation of television: A cognitive-affective analysis', in TANNENBAUM, T.H. (ed.) *The Entertainment Functions of Television*, Hillsdale, NJ: Lawrence Erlbaum Associates.

SINGER, J.L. and SINGER, J.D. (1983) 'Implications of childhood viewing for cognition, imagination and emotion', in BRYANT, J. and ANDERSON, D.R. (eds) *Children's*

Understanding of Television: Research on Attention and Comprehension, New York: Harcourt Brace and Jovanovich.

SMILANSKY, S. (1990) 'Socio-dramatic play: its relevance to behaviour and achievement in school', in KLUGMAN, E. and SMILANSKY, S. *Children's Play and Learning: Perspectives and Policy Implications*, New York: Teachers' College Press.

SMITH, F. (1978) *Understanding Reading: A Psychoanalytical Analysis of Reading and Learning to Read*, (2nd edition) New York: Holt, Rinehart and Winston.

SMITH, J. and ELLEY, W. (1997) *How Children Learn to Write*, London: Paul Chapman.

STUART, M., DIXON, M. and MASTERSON, J. (1998) 'Learning to read at home and at school', *British Journal of Educational Pyschology*, **68**, pp. 3–14.

SWEETMAN, J. (1998) *The Guardian*, 19 May.

TRELEASE, J. (1984) *The Read-aloud Handbook*, Harmondsworth: Penguin.

TRUGLIO, R.T., MURPHY, K.C., OPPENHEIMER, S., HUSTON, A.C. and WRIGHT, J.C. (1996) 'Predictors of children's entertainment television viewing: why are they tuning in?', *Journal of Applied Developmental Psychology*, **17**, pp. 475–93.

URQUHART, I. (1996) '"You see all blood come out": Popular culture and how boys become men', in HILTON, M., *Potent Fictions: Children's Literacy and the Challenge of Popular Culture*, London: Routledge.

VYGOTSKY, L. (1933) 'Play and its role in the mental development of the child', in BRUNER, J.S., JOLLY, A. and SYLVA, K. (eds) *Play: Its Role in Development and Evolution*, Harmondsworth: Penguin.

VYGOTSKY, L. (1962) *Thought and Language*, Cambridge, MA: MIT Press.

WALKERDINE, V. (1990) 'Some day my prince will come', in WALKERDINE, V. *School Girl Fictions*, London: Verso.

WEIGMAN, O., KUTTSCHREUTER, M. and BAARDA, B. (1992) 'A longitudinal study of the effects of television viewing on aggressive and pro-social behaviours', *British Journal of Social Psychology*, **31**, 2, pp. 147–62.

WELFORD, H. (1998) 'Is it a phase or is it a bully?', *The Independent, Education*, pp. 21–3.

WELLS, G. (1981) *Learning Through Interaction*, Cambridge: Cambridge University Press.

WELLS, G. (1985) *Language, Learning and Education*, London: NFER–Nelson.

WELLS, G. (1987) *The Meaning Makers: Children Learning Language and Using Language to Learn*, London: Hodder and Stoughton.

WELLS ROWE, D. (1998) 'The literate potentials of book-related dramatic play', *Reading Research Quarterly*, Jan–March, pp. 10–35.

WILCE, H. (1996) 'What's so great about reading?', *Times Educational Supplement*, 26 April.

WING, A. (1997) 'How can children be taught to read differently? Bill's new frock and the 'hidden curriculum', *Gender and Education*, **9**, 4, December, pp. 491–504.

WINN, M. (1985) *The Plug-In Drug: Television, Children and the Family*, (2nd edition), Harmondsworth: Viking Penguin.

YOUNG, B. (1998) *Emulation, Fears and Understanding: A Review of Recent Research on Children and Television Advertising*, London: Independent Television Commission.

ZIPES, J. (1995) 'Once Upon a Time beyond Disney: Contemporary fairy-tale films for children', in BAZALGETTE, C. and BUCKINGHAM, D. (eds) *In Front of the Children, Screen Entertainment and Young Audiences*, London: British Film Institute.

Children's Books

(The dates and publishers given are those of the editions referred to in the text. Date book first published noted in brackets [ ] if different from edition read)

APPS, R. (1990) *The Twitches*, Hemel Hempstead: Simon and Schuster Education.

BURNETT, F.H. (1994) [1905] *The Little Princess*, Harmondsworth: Puffin Books.

CROSS, G. (1982) *The Demon Headmaster*, Oxford: Oxford University Press.

CROSS, G. (1996) *The Prime Minister's Brain*, Oxford: Oxford University Press.

DAHL, R. (1995) [1964] *Charlie and the Chocolate Factory*, Harmondsworth: Puffin Books.

DICKINSON, C. (1997) *The Lost Diary of Tutankhamun's Mummy*, London: Harper Collins.

DISNEY LADYBIRD (1985) *Cinderella*, Leicestershire: Ladybird Books.

FINE, A. (1994) [1994] *The Diary of a Killer Cat*, Harmondsworth: Puffin Books.

FINE, A. (1996) *Jennifer's Diary*, Harmondsworth: Puffin Books.

FITZHUGH, L. (1975) *Harriet the Spy*, London: Lions.

FOWLER, M. (1997) *Puzzle Adventure Kit: The Footprint Files*, London: Usborne Publishing.

HORWOOD, W. (1995) [1993] *The Willows in Winter*, London: Harper Collins.

JUSTER, N. (1995) [1962] *The Phantom Tollbooth*, London: Harper Collins.

KING-SMITH, D. (1983) *The Queen's Nose*, Harmondsworth: Puffin Books.

LEWIS, C.S. (1995) [1950] *The Lion, the Witch and the Wardrobe*, London: Collins.

LEWIS, C.S. (1990) [1951] *Prince Caspian*, London: Collins.

PORTER, E.H. (1994) [1913] *Pollyanna*, Harmondsworth: Puffin Books.

POTTER, B. (1987) [1908] *The Tale of Jemima Puddle-Duck*, Harmondsworth: Frederick Warne.

POTTER, B. (1987) [1906] *The Tale of Jeremy Fisher*, Harmondsworth: Frederick Warne.

POTTER, B. (1987) [1905] *The Tale of Mrs Tiggy Winkle*, Harmondsworth: Frederick Warne.

ROWLING, J.K. (1998) *Harry Potter and the Chamber of Secrets*, London: Bloomsbury.

ROYSTON, A. (1991) *Eye Openers: Dinosaurs*, London: Dorling Kindersley.

SPYRI, J. (1994) [1880] *Heidi*, Harmondsworth: Puffin Books.

STORR, C. (1967) *Clever Polly and the Stupid Wolf*, Harmondsworth: Penguin.

STORR, C. (1970) *Polly and the Wolf Again*, Harmondsworth: Penguin.

STORR, C. (1982) *Tales of Polly and the Hungry Wolf*, Harmondsworth: Penguin.

STORR, C. (1992) *Last Stories of Polly and the Wolf*, Harmondsworth: Penguin.

TRAVERS, P.L. (1994) [1934] *Mary Poppins*, London: Collins.

URE, J. (1996) *Skinny Melon and Me*, London: Harper Collins.

WAUGH, S. (1997) [1996] *Mennyms Alive*, London: Red Fox.

WYLLIE, S. and PAUL, K. (1990) *Dinner With Fox*, London: Orchard Books.

Television programmes/series

The Demon Headmaster, 1998, British Broadcasting Corporation

Harmony's Return, 1996, British Broadcasting Corporation

Look and Read: The Legend of the Lost Keys, 1997, BBC Education, British Broadcasting Corporation

Look and Read: Spywatch, 1995, BBC Education, British Broadcasting Corporation

The Queen's Nose, 1996, British Broadcasting Corporation

Sesame Street, Children's Television Workshop (shown on Channel Four)

Teletubbies, British Broadcasting Corporation

References

Videos

Alice in Wonderland, 1951, Walt Disney
Cinderella, 1950, Walt Disney
Fly Away Home, 1996, Columbia Tristar
Harriet the Spy, 1996, Paramount Pictures
The Lion, the Witch and the Wardrobe, 1995, British Broadcasting Corporation
The Little Mermaid, 1990, Walt Disney
A Little Princess, 1995, Warner Bros.
Mary Poppins, 1964, Walt Disney
Matilda, 1996, Columbia Tristar
Muppet Christmas Carol, 1993, Henson Productions
Muppet Treasure Island, 1996, Henson Productions
Pollyanna, 1992, British Broadcasting Corporation
Prince Caspian, 1995, British Broadcasting Corporation
Sesame Street Bedtime Stories and Songs and Big Bird's Story Time, Children's Television Workshop
Sing Along Songs (Vol 9): Friend Like Me, 1993, Walt Disney
The Tale of Mrs Tiggy-Winkle and Mr Jeremy Fisher, 1994, Pickwick
The Tale of Tom Kitten and Jemima Puddle-Duck, 1993, Pickwick
The Willows in Winter, 1997, Carlton
Willy Wonka and the Chocolate Factory, 1971, HMV
Wizard of Oz, 1939, MGM

Children's Questionnaire

I am a lecturer at Goldsmiths' College, University of London and am conducting research into young children's use of TV, videos, computers and books. In addition to interviewing young children (aged 3–7) and their parents I am asking parents and young children to fill in questionnaires so as to gain a better idea about what parents and children think about videos, TV, computer games and books. *The responses will be anonymous and no names of children or adults need be given.*

It would be a great help if you and one of your children would fill in the attached questionnaires. If you have more than one child in the 3–7 age range please choose **one** child to fill in the children's questionnaire. You may need to help your child read the question, tick the boxes or write their answers but please try not to *tell* them what to write or say as you will have your chance to write what you think when you fill in the parents' questionnaire!

When filling in the parent's questionnaire please answer the questions in relation to the child you chose to complete the children's questionnaire.

When you and your child have completed the questionnaires please return to me using the attached SAE.

Thanking you in advance.

Children's Questionnaire

1. How old are you? ☐

2. Are you a girl? ☐
   Are you a boy? ☐

3. When you go home after school what do you like to do?

   ....

   ....

   ....

4. What things do you like to do over the weekend?

   ....

   ....

   ....

5. Have you got a computer at school?   Yes ☐   No ☐

6. What do you do on the computer at school?

   ....

   ....

   ....

7. Do you play on the computer every day? ☐
                      nearly every day? ☐
                        once a week? ☐
                        not very often? ☐

8. At school do you play on the computer on your own? ☐
                                    with a friend? ☐
              with someone your teacher has chosen? ☐
                    with two or three other children? ☐

9. What is your favourite computer game/programme at school?

   ....

10. Have you got a computer at home?   Yes ☐   No ☐

11. At home, do you play on your computer every day?   ☐
    Nearly every day?   ☐
    At the weekend?   ☐
    Not often?   ☐

12. What computer games or CD Roms have you got at home?

    ....

    ....

    ....

13. What is your favourite computer game or CD Rom at home?

    ....

    ....

    ....

14. At home, do you usually play on your computer on your own?   ☐
    With an older brother or sister?   ☐
    With a younger brother or sister?   ☐
    With your mum?   ☐
    With your dad?   ☐

15. Have you got a video at home?   Yes ☐   No ☐

16. Do you like watching TV?   Yes ☐   No ☐

17. Do you like watching videos?   Yes ☐   No ☐

18. What are your favourite TV programmes?

    ....

    ....

    ....

19. What are your favourite videos?

    ....

    ....

    ....

20.   Can you remember what you liked to watch when you were very little?

....

....

....

21.   Do you still watch any of these programmes?

....

....

....

22.   Does a grown up ever record TV programmes for you?   Yes ☐   No ☐
      Which ones?

....

....

....

23.   Do you usually watch TV/videos on your own?   ☐

                  With an older sister or brother?   ☐

                  With a younger brother or sister?   ☐

                           With your mum?   ☐

                           With your dad?   ☐

                        With someone else?   ☐

24.   Have you read any books because you have seen the video or TV
      programme?
                                    Yes ☐   No ☐
      If yes, which ones?

....

....

....

24b. If you answered YES to question 24 do you think that watching the video/film/TV
      programme:

      helped you read the book?   Yes ☐   No ☐

      helped you *understand* the book?   Yes ☐   No ☐

25. Have you read a book and then seen the video?   Yes ☐   No ☐
    If yes, which ones?

    ....

    ....

    ....

26. Can you think of any videos which are BETTER than the books?

    ....

    ....

    ....

27. Can you think of any books which are BETTER than the videos?

    ....

    ....

    ....

28. Have you ever watched a video, TV programme or film and wished there was a book
    to go with it?

    ....

    ....

    ....

29. Have you read a book and wished there was a video of it?

    ....

    ....

    ....

30. Do you think books are better than videos or videos are better than books?

    ....

    ....

    ....

31. Have you got any toys that are linked to TV or video?

   ....

   ....

   ....

32. Have you got any toys that are linked to books?

   ....

   ....

   ....

33. Have you got any computer games, computer programmes or CD Roms that are linked to books, videos or TV programmes?

   ....

   ....

   ....

34. Do you ever pretend to be someone from a TV programme or a video?

   If so, who?

   ....

   ....

   ....

35. Do you ever pretend to be someone from a book?
   If so, who?

   ....

   ....

   ....

36. Have you ever got ideas for games from videos, TV or books?

   ....

   ....

   ....

37. Do you have any story tapes at home?

    ....

    ....

    ....

38. Which do you like the best?

    Books □

    TV □

    Videos □

    Storytapes □

    Comics □

    Computer games □

39. Do you ever watch TV or videos at school?   Yes □   No □
    If yes, what do you watch?

    ....

    ....

    ....

40. What do you think grown ups think about children watching TV and videos?

    ....

    ....

    ....

Thank you very much for answering all these questions.

Parents' Questionnaire

1. How old are your children? Girls.............................

   Boys............................

   When filling in this questionnaire I am answering the questions in relation to:

   (✔ as appropriate)

   my daughter ☐   my son ☐

   who is .... years old

   and is at home ☐ nursery/playgroup ☐ Reception ☐ Year One ☐ Year Two ☐

At home

2. How often does your child:

	Never	Rarely	1–3 times a week	4–5 times a week	Every day
• watch videos?	☐	☐	☐	☐	☐
• listen to audiotapes?	☐	☐	☐	☐	☐
• use a computer?	☐	☐	☐	☐	☐
• *choose* to read books?	☐	☐	☐	☐	☐
• read comics/magazines?	☐	☐	☐	☐	☐
• watch live TV?	☐	☐	☐	☐	☐

3. Does your child watch:

   (✔ as appropriate)

   more TV than videos ☐

   more videos than TV ☐

   approximately equal amounts of TV and videos ☐

4. Does your child *usually* play on the computer:

(✔ as appropriate)

with their brothers/sisters	☐
you or another adult	☐
on their own	☐
not applicable	☐

5. Does your child *usually* watch TV or videos:

(✔ as appropriate)

with their brothers/sisters	☐
you or another adult	☐
on their own	☐
not applicable	☐

6. What do YOU think are your child's favourite TV programmes?

....

....

....

....

7. What do YOU think are your child's favourite videos?

....

....

....

....

8. What do YOU think are your child's favourite books and/authors?

....

....

....

....

9. What do YOU think are your child's favourite audiotapes?

....

....

....

....

(✔ as appropriate)

10. Do you record TV programmes for your child?   YES ☐   NO ☐
    If yes, please list names of programmes

....

....

(✔ as appropriate)

11. Does your child have cartoon videos?   YES ☐   NO ☐
    If so, please give up to three examples of current favourites

....

....

....

(✔ as appropriate)

12. Does your child have children's drama videos?   YES ☐   NO ☐
    If so, please give up to three examples of current favourites

....

....

....

....

13. Does your child have factual videos?   YES ☐   NO ☐
    If so, please give up to three examples of current favourites

....

....

....

(✔as appropriate)

14. Does your child have art and craft videos (e.g. *Art Attack*)?   YES ☐   NO ☐
    If so, please give up to three examples of current favourites

    ....

    ....

    ....

    ....

                                                                    (✔ as appropriate)

15. Has your *child* ever read a book on which
    a video or film is based (e.g. *Matilda* or *Noddy*)?   YES ☐   NO ☐
    If yes, please list examples

    ....

    ....

    ....

    ....

15b. If you answered yes to Q 15, do you think watching the video/film helped your child
     read the book? If so, how?

    ....

    ....

16. Have *you* ever read your child a book on which a video
    or film is based?   YES ☐   NO ☐
    If yes, please list examples

    ....

    ....

    ....

    ....

16b. Do you think watching the video/film helped your child understand the book(s)?
     If so, how?

    ....

    ....

17. Do you buy your child comics or magazines related to
    videos or TV programmes (e.g. *Tots TV*)?   YES ☐   NO ☐
    If yes, please give some examples of current favourites:

    ....

    ....

    ....

18. If your child is at school, what TV programmes and/or videos did your child like
    before they started school?

    ....

    ....

    ....

19. How often does your child

    (✔ as appropriate)

	every week	every 2–3 weeks	once a month	every few months	never
visit the local library?	☐	☐	☐	☐	☐
borrow books from the library?	☐	☐	☐	☐	☐
borrow videos from the library?	☐	☐	☐	☐	☐

20. Does your child ever pretend to be a TV/video character? YES ☐   NO ☐
    If yes, who has your child pretended to be?

    ....

    ....

    ....

21. Does your child ever pretend to be a character
    from a book?   YES ☐   NO ☐
    If yes, who has your child pretended to be?

    ....

    ....

    ....

22. I think ......

(✔ as appropriate)

	improves reading	has no effect on reading	is bad for reading
I think watching TV	☐	☐	☐
I think playing computer games	☐	☐	☐
I think watching videos	☐	☐	☐
I think listening to story tapes	☐	☐	☐
I think reading to children	☐	☐	☐
I think letting the children help with shopping etc.	☐	☐	☐
I think playing word games (e.g. Scrabble, word lotto)	☐	☐	☐
I think playing other games (e.g. Monopoly, snap)	☐	☐	☐
I think listening to and singing songs	☐	☐	☐

(Please turn over for questions related to school)

At school

23. Does your child watch TV at school?　YES ☐　NO ☐　DON'T KNOW ☐

24. Does the school use schools' TV　YES ☐　NO ☐　DON'T KNOW ☐
programmes?
If yes, what TV programmes does your child watch at school?

....

....

25. Has your child seen videos at school
as a treat (e.g. end of term)?　YES ☐　NO ☐　DON'T KNOW ☐
If yes, what videos has your child seen at school?

....

....

26. Do you think Schools' TV programmes

(✔ as appropriate)

Help teach your child about the world? ☐

Help your child learn to read? ☐

Help your child with their maths? ☐

Give your child a break from classwork? ☐

Are a bit of a waste of school time? ☐

27. Would you like the teachers to use more TV/videos in school?   YES ☐   NO ☐
If yes, briefly state your reasons:

....,

....

28. Would you like the school to have a video library
and allow children to borrow videos?   YES ☐   NO ☐
Please briefly state your reasons

....

....

....

29. If you answered yes to Q 28, what sort of videos should the school video library
contain?

(✔ as appropriate)

art and craft videos ☐

children's drama ☐

short cartoons (e.g. *Bugs Bunny*) ☐

Disney cartoons and films ☐

children's films (*Babe*) ☐

general interest films (e.g. *Jurassic Park*) ☐

information videos ☐

videos in another language ☐
(if this box is ticked please state which languages)

other ☐
(if this box is ticked please give brief details)

THANK YOU *VERY* MUCH FOR SPENDING TIME ON THIS QUESTIONNAIRE.

List of Transcripts

Transcript no:	*Activity recorded*
Transcript A (TSA)	Interviews with Year One children
Transcript B (TSB)	Interviews with Year One children
Transcript C (TSC)	Interviews with Year One children
Transcript D (TSD)	Interviews with Year One children
Transcript E (TSE)	Interviews with Year One children
Transcript F (TSF)	Interviews with Year One children
Transcript G (TSG)	Interviews with Year One children
Transcript H (TSH)	Interviews with Reception children
Transcript I (TSI)	Interviews with Reception children
Transcript J (TSJ)	Interviews with Reception children
Transcript K (TSK)	Interviews with Year Two children
Transcript L (TSL)	Interviews with Year Two children
Transcript M (TSM)	Interviews with Year One children
Transcript N (TSN)	Interviews with Reception children
Transcript O (TSO)	Interviews with Nursery children
Transcript P (TSP)	Interviews with Nursery children
Transcript Q (TSQ)	Interviews with Reception children
Transcript R (TSR)	Interviews with Year One children
Transcript S (TSS)	Interviews with Year One children
Transcript T (TST)	Interviews with Year Six children
Transcript U (TSU)	Interviews with Year Six children
Transcript V (TSV)	Interview with Primary teacher
Transcript W (TSW)	Interview with Primary teacher
Transcript X (TSX)	Interview with Nursery teacher
Transcript Y (TSY)	Interview with Primary headteacher
Transcript Z (TSZ)	Interviews with parents
Transcript Aa (TSAa)	Interviews with parents
Transcript Ba (TSBa)	Interviews with parents
Transcript C (TSCc)	Interviews with parents
Transcript D (TSDd)	Interviews with parents

Appendix D

Transcript of Rehana's *Wolfie Stories* (Puppets)

Context: Playing with magnetic theatre made at school — three characters made from corks — Polly, Wolf and mother. Rehana began moving the characters round the stage and gradually a story began to emerge. She had a number of backdrops which she used during the course of the story. (Age 7.5.)

In the following transcript / indicates the point at which Rehana changed the backdrop. When Rehana is 'in role' the character's name appears on left. When narrating or speaking as herself, her own name appears on the left.

[Untitled as the story emerged from her play]

Mum:	Now, I want you to be really, really careful.
Polly:	We will.
Mum:	I mean really, *really* careful.
Polly:	We will, Wolfie is going to look after me.
Mum:	I want you to be really, really careful.{voice fades}
Rehana:	Her voice faded as they / disappeared into the sinister forest.

[The wolf and Polly venture into the woods and this is demonstrated by Rehana changing the backdrop to indicate they are moving from scene to scene. The wolf and Polly finally arrive at a spooky house.]

Rehana:	They looked around and there were spider webs everywhere.
Polly:	Ugh, Yuk!
Rehana:	There were dead flowers.

[Polly is moved centre stage]

Polly:	Oh, fish and chips! Yum!
Rehana:	She opened the lid and there was a fish swimming in a jar and a potato! They ran off holding hands and screaming for their lives. They ran past the spooky house / through the deep, dark forest / and all the way back to home. Just then Polly's mother came home.
Mum:	Oh, you're safe Polly! How was your day in the woods?
Rehana:	Polly looked back at the darkening trees and the red setting sun. The wolf looked as well. The path that was going up was the path to the fearsome woods.
Mum:	Well? How was your day in the woods?
Polly:	Oh, it was fine mother! We had a beautiful walk and everything, coconuts, collecting coconuts!
Mum:	Oh yes, well where are they?

Polly:	We dropped them.
Mum:	Oh why? We could have planted a coconut tree.
Polly:	They don't grow like that.
Mum:	Oh don't they indeed? [Pause] Well, I must go into the house and have a little rest.
Rehana:	And she trotted off the back stage, look Mummy, look! And this is where they go in. She trots off back stage.
Polly:	Wow, that was an adventure!
Rehana:	'Yes it was' said the wolf
Polly:	D'you think we'll ever go on another one?
Rehana:	'I don't know,' said the wolf, 'I really don't know'.
[Pause].	
Rehana:	Mummy, I'm going to make another character and he's, she's going to announce the things and stuff.

[10 minute break whilst she made another character for the stage and then played with her new character]

Rehana:	The next story is called The Magic Road.

[When the new props were completed she gathered together a range of backdrops.]

Rehana:	OK. Um . . . um . . . [raises sign with title] The Magic Road.
Polly:	Mummy, *please* can I go up that beautiful road? [Character indicates a golden yellow road drawn on the backdrop] Please can I go up that beautiful road to see what's at the top?
Mum:	Darling, loads of people say it's dangerous so *please* don't go.
Polly:	Oh Mummy, *please!*
Mum:	[Pause] OK just so long as you're careful. Be c-a-r-e-f-u-l! [The last word is drawn out and the end is barely audible]
Rehana:	Her voice drained away as Polly walked further and further out. First she had to go . . . /through a wood then she went up a big path. Suddenly she came to a wolf and the wolf said 'Hallo little girl, would you like to come with me and I'll give you some sweeties?'
Polly:	Oh yes please!
Rehana:	No, no, no, actually no, I don't want her to say that.
Wolf:	Oh come on. Come on! Come on!
Rehana:	Finally the wolf dragged her away until she couldn't put up any more. Suddenly she found herself outside a great big castle. '/ Heh,heh,heh' said the wolf, cackling evilly. /She went inside. Well she couldn't help it, the wolf was dragging her!/
Queen:	Oh you've done a good job Wolfie.
Wolf:	Thank you oh Mighty One.
Rehana:	The wolf went to stand to one side [moves wolf to one side]. There was a mean looking house [indicates a house on the backdrop]. There was spider webs and ivy climbing up and a grey house with a brown wooden door and it was terrible.
Queen:	Take my advice little girl, go further into the um, castle and you will be able to SEE [starts high pitched singing] THE GREATEST EVER . . . !
Wolf:	Shut up! The audience wont like your singing.

Queen:	[Still singing but more quietly] . . . To see the greatest ever thing.
Rehana:	Polly couldn't resist. Anyway the wolf had grabbed her again — he had a great thing with grabbing — and he pulled and tugged her into the next room. /This was lightly lit by two candles . . . had a wooden floor and an arrow slit and another arrow slit.
Queen:	Blow that candle out.
Wolf:	Wh..wha . . . What? Sorry, I was sleeping. What did you say?
Queen:	I said 'Blow that candle out,' what d'you think I said?
Wolf:	[noisily blows candles out] Oh no, it's too dark to see now, oh no, oh no, oh no!
Rehana:	I know. Are you ready? [Makes blowing noises and turns off light in bedroom]
Queen:	Oh no, we can't see now. Light them again!
Wolf:	But you *told* me to take it off
Queen:	Oh come on, just light it!

[Turns light on again].

Wolf:	Ow! I burnt my paw and it's all your fault!
Queen:	Oh stop being so stupid. Come on little girl.
Wolf:	I don't know, you asked me to take the candles out in the first place.
Queen:	Come on [to Polly]. You Dumbo, I *told* you.
Wolf:	Look, I'm not a Dumbo, I haven't got wings.
Queen:	Tch! [sighs] Come on little girl, we shall be going . . . into another room. /This other room has prison gates.
Rehana:	She was scared of going in but the wolf unlocked the gates and pulled her in. Well the wolf was quite surprised. It was the most amazingest room you have ever seen. I had a school, an office . . . office one and office two. [Backdrop shows a street scene with a school and two offices]
Polly:	Do you really work here?
Queen:	Oh don't be a stupid idiot, of course we don't work in school.
Wolf:	[In silly voice] I do!
Queen:	That school is just to make it look decorative well. . . . I work in office one, because I'm the best and he works in office two because he's the second best.
Wolf:	Hey, excuse me, my office has stained glass windows. Don't *touch*!
Polly:	Sorry
Queen:	This is where we work and do all our . . . thinking.

Wolf [Indistinct]

Queen:	What shall we do with her d'you think?
W:	Keep her as a slave, I love the idea of *slaves* hee-hee.
Queen:	You're *my* slave.
W:	No I'm not.
Queen:	Yes you are.
W:	No I'm not.
Queen:	Yes you are.
W:	Well, we could keep her to catch other people.
Queen:	*Y-es!* What a great idea, yes, good idea! [Wolf pats Queen on back] I'm not joking!
Wolf:	Sorry, I was just patting you on the back in case you were.
Queen:	OK. You go out and find . . . another *ch-hild*. I shall come out, no . . .

Wolf:	*I* shall come out with her just to make sure she doesn't do anything she's not supposed to.
Rehana:	He grabbed Polly's wrists and led her away. / They walked through the deep forest. Soon they came to a girl sitting down at the back.
Wolf:	[fiercely]Come on, you're coming with me!
Polly:	I'm not on their side!
Wolf:	Come with me little gi-rl.
Rehana:	/ They came up to the castle and he took them through into the first room / and the candles were carefully lit just in case they fell off. He grabbed their hands and then they / walked into the next room and opened the prison gates / And there was the witch standing quite nicely in the way, waiting.
Queen:	Oh! We've got another girl here. Now we've got two for now, Now we can use them as slaves.
Polly:	No!
Girl:	No!
Polly:	No!
Girl:	No!
Polly:	No!
Girl:	No!
Polly:	No!
Girl:	No!
Rehana:	They said, they ran off, past, um / through the door / out of that / and then up the road / through the forest / they ran home. And then they both separated and ran their different ways home

[Girl puppet leaves stage left and only Polly is left on stage]

When *Polly* got home . . . [mother puppet appears].

Polly:	Oh hallo mother!
Mum:	Darling, you took so long, what happened?
Polly:	[To audience] D'you think I should tell her?
Me:	No.
Polly:	No? I'll tell you later mummy, mother, mum, I'll just go and make us a nice cup of tea. Come on, let's go along this gravel path.[mother puppet leaves stage left]
Rehana:	When her mother had gone in through the door she stood and had one last look at the yellow, pebbly road and thought of the adventure she had had there.
Mum:	[Shouting off stage] Polly! The tea's getting cold!
Polly:	Okay, okay, okay! And the forest and the play she had done before and of the adventure with a *good* wolf.
Mum:	[Shouting off stage] Polly! Come on, the tea's getting cold!
Polly:	Coming Mum! [Polly leaves stage left saying 'Bye!' to audience as she leaves]
Rehana:	And then they all come onto stage. Right, clap them and whoop them.

[Polly and Mum are moved forward to take a bow. The Queen and the wolf move forward]

Rehana:	But what about these two? Boo them!

Transcript of *The Faraway Tree* (Oral story)

The Faraway Tree. Once there lived, once lived a little girl she was nine. Her name was her name um..her name was Charlotte. She had long blonde, no, fair hair down to her shoulder and she was tall for her age with freckles. She had a wimpy little brother who was three, yes, he was three. He was called, um, William and he had short brown hair. He had short brown hair and *he* was quite *small* for his age. One day they went outside and played, and were playing. They climbed up a tree and sat on one of the branches. Suddenly there was a swooping sound and they got swallowed up. They went falling down, down, down, tumble, tumble, tumble. Her little brother screamed but she thought it was exciting that um, Charlotte thought it was exciting. When they got to the bottom William said. 'I don't want to be here. I want to go home'. 'No' said Charlotte, 'I want to have an adventure' so they did. There was a trap door and a rope coiled up. She opened the trap door and uncoiled the rope and threw it down. It fell down and she clung on to it and slid down with her brother following. Then there was another trap door, she opened it, got the other coiled rope, threw it down, slid down it and the other brother, her other, her brother did as well. When they got down they went along a very big, they went along a stone road, then they went up some steps, down a hill, up some more steps, down the steps, up the hill, down the hill, up the steps and up another hill. When they got there, wherever they were, they stood and they were amazed. There was a tree trunk about as tall as a car and as long as a car, for exhaust pipes there was um, little leaves sticking out and they were on *wheels*. They had little cuts, they had been cut at the sides to be windows and for seats they had big knots that you find on trees, they had big knots that you find on trees. They were driving along, no, other people were driving in them. Soon they found one unoccupied, it didn't belong to anyone so they hopped in, no, well, actually only Charlotte hopped in she had to yank her brother in with her. Her brother sat down and squatted down actually and they drove off. There were *millions* of other ones, they had to be careful not to crash. Soon they came to a little road where it said you may go fast so she trod down on one of the other another knots where the feet where your feet go and it was squashy and you zoomed along. There was a sort of, there was another, there was a wooden plank and it said on it green no, orange for go, green for stop and yellow for ready, get ready. It was, it was the right colour to go and they went zooming off again. Soon there was a little, there was a tall big mansion and they parked outside. Um, Charlotte and her wimpy little brother William went in. There were spider webs everywhere and when they went in the door creaked open, the steps were steep. They went along a long, narrow corridor. Charlotte was a bit nervous but William howled and howled and howled. Soon she said to him 'Oh, be quiet' and they came along, soon they came along to a lit — a big wooden door. She opened it, there was another passageway but this time it was sloping. She went up, down the steps, along the straight and then there was a stone door. When she opened it it clanked back because it banged against the stone wall. She went in. To her shock, surprise plus horror there was a little wooden table with stone legs and little knots of trees for stools. Sitting down on them were three witches. There was a witch in purple, there was a witch in blue and there was a witch in green. They all had the same clothes on except for the colour. They all had cackly, horrible um, um, laughs and voices. They were very tall. On the table were little cups of green liquidy stuff. It was yuk. In the right hand corner there was a sink and cat was doing the washing up with an apron on. On the left hand corner there was a fro — no, there was, the cat was cleaning the plates and on the other side was another cat drying the plates. And the witches were talking. Next to them was another, no, a little wooden box, on it, on it the pattern was like a tree, it looked like a tree bark because it was, well it looked like a tree bark. On top of it was a tablecloth with frogs on it and on top of that was a big, black cauldron. Inside it was some whitey, greeny, turquoisy, reddy, bluey liquid bubbling away. They ran back and thought we'll go back there later to sort out what they're planning to do. They went through another path, up a slope, down the steps, through the corridor out of the stone door, which didn't clang because they were careful, along the corridor, up the stairs, down the slope through the wooden door and then there were two ways. One way which was the way of the witches and on there they had been such in a rush they had forgotten to see the sign on the door there was a big plank and it said bad world, and that was where they just went in, and on the other side there was another door and it said good world and on the other side there was topsy-turvy world, there was a square room on the other bit was the topsy-turvy world and on the other side was a sensible world. They decided to go in the topsy-turvy world. When they went in it looked as though they were standing on the ceiling but luckily they weren't. There was this chairs and stuff fixed onto the ceiling and there was also chairs and stuff fixed onto the floor. A man came along and said, 'Well, well, well, what *do* you want?' They didn't say anything. 'Oh well', said the man, 'I can't help some people these days,' and disappeared. They went out through a door and there was a big house with four doors. On the front there was a door that said, um, um, sensible man, on the other side funny man, the other one was silly man and the other one was nice man. They opened each door in turn but when they went in all they saw was one man. Now, what it, the man said, no, no,um, Charlotte said, 'But I thought there were four men in here.' 'Ah, no, no, no, no, no. I have four doors because it depends what sort of mood I'm in. I go to the door when I'm feeling good, I go to the sensible door when I'm feeling sensible and I go to the silly door when I'm feeling silly and then I go to the other door when I'm feeling what it says on there.' 'Oh,' said William a bit shocked. 'Come on, sit down, have a nice cup of tea,' said the man. Um, 'OK,' said Charlotte and William at the same time so they sat down. The man plodded into the next door and seized up a bubbling, frothy bottle of a frothy sort of yellow something, didn't know what it was, poured it into three cups, put the three cups on the tray and carried it carefully into the room where they were sitting. He put them on a little table and sat down. 'Here you go, bubbly, frothy, yellow drinks, lemon bubbly, frothy drinks,' he said. And Charlotte said, 'I don't know what these are and neither does William, he's my little brother and a bit wimpy.' William was very shocked by this but he didn't, he was very annoyed by this but he didn't get cross. Anyway, 'These you'll really like them,' said the man.' 'Oh alright then' said Charlotte and had a little sip, it wasn't very pleasant but then when she had a bit more she decided that she liked it even more and she kept on going and kept on slurping it all up and then William started slurping all his up. The man said, the man said, the man said, 'Do you like it?' and Charlotte said, 'Mmm, yeah.' 'Good' said the man and the man seized up the drink before they had finished and threw them into the sink which was in the other room and came back. 'We'd better be going,' said Charlotte, 'We'd better be going to sort out what those witches are doing.' 'Oh, good luck,' said the man and he disappeared. They went out of the topsy-turvy door and

then they went down the path, up the path, through the wooden door, up the stairs down the slope, through the stone door and then, there was the door saying bad world. Charlotte was tensed but they both stepped in. They went along the corridor. Then they saw the witches again. The cauldron had got filled up even more. They managed to catch a snip of what the witches were saying. They said, 'If we can, if we turn the whole kingdom into frogs heh heh heh heh we will be able to take it over.' 'Oh no,' thought Charlotte and then she said that to William. Luckily the mixture had now turned to white. 'Now,' 'said the witches, 'We'd better just go away while these bubbles set. We'll go somewhere else, we'll go on a trip.' 'Okay' said the other witches, 'But remember we must do it when they are asleep.' 'Of course I will, Dummy,' said one of the other witches and off they went. The colour of the cauldron was a milky kind of colour. Charlotte went over to the sink and there were two taps, one of them says milk and the other says water. She turned on the water tap but only water came out. She turned it off. She turned on the milk tap and the *exact* colour of milk and *exact* colour that the cauldron was came falling out. She tipped all of the contents of the cauldron down the sink as the cats had gone as well and she put the cauldron under the tap and so it filled up with milk. Then she put it down, she put it down on the table and went back to the door to see what would happen. 'Now they will only feed them milk in the night and they're sure to wake up,' she said and they went to hide behind a big coal box. So, the witches came back, They said, 'Heh, heh, heh, heh, heh. It's getting late into the night so we may now um, um, we may now do our plan.' They went out carrying the cauldron with them and some cups. Then Charlotte and William went running back and tried to find their way back. Now, they found the trap doors, climbed up the rope and shut the trap door and coiled the rope up. They went up the next rope that was hanging down because what they used, climbed up that, shut the trap door and coiled the rope up. When they got to the top Charlotte said, 'Oh no, Mummy will be worried about us, and Daddy.' But when they got out she looked at her watch and back in the thing it had said nine o'clock pm but now it said exactly the same time that they had left. They went back to the house and the mummy said, 'You were very quick.' And Charlotte said, 'Oh, well, um, er, we decided not to play, we decided to back again.' And they just went up to their room and never told their parents what had happened. The end.
[Rehana, aged 7.5]

Transcript of Retelling of *Pollyanna*

Story of Pollyanna as told by Rehana, aged 5.6.

First story of Pollyanna

Da,dada, daa, da, da, daa, dada, da, dada dada daa *[Sings made up tune as introduction — as on many story tapes and on the video of Pollyanna.]*

Pollyanna was a girl who lived all by herself. Pollyanna was a girl who lived all by herself in a little cottage where she had lived when her mother and father met their death because her mother and father were still dead, were dead and her other brothers and sisters — she had at least had about seven and she was the eighth one and luckily she didn't get killed, but get um, got, was, as old as them because she was the youngest daughter. And all of the other seven, all of her brothers and sisters had died and her mother and father had died too. So, she was a little girl in a pretty little cottage surrounded by flowers and beds, beds of flowers and she was thinking. 'Now, shall I go to my aunt's house or shall I not? Shall I or shall I not?' she was saying over and over again all day. And then, just then she realized she would and so, she got a piece of paper and wrote, Dear Auntie and then she thought. Dear Auntie I'd like to come round so you can look after me. At least look after me but not my mummy and daddy or my seven brothers and sisters because they're all dead so that's why I want you to look after me. Yours faithfully, Pollyanna. Eight, oh, nine, nine, nine. And so she sent it in a little envelope to her aunt.

And then she went out walking and walking with her bruised, scratched legs and with her beautiful straw hat on, her beautiful checked skirt on and her beautiful checked blouse on. And she walked and walked and walked and walked until she came to another little cottage in the woods, in, in the, in the fields I mean. And, but the aunt hadn't read it before she could come and so she walked through the woods to a little other little cottage in, with the flowerbeds all around, just like her own little cottage but much fancier. And she walked down the garden path which was curved like in the swimming pool when you go round and you see a big crowd in the swimming pool but it was like the path in the swimming pool and it could be curved, it was all curved. And on that side of the curve was a big, thin woman looking out for her, at least that's what she thought. And there was Nancy, the cook, um. I mean Nancy was looking out and that was the cook but she was about seventeen and she was quite old. And she said, 'Hallo, Pollyanna. You must be Pollyanna the niece.'

'Yes I am' said Pollyanna, 'And my father and mother are dead.'

'Yes, well never mind. Now let's come in and introduce you to your aunt.'

'Thank you Nancy um, thank you um, servant.'

'My name is Nancy. You shall call me by the name of Nancy.'

'Thank you. Nancy, I'm sorry can you introduce me to my aunt?'

'Of course I will.'

And with that she followed Nancy into the kitchen through the passageway, down the passageway, up the passage way, then down the stairs, up the passage way until they came to a little room where she thought she might be, said Nancy. And she said, 'Shhh! Your aunt might be sleeping.' And so they looked in but no, the aunt wasn't sleeping she was perfectly, perfectly cross, sitting up cross-legged, folded arms, nose in the air and mouth shut and pursed lips. And, and, 'Pol...Aunt Polly...Miss Polly. Miss Polly,' said Nancy, 'This is your niece' and she pushed Pollyanna forward to meet her. And suddenly, her pursed, Miss Polly's, Aunt Polly's pursed lips opened, her arms set free, her legs uncrossed, her arms uncrossed and a smile began to curl up and then vanished. 'Pollyanna, I annore you not. I ask you not to go on my knees when you're in private like this, thank you.' Do you know why the aunt was so grumpy? I'll tell you. Er...many years ago she was, she was wanting to marry a man and the man didn't want to marry her because he didn't love her anymore and so, ever since then she was sad and lonesome. It was only the servants, who didn't really like her very much, didn't really like her very much and the people who went along the road who used to say, 'Good morning Miss. Good morning missus.' And she said, 'I'm not a Mrs. I'm a Miss. Anyway, I used to be a Miss,' she would say as she walked on with her basket in the woods. And then she said, 'I'm going to show you to your little attic room, little attic room, to your little attic room.' And with that she marched upstairs with Pollyanna by her heels.

Da,dada, daa, da, da, daa, dada, da, dada dada daa *[Sings made up tune to signal end of episode]*

Chapter Two: The Game
Da,dada, daa, da, da, daa, dada, da, dada dada daa *[Sings made up tune to signal start of chapter]*
Chapter Two: The Game

Nancy was in the kitchen while, um Pollyanna was tidying her bedroom. She had a little wardrobe at the front, a little bed at the back, and a little [indistinct] and she thought, she thought I'm going to go down, I'm going to open the window and ju...I'm going to climb down the tree and walk out, out into the fresh air, fresh air, fresh air, she said over and over again to herself. So she walked along the little alley way, up some little stairs to the window. *[Tapped table to make sound like steps and whispered 'That's the little steps']* And she thought I'm going to hold my nose and go down that tree. She holded her nose, closed her eyes and climbed down that tree with only one arm and none eyes. And she walked along and climbed up a little stone and looked about and then Nancy came and said, 'What are you doing?' And I said, she said, 'Well, you know why I'm always cheerful? That's because my father told me game.' Nancy looked puzzled. 'What game?' 'Well first I wanted a doll but they said no doll had arrived so they sent me a pair of crutches instead.' And Nancy said, 'I can't see any happiness in that if you wanted a doll and you got a pair of crutches!' 'I didn't see that either but unless when Father told me.' Suddenly, um, suddenly, um, Pollyanna turned off very quickly and thought. Then she opened her mouth again to speak and said, 'Well what you do when you need some thing to be glad about, but what to be glad about? Well if you sleep up in a little attic room then you got to say that you're glad you went in an attic room.' 'But you're not supposed to open the window.' 'Oh aren't I? Oh, never mind.' 'But the drapes, but the um, screens haven't come yet'. 'Haven't they? Oh never mind.' And then, just then the auntie came out and said, to um, Pollyanna 'Pollyanna, Nancy, I'm sorry if I behaved badly. The new screens will be coming for the windows. Pollyanna come here, into your attic room and down the stairs into my bedroom. You may sleep with me tonight.'

'Oh really? Good, good, good, good, good,' said Pollyanna. And with that her uncle, who I hadn't mentioned, her uncle and auntie picked her up and gave her a huge cuddle. The end!

Da,dada, daa, da, da, daa, dada, da, dada dada daa *[Sings made up tune to signal end of story.]*

Index